IN THE WILDERNESS

In the
Wilderness

COMING OF AGE
IN UNKNOWN COUNTRY

KIM BARNES

ANCHOR BOOKS
A DIVISION OF RANDOM HOUSE, INC.
New York

First Anchor Books Trade Paperback Edition, March 1997

Copyright © 1996 by Kim Barnes

The Library of Congress has cataloged the Doubleday
hardcover edition as follows:
Barnes, Kim.
In the wilderness : coming of age in unknown country / Kim
Barnes. — 1st ed.
p.   cm.
1. Barnes, Kim—Childhood and youth.   2. Women poets,
American—20th century—Family relationships.   3. Women poets,
American—Idaho—Family relationships.   4. Barnes, Kim—Homes
and haunts—Idaho.   5. Idaho—Religious life and customs.
6. Idaho—Social life and customs.   7. Wilderness areas—Idaho.
8. Pentecostalism—Idaho.   9. Family—Idaho.   I. Title.
PS3552.A6815Z467   1996
811'.54—dc20
[B]   95-24889
CIP

ISBN 0-385-47821-6

www.anchorbooks.com

Printed in the United States of America

13   12   11   10   9   8   7   6   5   4

In consideration of their privacy, the names of some of the people appearing in this text have been changed.

An earlier version of Chapter Four was originally published in *The Georgia Review*.

Acknowledgments

There are many people without whose support I would never have found my way back: Mary Clearman Blew, who shared with me her vision; Claire Davis and Dennis Held, who offered friendship no matter the season; and Robert Johnson, upon whose quiet belief and confidence I could always depend. Thanks to Robert Wrigley for seeing me through; it is my hope that our children—Philip, Jordan and Jace—will add to this story their own. I would also like to thank Keith and Shirley Browning, Margaret Bremer, Ripley Schemm, Annick Smith, Bill Kittredge, Judy Blunt, Julia Watson, Dee McNamer, Renée Wayne Golden, Bruce Tracy, and all the others who offered their encouragement and direction. Thanks, too, to the Idaho Commission on the Arts and the PEN/Jerard Fund.

I am also grateful to those who have dedicated their time to uncovering and retelling much of the local history, which might otherwise have been lost. Among many upon whose knowledge and research I depended were Lalia Boone, Cort Conley, Ladd Hamilton, Louise Shadduck, Ralph Space, Sandra Taylor, and Johnny Johnson.

In attempting to acknowledge the inevitable disparities between my recollection and that of those who might tell this story otherwise, I recall a line attributed to Barbara Kingsolver: "Memory is a complicated thing, a relative to truth, but not its twin."

For my husband, Robert Wrigley,
my saving grace

In memory of Nan,
whose wisdom and courage
continue to sustain me

And for my parents

Willows never forget how it feels
to be young.

Do you remember where you came from?
Gravel remembers.

Even the upper end of the river
believes in the ocean.

Exactly at midnight
yesterday sighs away.

What I believe is,
all animals have one soul.

Over the land they love
they crisscross forever.

—WILLIAM STAFFORD
"CLIMBING ALONG THE RIVER"

Until the spirit be poured
upon us from on high, and the wilderness
be a fruitful field, and the fruitful field
be counted for a forest. Then
judgment shall dwell in the wilderness. . . .

—ISAIAH 32:15,16

IN THE WILDERNESS

CHAPTER ONE

Past the Clearwater Timber Protection Association and the "Fire Danger" board, across the creek and before the dump, the small house squatted in a pocket of red fir and pine, not visible from the road. The locals called the hollow Dogpatch. The Joneses lived nearby, and Gerty Buck and her son, who owned a motorcycle, and someone else across the way who had two German shepherds chained to a clothesline. The dogs were the first things my younger brother, Greg, and I saw when we stepped off the bus after school. They barked ferociously, racing back and forth between the two T-shaped poles, until we disappeared down the steep path leading past the woodshed and root cellar to a small piece of flat ground surrounded by trees.

Beside our house, painted the same umber red as other

shacks built by local loggers on company land, flowed the spring, and from its constant source we took our water. Each day the train, pulling its load of logs, ran the route from Headquarters to the mill at Lewiston and back, and my brother and I, feeling the tremor of its coming before we heard the engine's rumble, ran to the rear of the house and through the trees to wave at the brakeman and engineer. When not in school, we filled our days exploring the near woods, digging after ground squirrels, amassing piles of found treasure: feathers blue as river water, bones of deer, old buckets and chains, nests stitched through with colorful bits of moss.

A narrow footbridge crossed the spring to the path leading to the outhouse. Several years before his death, one of my great-uncles, Ed Swanson, had added a small bathroom off the kitchen, but the pipes froze in winter and clogged in summer. The outdoor privy seemed familiar, made comfortable by a tightly closing door and a genuine toilet seat. Behind the outhouse the trees grew dense, and the little building seemed the last safe place before the forest closed in. It was a corner boundary for my brother and me—home base for hide-and-seek, our secret meeting place where we could be hidden from our mother's eyes.

On the other side of the spring, the root cellar squatted deep in the bank beneath its cowl of sod. It had begun its service as a bomb shelter, dug out in one day by Uncle Ed during the Cuban missile crisis. I cannot imagine why the shy Swede believed Castro might target him and his family deep in the wilds of Idaho, but his panic and furious excavating became the stuff of family legend. He leveled the dirt floor, built the walls and roof of rough-cut cedar and hung a door so heavy the hinges shrieked when it opened. He filled the shelter with tins of food and brown Purex bottles of water. Finally, he cut a hole in one wall and added a large crank air vent. It reminded me of the meat grinder my mother used to make sausage, and when my brother and I together turned the handle the wind sang in fresh and cold.

By the time we came to live in the hollow, the shelter had become a catchall for old clothes and empty boxes. We hauled case after case of pop bottles over the hill to Headquarters, pulling our wagon along the one-mile stretch of road, stopping each time a logging truck geared for the rise. When we gave a high, imaginary tug, the driver let loose a brawling blast from his air horn and we'd howl with pleasure. In Headquarters, the store saved its outdated comic books, covers torn away, in a pile behind the fishing gear. With the dimes from our turned-in bottles we could each head home with two comics and a chocolate cone, our wagon rattling empty behind us.

Across the track was the dump with its brown corked bottles, the bits of metal and porcelain we carried home like booty. The deer bed was there, fragrant grass crushed beneath an overhanging branch of yellow pine. We would lie down and smell the musk, pick tufts of hair from the needles, imagine the warmth of a fawn nestled tight in the curve of its mother's flank. We hunted the grouse that roosted near the house. Sometimes my brother and I would find them huddled in the woodshed. "Fool hens!" we'd shout, pumping our pellet guns, shooting them near the shed, where their wings beat against the metal siding.

We fished no matter the season, first testing our luck in the shallow spring, then in Reeds Creek, cutting through the meadow a half mile south. We knew each shadowed pool and the fish that stilled themselves there: many times we jerked them free of the water, only to see them sail from our hooks like silvery kites. Always, we knew, they would return to their favorite bend, where grasses hung down and fat grasshoppers fell.

The meadow spread out from the creek on either side, a marsh, really, spongy and thick with cattails. Deer fed at its edges and once, just as the big rainbow I had caught and lost five times before gave in to my patience and took the worm I let drift one last time by its hole, from the corner of my eye I saw the ground shift and settle. In a nesting of dry fern lay a fawn, curled against itself and nearly invisible. The rod jumped in my hands but I could not look from that spot. I was afraid the shape might disappear, my sight might deceive me, though the fawn huddled so close I might cast my line across its dappled back. As still as it was I could see the body tremble, the nostrils flare with the scent of me.

I knew I'd lost the fish. The tension in the line was gone, and the rod no longer quivered as though it held life of its own. I backed away, looking up the trail toward home only after I had lost the white spots and dark eyes to the tall grasses. There was a secret there, more mysterious than the fish sleeping without air in beds of gravel. I wanted it to stay.

I remember the late autumn evening my brother did not come home, the snow beginning to fall, my mother standing in the yard, hands cupped to her mouth, his name echoing back, all the love and fear in her voice repeated again and again. We knew better than to try and find him in the dark and could only wait, shivering in the cold, for my father to come home.

I think of us there, a woman of twenty-nine, a girl of eleven, both imagining a life without this other—son, brother —both believing that the one who could save him would arrive at any moment, bringing with him his strength and sense of the woods. My father, we believed, might see through the blackness, his eyes so blue they seemed clairvoyant. We believed he might feel in the air my brother's lost breath, trace with his fingers the heat left by his body. If only he'd come, *now, now.*

But by the time he came home Greg was stumbling from the trees, clutching the scruff of our dog's neck, nearly deaf from the cold. He screamed as my mother rubbed his fingers into life, her prayers and scoldings a constant chorus. I stood ready with warmed blankets, feeling outside something dark slip away, taking with it its hunger.

I recall my father's absence in that place more than his presence, the sound of logging—his saw, the clanking choker —more than the tenor of his voice. So much had changed since the first years of my life spent living in the woods, years when we moved from one logging site to another, my father and uncles hitching our wooden trailers to the backs of self-loaders and surplus jeeps, filling the cars with cardboard boxes, stashing our treasure like gypsies. Those were the years when my parents seemed happy to live hand-to-mouth as long as the hand that held the food, as long as the mouth that received it, was that of the other. I think of their traditional wedding pose—my father eighteen, my mother sixteen—each holding to the other's lips the sweetly frosted cake.

The year we spent living in the hollow, the year I turned twelve, was the last year we would live in the woods, the last year I would sleep beneath the soft brush of pine against the tin roof, the last year I would remember our family as somehow whole. From that house we would take nothing that did not fit into the trunk of our car and make our final trip down the river road to town.

My life would change in ways I could no more dream than a far-off soldier might imagine an enemy hidden in a shelter beneath the mounded forest floor, or a young girl, fishing the shallow stream, might for a moment believe a heart other than her own beat in the meadow's thick grass. Who is that girl, the rod still quivering in her hands, rapturously balanced between two worlds? I sometimes think that if I could go back, follow the driveway down, past the woodshed and out into the meadow, I might find her—I might find what I have lost. Like my brother wandering in the wilderness, I might find home.

CHAPTER TWO

I begin in Oklahoma, in the late 1920s. In a one-room farm-house near Stigler, my father's mother sleeps on a makeshift bed of muslin-covered cornhusks with her seven brothers and sisters. They are used to sleeping this way, and the warmth their bodies generate is a great comfort. Outside, the wind sweeps the leaves and straw from the dirt yard. In the morning when they wake, the soiled blanket covering them will be frosted with their moist breath.

Only one child stirs, my grandmother's eldest sister, Daisy. Since the death of their mother, and then their stepmother a few years later, it has been Daisy who has kept them clothed and fed, who has shielded them from their father's drunken rages. She's a beautiful girl, her light blue eyes brilliant against the smooth brown skin inherited from her Cherokee grandmother. She sits up slowly and sees her father slumped in his chair, sour with whiskey and sweat. Raising her arms above her head, she winds her long hair into a bun, then slides carefully from between the other children. Quietly she begins to work her way around the single room, knowing he'll whip her raw if he wakes to find her gathering her shoes, pulling on her two pairs of rough stockings, pulling first one and then the other of her cotton dresses over her flour-sack slip (even in the cold she is wet with sweat), then her winter coat.

She reaches to take the hard biscuits wrapped in a clean tea towel from the cupboard, but decides it will be a last offering, something the youngest can chew on while her father calls her name across the fields. The door squeaks on its leather hinges, and she thinks to run but takes a breath and steps out onto the packed red clay. Cold air cuts her lungs as she walks toward the corn rows, stopping to squat one last time, feeling the weight of her clothes, all she owns, but never once looking back.

How did she survive her journey that night? She had seldom left the isolated farm, had seen the city only a few times, had never left the county she was born in. A girl, maybe sixteen, bundled in beggar's clothing, no luggage or purse, walking, perhaps hitchhiking, her way across the state line into Texas, kept warm by fear and shame, kept going by the exhilaration she felt whenever she remembered she was free. In Texas, she believed, she could find a way to live on her own. In Texas, there was oil, money and, if she were lucky, a man who would find her comely enough to make her his wife.

She found a job working early shift in a small cafe in the panhandle. She knew the first time he came in—square-jawed, lips set—she'd marry him. He was going somewhere, maybe not in oil, maybe not in Texas, but somewhere. She could see it in his shoulders, the way he focused on his food, how his hands weren't still—not nervous, but always moving, stirring sugar into the black coffee, rubbing water rings off his fork, smoothing the napkin's edge between his fingers. He didn't smoke, and she liked that about him. There were things he wanted to do, and he wasn't one to waste his time. Within a month they were married, and it would be his ambition that would lead my great-uncle Clyde Knight into the Idaho wilderness, and it would be his lead that my family would follow.

But first I must go back to that shack where the children are waking to find their sister gone. My grandmother, because she is the second-eldest girl, moves around her sleeping father and stirs the ashes of last night's fire, looking for an ember to breathe on and bring to life. She thinks Daisy may be out gathering more wood, but there is a stillness in the house that doesn't feel right. Why isn't the water heating? Their father will expect it when he wakes, and she trembles to think of his anger should he not be met with warmed biscuits and the pale liquid drawn from the grounds of yesterday's coffee.

She opens the door. Even though the wind whips her bare legs and makes her teeth chatter, she wishes for the three-mile walk to school. She misses the books, the room and its little stove, the smell of drying wool and chalk dust. But her father has said she must stay home: sixth grade is enough learning for any girl, and the other children must be looked after.

She looks across the flat fields and pasture for Daisy. She knows firewood is getting harder to find, but she cannot imagine why Daisy would wander so far from the house in this weather, knowing that in his state their father would want her to keep the baby quiet.

She picks up the few remaining sticks of oak left by the door. Her younger brother Lee is awake now, stretching his bad leg, rubbing it at the knee. Like her, he limps across the room: both have been crippled by TB. She doesn't even think of it anymore, compensating for the difference in the length of her legs by walking on the toe of one foot. Already, her hip is enlarged and her back curved from the stress.

They go about their chores as though in a church, cushioning each step, hushing the four-year-old when he calls for milk. But as the others wake and begin clattering from the bed, they see their father stir. He notes the fire first, then turns his reddened eyes toward the cookstove.

"Where's Daisy?" His voice is coarse with phlegm. He coughs and spits into the fire.

"Don't know, Daddy." Even as she says it, she cringes away from his chair. Daisy is the one he depends on to rub his feet and fix his meals. Even as young as Daisy is, she's had suitors, and he has run each of them off with threats, a gun in his hand.

Immediately he is suspicious. Hadn't she tried to run away once already? Raising himself from the chair, he stumbles toward the door, groaning, made angrier by the pain in his head. He shouts her name once, then, still standing on the threshold, opens his stained trousers and pisses a long stream onto the red dirt.

"Daisy! I'll whip you good, girl!"

My grandmother gathers up the baby and sways to keep her quiet. She watches the man walk toward the barn, still calling, his stride becoming more purposeful. He disappears into the barn and she turns to the stove, knowing he's leaving and may be gone for weeks. It is not the first time. His trips into town to drink and gamble are common enough, but before he has left them with enough cut wood, meat, flour and sugar to get by. The children crowd to the door, watching the wind bend the dry corn stalks to the ground, their bellies already aching with hunger.

My grandmother and Lee fed the children the hard biscuits, soaking the baby's in the last of the milk from town. They had no food, and no wood to keep the fire burning. At thirteen, my grandmother was older than Lee by a few years; as their eyes met above the heads of their brothers and sisters, they knew that survival depended on them.

Together they scouted the ground for wood, but what could be broken or easily carried had already been scavenged and burned. They ventured out farther, wrapped in flour sacks and their father's shirts. A quarter mile from the house they found a small fallen blackjack. Calling for some of the others to help, they dragged it home, feeding it a foot at a time into the fireplace.

There was food: the crippled calf, grazing in the corn rows. The younger children watched as their older brother and sister chased the bawling calf, all three—the boy, the girl, the bony animal—limping across the frozen ground. But they were children, and even the life-and-death chase brought them to cheers and laughter as the calf slipped between them, one or the other skidding along behind, hanging on to its tail.

Finally, Lee found a rope and lassoed the calf, then straddled its belly while my grandmother slit its throat. They'd lived the farm life long enough to gut and skin with the grace of old hands, and throwing their combined weight to the rough rope, they winched the small steaming carcass to the low rafters of the smokehouse. Sawed off a hunk at a time and roasted over the coals of the saving tree, it was enough meat to last them until their father came home.

• • •

My grandmother took Daisy's place in that ramshackle house, enlisting the help of her younger sisters to make the meager meals, to cut and sew the flour sacks into baggy dresses and shirts that raked their skin. The bitterness she harbored against her sister kept her jaw tight and her direction set: she would not leave the others as Daisy had, nor would she ever admit that she longed to do the same and be gone from the house that reeked of kerosene and urine.

Years later, when a drinking partner of her father's, Pat Barnes, a tall, lean red-haired man, began courting her, she allowed herself to imagine another life. The children were older now. Certainly her younger sisters were grown enough to cook and clean. Her father didn't like it, and although he teased the man about flirting with his daughter, he forbade her to see him, and threatened to beat them both if she disobeyed.

When she turned eighteen, they asked for permission to marry, and when her father said no they eloped. They lived first with my grandfather's sister, a shrewish woman whose only use for my grandmother was as a milker and maid. When my grandmother became pregnant with her first child, she craved one delicacy: a full, sweet plum from her sister-in-law's tree. This the woman denied her, taking special pleasure in the smallness of her cruelty. Because of this, my grandmother believed, her daughter was born with a birthmark on her hip, the exact size and purple shade of the plum she had longed for.

Even after she and her husband found their own piece of land to sharecrop, her life seemed little changed from the one she had left. Except for this: she loved the man who worked the packed sod and came home to her each evening, a wide smile on his dusty face. She would give birth to four more children, the next to the last my father.

On their little acreage of leased land, they grew cotton and broomcorn. They raised a few hogs and a milk cow, enough to keep food on the table and land under their feet. My grandfather never really gave up fighting the heat, the hailstorms and tornados. A man bred to the life, his fair skin fissured and toughened, his eyes permanently squinted against the dry silt wind and sun, he might have made it if the country had given just a little, offered up something he could depend on from one season to the next. But this was the time of dust, and what sustenance he could not draw from the seed and furrows he drew from the still: the one thing he could count on in that land of baked soil was alcohol, and he gave himself to it more and more.

His is an old and familiar story in the too-often romanticized myth of the twentieth-century pioneers—the story of men broken by the land's promise and the government's lie that said borrowed money, hard work and patriotism would see the country through. And alongside this story is the quieter story of the women, who sometimes endured but more often did not, twice betrayed, first by the land and then by the men who worked it.

There was one year they all remember as good, the year things took a turn for the better. Prices were up, and harvest had gone well. Their house had a wooden floor and two rooms big enough so that Coleen, the oldest and only girl, could have her own bed instead of being piled together with her four brothers.

That year they bought a new couch. My grandmother hung curtains on the windows, pleased with the colors that brightened the fading wallpaper. My grandfather bought himself a new fiddle, a true extravagance. They were all musical, and it is the music my father speaks of now as holding the best of his Oklahoma memories: summer evenings when the heat eased and they could sit on the sagging porch and play their fiddles and guitars and sing.

It was my father who hunkered inside the house one day, beneath the open window, four years old and flush with his secret—a box of wooden matches left beside the stove. His brothers and sister were at school, except for the youngest boy; the creak of the porch slats let him know that his mother was rocking the baby to sleep.

I imagine him as he slid open the cardboard box, breathing in the sharp smell of sulfur. Several of the matches fell into his lap, and he gathered them up quickly. He wanted only one, just to feel the magic of friction and fire, to hold in his hand the instant bloom of light. He struck it slowly at first, then faster and harder, and the match's tiny explosion took his breath away. He held it gingerly, letting the rest drop from his lap as he raised to his knees, holding the match before him like a gift.

Above him, his mother's new curtains drifted in the spring breeze. A corner brushed the boy's hand, and suddenly the flame was no longer his but something alive and growing, climbing the curtain and spreading fast until the window was framed by fire. He grabbed the box, spilling matches over the floor. They rolled across the linoleum, beneath the table and chairs. He crawled after them, thinking that if he could just get them back in the box, put the box back on the counter, and walk out the door onto the porch where his mother sat nursing the baby, no one would know it was he who had been bad. He reached beneath the couch, where one had rolled, and touched instead the smooth black case of his father's new violin. The peeling wallpaper caught, its pale pattern disappearing as the fire ate deeper, through the newsprint insulation and into the walls. He stood up but did not scream, did not run outside to his mother, who might yet believe him the best boy—the quietest, most thoughtful, the wise and responsible one.

Perhaps then he heard his name, his mother's voice screaming at him from the door. He turned to her slowly, the smoke filling the room so that his eyes watered, and he saw how she held his brother at her breast and how the child still suckled, greedy and pawing. Only when his mother started to limp toward him did he move. He grabbed her hand and together they stumbled from the porch, falling to their knees on the hard-packed dirt, coughing for breath as the baby began to cry.

When the fire grew too hot to endure they moved, heading for the field. Only then did the boy think of his father, how in times before he might have seen the tall man jump from his tractor and come running to save them. He imagined the ground his father could cover, arms pumping, fists doubling with each stride. But the man was not in the field. He was in town, not to buy food or sell the heavy skimmed cream, but to drink.

From the muddy bank they watched bits of paper and blackened cloth rise on dark columns, knowing the neighbors would see the smoke and come running with their buckets and shovels. But it would be too late. It always was. The women would comfort the wife. The men would stand silent, spitting in the dirt, already planning their own run for whiskey.

My grandfather's drunks got longer and more frequent. The fire was not the reason: they had endured so much by then that fire seemed only a purer form of loss. The man remembered by his sons for his quickness and agility seemed to buckle as he walked. He had been known to jump from a moving tractor, come up holding a copperhead by its tail and be back in his seat before the snapped-off head hit the ground. The only singing he did was at the bar with the other men who could not face sober another season of stunted crops and government handouts. He often drank with his wife's father and her brother-in-law, and the four of them would disappear for days, finally staggering home filthy and hungover. My grandmother made him sleep on the porch and would not feed him until his chores were done. He was sheepish then, shamed and sorry, and worked like a man possessed, breaking the clay into rock-hard clods, filling the empty larder with fat squirrels and partridge.

The daughter married and moved away. The older boys became vigilant, protective of their mother, who sent them into town to search for their father in the beer joints. When they found him, they carried him to the old pickup and rolled him into the bed, where he slept the rough road home, bouncing about like a dead man.

In the spring of 1955, my grandmother stood on the porch, blocking the fierce Oklahoma sun with her raised hand. She peered across the field where the old creek bed ran. She had been waiting for her husband's drunken arrival when the noise had reached her—the muffled *whump* of earth and metal colliding.

Had the fools run off the road? She refused to allow herself fear, believing they were probably hanging from the doors even now, laughing and deciding it was as good a time as any to take a pee.

She waited for several minutes, then called Roland from

the house. With Ronnie, the oldest, in the service, it was Roland she relied on to handle her husband. Roland was not afraid of his father, and if need be, he could outrun the staggering man and hide until his rage died.

She watched Roland climb into the car and take off down the road, disappearing over the hill's crest, then saw him again as he crossed the bridge and dropped out of sight behind the trees. She stood there, feeling the cooling wind catch the thin skirt of her housedress, feeling the sweat run from beneath her arms and pool at her belted waist. When she saw her son again, his face was white behind the wheel. Even from a distance, she could see the red blotches covering his arms.

The boy staggered from the car. He was crying.

"What is it? Tell me. Are they dead?"

"Daddy's hurt bad. Real bad."

"Go fetch Uncle Everett. Do it now! Run!"

She turned and saw her youngest boy looking at her, his mouth drawn tight. "Get in the house. You go sit and be still, you hear?"

He was staring. Across the front of her, handprints bloomed like bloody roses.

My father wasn't there. He was a high school junior, gone to Lawton on a class trip. But when he stepped off the bus, he knew what the girl who waited for him, the one who worked as the local telephone operator, would say. He had dreamed it already: his father was dead.

The accident that killed my grandfather also killed my grandmother's father. Her brother-in-law, who had been driving and missed the bridge, sending the car nose-first into the dry creek bed, was injured but survived. What did my grandmother have left to sustain her? When the letter came from Idaho, they all agreed it would be a new start, a way for the boys to learn a trade. Clyde guaranteed them food and shelter, and that was more than she had ever been promised. Roland would stay behind until everything was sold—furniture, pickup, farm equipment, my grandfather's beloved hounds—and Ronnie would follow the next summer when his stint in the service ended. My father and his youngest brother boarded the train with their mother and headed for the Northwest.

Many times I heard my Uncle Clyde say, "I looked to those hills and thought, No man should ever go hungry here." Deer, elk, partridge, fish thick as a baby's leg from the smallest stream. And the trees, stretching from the Snake to the Clearwater, Lochsa and Selway, from Oregon and Washington to Montana. With hard work, guts and ingenuity, a man could feed his family and make money besides.

He had begun working for his brother at Waha, sending logs out by train north to Lewiston. He saved his money, took extra odd jobs, asked the markets for their old produce and bread, scavenged from garbage bins. Every fall, he shot one elk, one deer. Every summer, he and Daisy fished, filling milk cartons with rainbow trout, freezing them in solid blocks of ice. They harvested blackcaps, huckleberries, plums, cherries, apples, apricots, anything and everything they could gather or glean. With some of the fruit, she made pies and sold them to the cafes.

For one winter and one winter only, Clyde worked for Potlatch Forests Incorporated, mushing into the isolated logging camps along the North Fork of the Clearwater River with Daisy and their daughter, Peggy, bundled tight in the dogsled. The only women in the camps were prostitutes, whom Daisy, in her role as head cook, immediately put to work as flunkies serving three meals a day to long tables of hungry men, washing stacks of dishes, wringing from the plaid wool shirts and denim pants gallon after gallon of ambered water.

Clyde bought used and broken equipment, military surplus he rigged with booms and hitches. He was a genius with tools, gears and ratchets. What parts he couldn't buy, he made. He knew that his small wages were nothing compared with the profit gained by the company, and when after that first year he came out owing them money, he was determined to strike out on his own, to become what the loggers called a gyppo, independent of corporate ties. With a good crew he could do it.

By the time my father and his family came to live in the Clearwater National Forest, Clyde had cleared a site along Orofino Creek, within fifteen miles of Pierce, a town (population five hundred to one thousand, depending on the season) located ninety miles east and slightly north of Lewiston. He gave my grandmother her own shack, put the boys in another. For eight bits an hour, they cut and skidded, dodged wind-snapped crowns and barber-chaired fir, kicked-back saws and heart-rotted cedar. They spent the evenings gathered in the narrow room, laughing at how bad the injury might have been, how narrow the escape, how close Death got before they poked Him in the eye with a peavey, stomped His toe with spiked boots, buried Him beneath tons of piss pine. They laughed at their own foolishness, eight bits an hour while the old man got rich.

My father laughed loudest. When his brothers fought a frozen saw, cursed and kicked a jammed winch, my father laughed. He laughed as they tumbled over stumps, madder at him than the machinery. When he stripped a gear, knotted cable, caught an ankle while decking logs, he reacted calmly, taking one last drag off his Camel before bending to survey the damage, to undo what needed to be undone. There was nothing he couldn't make sense of, no breakdown or injury that couldn't be learned from.

"People kill the things they most love," said A. B. Guthrie, who knew as much as anybody about love of land. Day after day my father sawed, fell, limbed, skidded and burned what he lived for. The money, what little he earned, meant nothing. The woods, he said, had gotten in his blood.

In 1956, when my father called his high school sweetheart and asked her to marry him, the logging camps lay surrounded by hundreds of miles of uncut forest. The sites themselves consisted of five or six eight-by-twenty-foot clapboard trailers circled like a wagon train amid the new stumps and slash piles. Each trailer held a bed, woodstove, table, and two straight-back chairs. A few were equipped with primitive plumbing—a single sink that drained onto the dirt below.

When my mother came to Idaho, she was a young and lovely woman making her own escape into the wilderness. She told her grandmother with whom she lived that she would be back the next fall to finish school. She climbed into the car with Roland, her future brother-in-law, who had bartered and sold what was left of the family's possessions and was headed for the woods. It would be years before she returned, holding me by one hand, my brother straddling her hip.

She has told me the first months were hard, even though she loved my father and wanted to be with him. The weeks before the wedding, she stayed in my grandmother's small shack, sharing the double bed with her future mother-in-law. Unlike my father, she had no siblings, and the unaccustomed closeness of another left her unable to settle into sleep, fearing the movement of her own dreaming body.

As cramped and self-conscious as she was, she still believed herself lucky. She had spent much of her childhood in Oklahoma City. Her father was a professional gambler, a grifter, and their conditions were determined by his winnings. One day they would be rich; the next they would spend in a cheap motel where she and her mother waited the long hours for my grandfather's return. She remembers a period of several months, when she was four or five, spent in California, in a hotel whose lobby was draped in red velvet. There, while her parents slept late, she would wander the halls, accepting candy and coins from the bellboys and an old black porter, who placed in her palm each morning a new and shiny dime. She explored the surrounding avenues and stores, taking Princess Diamond Jill with her, the champion-sired English bulldog won by her father in a card game.

Princess moved with them to the house my mother remembers as a mansion, and in my own imagination the home and its contents have taken on fairy tale proportions: in the closets the relinquished clothes of a wealthy lawyer and his wife; brocade furniture; china plates and silverware and a pantry full of food; my mother carrying each dish from kitchen to table with painful care, feeling the fragility of crystal, trembling with the weighty roasts and brown gravy, while Red, as my grandfather was known, settled comfortably into the captain's chair, pulling from his pocket the heavy gold watch won from the man between whose elegant and ironed sheets he would soon sleep.

Then one night her mother woke her, wrapped her in a blanket and led her to the car—a shining Mercury with plush upholstery. No matter what else her father might win or lose, he always had a fine new car.

They left the house as they had found it—clothes neatly pressed and hung, the dishes nested in their windowed cabinets—as though their presence there had been weightless. Her father hunched behind the wheel. She could smell on him the hot bar smells—the sawdust mixed with spit and spilled beer, the rank whiskey, the perfume of someone she did not know. They headed west out of town. She watched the lights of Oklahoma City fade, and when she could see them no more, she laid her head against the window and gazed into the starred night sky, gently stroking the strong, broad back of the dog.

From California, they moved back to Luther, a small town southwest of Tulsa, where her maternal grandmother kept a small herd of dairy cows. After a time, her parents drove away, leaving her to a more stable life, normal in ways that seemed to matter: regular schooling, solid meals, a bedroom she could wake to each morning and believe herself home.

Certainly they made a wise decision. During the few periods my mother returned to live with them, she would sometimes stay at the bar they were running, eating when she felt like it, going to bed in the back room when she pleased, long before the last drinkers had stumbled out into the Oklahoma air, thick with the whir of cicadas. She watched the headlights trail across her walls, still hearing the clink of glasses, her father's rough laughter pushing her into sleep.

It's easy to romanticize my grandparents' ramblings, easy to see them as exquisitely lost in the economic and political wreckage that was our country during those years. Oklahoma has always symbolized hardship and grit, peopled by the disenfranchised and disillusioned. Anyone who could survive the hostile weather, could scratch out a living from the hard red clay, was made of something extraordinary, like the blackjack oak growing from the creek bottoms, twisted by wind and stunted by drought, strong as steel at the core.

But for my mother, there was nothing novel about her

parents' absence, nothing humorous in the stories they told of their adventures on the road. She distanced herself from them, went to school, took care of her aunt Sarah, Granny's youngest daughter, born nearly ten years after my mother, and did her farm chores. One day, she came home to find Princess missing. She searched the barn, the creek bed, crawled beneath the house, where the cat lay blinking, nursing her newest litter, and called until her voice cracked and the sky darkened.

Several years ago, I overheard a relative say that my grandfather had needed money to pay a gambling debt and sold the dog. As tough as Granny could be, I imagine her telling my mother that Princess had been hit by a car, holding her while she cried, stroking her hair, shushing her. "We'll get you another dog, now. Don't you worry." And then to herself, the words I myself have heard her say: *Always knew he was a snake in the grass. Man never was no good.*

What my father and his family left to come to Idaho was economic hardship and the painful memory of a man who had once been a caring husband and father. My mother left even less—a family connected only by blood. That first camp my parents shared was made up of orphans—my father and his brothers; my mother, running from parents already dead to her; my grandmother, at once widowed and made fatherless; her sister; and my uncle Clyde, raised by his sister after losing his parents in a flu epidemic. That circle was more than a practical formation of community: it held all their pain and remaining strength, the combined belief that they could survive.

My mother was drawn into the circle by my father's love, and what remained of his life became hers. My grandmother,

whom everyone called Nan, cast herself in the role of matriarch, and the relationship they had was both fiercely intimate
and silently combative. From the beginning, Nan, whose
strong nature had given her an indomitable will and a ruling
tongue, took on the task of turning my mother into a fit and
proficient wife and daughter-in-law. Since my father had no
money of his own to pay for the wedding, having given it all
to Nan, it was she who paid for—and picked out—my
mother's wedding dress: a blue wool suit, simple white blouse,
and pillbox hat. My mother wanted a traditional gown, but
Nan scoffed at the idea of spending so much money on something that could never again be worn. The suit, she reasoned,
would do for church and funerals as well.

As disappointed as my mother was, the only emotion that
showed in her face as she prepared for the wedding was joy.
The photographs catch her tucking in her blouse, elbows
akimbo, nearly knocking the walls of the small shack. Her
elegance belies her age—sixteen—and the suit gives her an air
of sophistication. Tall, with a thin waist and shapely legs, she
resembles the movie stars her own mother as a teenager had
cut from the pages of magazines and pasted in a scrapbook,
one of them, Claudette Colbert, her namesake.

When the short ceremony ended, my uncles chased my
parents through the streets of Pierce and down the hair-
raising descent of Greer Grade (Roland passing on the right,
making my flatlander mother nearly faint with fear that he
would sail off the road and plunge into the canyon below) to a
little tavern on the river. There, they drank and laughed till
nearly dawn, then drove the grade back to the dirt roads rutted by logging trucks and into the woods, speeding alongside
the creeks and onto even rougher roads before arriving back at
camp, where they stepped out of the car and my father lifted
my mother over the steps made of bucked-up cedar and into

their own small trailer, still warm with the familiar heat of August.

Two years after moving her belt-lapped suitcase into my father's one-room shack, two years after being married by the Pentecostal minister and his preacher wife, my mother packed her bag again, then sat on the trailer's threshold and shaved her swollen legs. It was May, one week before her due date. She had rearranged her few articles of linen, bleached her hair, painted her nails a snappy pink, and said a prayer of thanks each night for the weight of her husband's hand resting on the shelf of her stomach.

Six days later, when her water broke, Aunt Daisy left a message for my father—"Tell him it's time"—and drove my mother to Nan's, who had remarried and moved to Lewiston. She soaked in the tub, hot running water a luxury, the tub even more so. When the pains started, she loaded her bag in the backseat and drove herself and Nan to the hospital.

The labor was hard and fast. Nan remembered my mother, eighteen years old, her own family a thousand miles away, bravely preparing her mother-in-law for the worst: "Nan, I might have to scream." And then, after enduring the labor, after pushing her baby from its watery chamber until its head bore down against the hard pelvis, just as the pain turned to an urge, a desire so strong she lunged toward her own spread knees, just as the baby was about to become real—flesh and bone, dark hair, blue eyes, a girl like she wanted, the first one a girl—the doctor breezed in, nuns tying strings, snapping gloves, and covered her face, filling her lungs with the stench of ether to stop the pain he could not imagine, thinking to save her from that wrenching moment when I slid into the hands of a stranger and began to wail.

CHAPTER THREE

In late fall kokanee the color of rosewood crowd the shallow tributaries of the North Fork of the Clearwater River. Land-locked salmon, they have made their way from deeper waters to spawn, and the beautiful mass of red they become is the result of their bodies' decay.

We lived for years along the banks of these creeks—Orofino, Weitas, Kelly—our destination determined by what timber sale my great-uncle had bid upon and, finally, by the lay of the land: we leveled our trailers atop the flatness of meadows, or maneuvered them between the stumps of a clear-cut.

Perhaps because I was so young, what remains with me about those camps is not the trees and mountains, not the streams pulsing with red as the days shortened; what remains is a sense rather than a memory of place, a composite of smells, sounds and images: the closeness of my parents as they slept beside me when the temperature dropped below zero; my mother's hair tightly curling around my fingers; cigarettes, coffee, sweat, diesel, the turpentine scent of pine.

In winter, our shack darkened by early dusk, the single kerosene lantern illuminated my mother's face as she worked biscuit dough across the oilcloth table. The door would open and my father step in, shedding sawdust like snow. He'd lay down his black pail and steel thermos and grin at my mother as though he had something wonderful to tell, something to make us jump and clap, something so good she'd wrap her arms around his neck and he'd swing her in circles, knocking down chairs, tilting the nail-hung cupboard, causing the flour to fly.

He'd lean over the table, careful with his diesel-stained clothes, never moving his calked boots from that one spot on the wooden floor, a place pocked and gouged, soft as tenderized meat. They would kiss, once, twice, and then he'd turn to where I played on our shared bed, nesting my doll in flannel shirts, covering her with tea towels, waiting for the grace of his smile.

Even now, my parents speak of those first years in the woods as somehow magical. As poor as we were, we ate well. In summer, we picked huckleberries big as cherries, jerked trout from the shadowed bends of creeks, wrapping them in leaves of skunk cabbage. For Nan and Aunt Daisy, the cold-water char were a delicacy, so different from the muddy catfish they lived on as children. Fried in cornmeal and lard, the small brookies turned golden. Each year until 1988, when my grandmother died, I took her my first catch of the season. She added nothing, only the fish neatly arranged across her plate —no fork or knife, only her fingers pulling from the bones sliver after sliver of pure white meat.

The men could step a few yards from camp and take their limit of deer and elk, enough to fill several town lockers with stew meat and roasts. I still associate the smell of blood, the mounds of entrails steaming in new snow, with fall. One season, it was a bear they hung from the loader's boom. Gutted and skinned, it swung in the cooling wind, pink and muscled as the body of a man. It was the one thing my mother could not eat, sweet and tallowy, like the mutton she despised as a child.

My mother found herself surrounded by mountains. The friends she had left in Oklahoma had by now finished their schooling. Most were having babies of their own, keeping house in Tulsa or moving into Oklahoma City to clerk at Woolworth's. The few letters she received she kept tied in a ribbon, tucked away in some secret place.

She rose before dawn each morning to fix my father's breakfast—venison steak and eggs, home-baked bread toasted on the cast-iron stove top, coffee boiled black in its aluminum pot. While he ate, she packed his lunch, filling the dented bucket with sandwiches and fried pies—golden half-moon pastries made with dried apricots. His work clothes hung from the beams, the thick flannel shirt and black pants washed the day before and ironed to a shine.

After his kiss at the door, she watched him climb into his truck, its blue exhaust disappearing into the dark sky like a heaven-bound spirit. When I awoke, she lay sleeping beside me. The kerosene lantern still burned, its reflection lost in the sunlit window.

We hauled laundry to the wash shed, where the gas-powered wringer washer sat like a giant toad, all belly and noise. Uncle Clyde had connected a large reservoir to the woodstove there, and by building a popping fire, we had enough hot water to wash our clothes and bathe. While I splashed in a small galvanized tub, my mother hummed in the makeshift shower stall fed by pipes running from the water tank.

When Nan first arrived in Idaho, Aunt Daisy had immediately set about matching her younger sister to one of the numerous eligible loggers. She settled on Elmer Edmonson, a widower, known locally as the Little Giant. His small stature belied his strength, and his reputation was that of a hardworking and fearless lumberjack. He and my grandmother moved out of the woods to Lewiston, into the house he had shared with his first wife, who had died of cancer. Nan set up housekeeping with the dishes and linens of another woman, grateful to have what was given her.

Soon after their marriage in 1956, while working a site near Craig Mountain, my step-grandfather was severely injured ducking beneath a log to secure a choker cable. The log rolled, crushing his skull. By the time they got him to the hospital in Lewiston, his head had swollen to the size of a watermelon, the flesh split from the pressure, yet he never lost consciousness. My parents shudder when they speak of it. No one less strong and determined could have survived, they say.

My grandmother nursed him constantly, and it was only as an adult that I was told how the kindly, shaking old man could turn suddenly manic, returning home from the grocery store with gallons and gallons of ice cream or giving away every dime in his pocket to strangers on the street. He had violent seizures and hallucinations, and the family would have no choice but to commit him to the state mental hospital at Orofino until his episodes subsided.

I don't remember his bizarre behavior or sudden, unexplained absences. Instead, I remember the evenings spent visiting Nan, waiting for Grandpa to come home from his rounds as a salesman hawking Rawleigh spices and liniment door-to-door. He would draw from his pocket a rolled purse of soft leather, jingling with coins that I dumped onto the floor, stacking the dimes and quarters into towering columns, breathing in the blood-sharp smell of copper.

In the camps, my mother was left with Aunt Daisy, who gave her little attention, believing that a woman's duty was to provide her husband with every bit and moment of herself, so that even in his absence her hands were busy making his meals, scrubbing the pitch from his clothes, snapping and smoothing fresh sheets for his bed. She counseled my mother to do the same, reminding her that the needs and love of a child must come second to the ties between husband and wife. She offered another piece of wisdom: the only power women have in this world is sex. A smart wife knew when to offer herself and when to hold back. There was little a husband wouldn't do if teased and denied enough.

By the time my father arrived home, my mother had cleaned the shack's every corner. Brown beans bubbled on the stove, and the room seemed honeyed with the smell of cornbread cooked in a cast-iron skillet. Her hair was neatly curled and combed, her fingernails painted. My own long hair she drew up in a bow so that my father might be pleased.

The trailer's size made it impossible to gather more than a few people in at once, but on weekends my uncles squeezed around the table for a game of cards. The bed was mine, an oasis of softness and warmth where I played with my dolls and listened to the men's stories. Their days were full of giant things—machinery and trees, the noise of saws and snapping cables. They wore their wounds, deep cuts and bloody gouges, with the nonchalance of immortals, doctoring themselves with turpentine and alcohol. I fell asleep, protected from the outside world by my father's strength, by his laughter, louder than the screech of tree against tree as the wind whipped the darkness.

Injuries in the woods are common and expected: deep punctures from snagged limbs, twisted ankles, bruises from falling off decked logs—traumas so small they rarely warrant mention. The real danger lies in the dance of machinery and wood. In the hands of a seasoned logger the saw seems tamed, teeth directed easily toward a precise and efficient cut. But green wood cannot be predicted, nor can the saw's instantaneous reaction to what lies hidden in the heart of fir, tamarack and pine. Kickback—the saw ricocheting off a knot or warp deep in the tree's interior—seldom leaves the logger unscathed. If he's lucky, he has no time to turn his head, and the razored chain cuts only his face. If instinctively he does jerk away, the teeth find a truer mark—the neck. Even with good roads and helicopters, help cannot reach a man fast enough to staunch the flow of blood from a severed jugular.

One local logger decapitated himself, slipping from a log, his chainsaw still running. Another died when a cable snapped and the loader's boom plummeted. Some are killed, simply and predictably, when the tree, set loose from its base, twists in an unexpected way. A tree will sometimes "barber-chair"—splinter vertically from a perfect half-cut, catching the faller squarely in the chest with enough force to crush or impale him against the next nearest trunk. Bulldozers roll. An unstable slope gives way and sends the logs, loader and man tumbling down the mountain.

The year I turned four my father lay housebound, a cast from armpit to hip. He had ruptured a vertebra that winter while trying to turn a pole with a peavey. After his surgery, we moved to Lewiston, in with Nan and Grandpa Edmonson for the six months it would take for his back to heal.

Workman's Compensation paid only forty-one dollars a week, so while my father recuperated, my mother worked morning shift at Kube's Korner Kafe. I had never seen so much of my father. The smoke from his cigarettes filled the small house. He read every western he could get his hands on, played solitaire and watched without comment the dramas of other people's lives unfold on daytime television. What I recall most is the card table set up in the kitchen for his puzzles— thousands of intricately cut pieces sorted by edge and color, which he patiently worked into perfect pictures of mountains and wildflowers—near replicas of the landscape they had hauled him from.

He showed me how the pieces fit, taking my wrist in his fingers, swiveling my hand, redirecting a corner. He smelled different—still smoky, but less like earth than pot roast and my grandmother's sacheted linen. I forgot to miss that other father, the logger who came home in twilight, bringing my mother wild iris, bending easily to kiss me.

Even though he walked with a noticeable hitch and lifting a saw made spasms ripple my father's rib cage, when the cast was off we headed back to the woods. This time we settled into a small green house in Pierce proper. Pierce was named for Captain Elias D. Pierce, a California prospector who discovered gold there in 1860; within a year of his discovery, the townsite had been cut and cleared, making room for the miners, gamblers and prostitutes who lived, at least for a short time, in the booming heyday of the town. Along with them came a large influx of Chinese workers, and for many of them the West and its riches also held horror: three miles southwest of Pierce is Hangmans Gulch, now a designated historical site. There, in 1885, five Chinese unjustly accused of brutally murdering a local businessman were dragged from their cells by vigilantes and hung on a makeshift gallows.

Placer mining came first, and soon the hills were pocked with lode claims and ore mining, sites with names such as the Democrat and the Mascot, the American, the Dewey, the Pioneer, the Ozark, the Crescent and the Wild Rose; the Oxford, the Klondike on French Creek, the Rosebud. Then came the dredges with their greater capacity to scoop the gold from its bed, working the waters of Canal Gulch, Rhodes Creek, the Orogrande.

My father remembers the early days in Pierce, when the road was mud in spring and dust in summer and boardwalks fronted the bars and the single hotel. Now we had the luxury of a sidewalk down both sides, which the merchants kept shoveled and salted in winter to encourage business. Rape's Grocery Store and Meat Locker, Durant's Dry Goods, a beauty shop, bar and the post office lined the street's north side. Across was the Clearwater Hotel and Cafe, where old-timers sat for hours behind the large front window, still uniformed in black denim and red suspenders, spitting into Folger's cans. Some wore hard hats. When they waved, light shone through where fingers once had been.

We settled into the boomtown gone drowsy, our rented house only slightly larger than the camp shacks. Perhaps this was done thinking that my mother would be happiest living in town, closer to stores and the company of other women, especially since my brother had been born and she now had two children to contend with. And maybe she was happier. Maybe it is only my own feelings I remember in that house—of being closed up, kept behind doors with locking latches.

We were less isolated—neighbors often stopped by for coffee, and ready-made bread and fresh beef were as close as Rape's store—but some part of the magic was gone. Unlike my mother and my aunts, "Pierce women" (as I heard them referred to in the coded kitchen conversation) did not live in the camps with their husbands, but took up permanent residence in town. Most were born and raised in the area and had married into other logging families. They learned to dress and order their households in deference to the mud and deep snow. They often wore their husband's clothing, as did my mother, but I remember them differently: their shirt cuffs hung unbuttoned; their pants sagged in the seat. They cut their hair into no-nonsense bobs permed tight to their heads, and their only makeup was an occasional slash of red applied haphazardly in the pickup's rearview. They sucked at their cigarettes like old men, eyes crinkling against the smoke.

My mother must have missed those first few years in camp, when she and her new husband slept snugged together on their single cot, never minding the thin mattress and close edges, forgetting there ever was another world. My father's injury made her realize how easily she could be left alone, and she awaited his return each evening with growing uneasiness. She listened to the stories other women told—how the wife had opened the door, already knowing with the first knock, already disbelieving the words she had always feared to hear: the dozer rolled; the chain snapped; that one tree, the *widow-maker*, gave in to the wind it had withstood for decades and came down like a javelin. Always, they told the grieving wife, death was quick, the one belief she could hold on to as she passed into her life like the newly blinded—feeling for thresholds, leaning heavily on the counter's edge.

When one day our town neighbor came running across the muddy yard, fear on her face that could mean only one thing, my mother fell against the window, clutching the curtain to her breast. In those few moments before the woman burst in, half her head still in curlers, the other half sprung loose in ribbons of hair—my mother donned the shroud of a widow.

But it was not my mother the woman mourned for but Jackie Kennedy, and as we all sat before the neighborhood's only television, my mother cried for the country, for the slain president, for the widow in her brain-spattered dress, for the long hours she herself had yet to endure, waiting for my father to come home.

There is a trileveled hierarchy in woodswork. True logging—falling, limbing, skidding and hauling timber to be made into lumber—is at the top; making shakes and shingles is at the bottom, and only those who for whatever reason cannot find work as lumberjacks split cedar. Between these two is pole-making: the cutting, skinning and hauling of cedar trees straight and uniform enough to be made into telephone and electrical poles. Uncle Clyde found that, with the help of his nephews, he could cut and skin record numbers of poles, taking advantage of an opportunity left open by the prejudice of others. Buyers were amazed by the loads hauled off the steeply pitched mountains—the long, thin trunks still whole, not cracked or snapped by carelessness—and paid my great-uncle well.

One summer, he bet my father and uncles a town dinner that they couldn't clear the pole sale on Mockingbird Hill in a single week. They began cutting at dawn, urging each other on, giving everything they had to beat the old man's bet, even though they knew the smallness of his wager. They worked steadily until the light drained from the trees and their backs ached with the weight of peaveys and saws, then drove back to camp to eat and sleep, happy as they had ever been in their lives.

They won the bet. Uncle Clyde took them to Lewiston and treated them to a platter of sweet red spaghetti at Italian Gardens. My father still laughs with pleasure at the memory of them all there together—four young men, boys, really, the oldest just twenty-five—working their way through the dense underbrush, clearing and skidding with the skill of seasoned lumberjacks, at home in a land the folks back in Oklahoma could imagine only as full of bear and cougar, a wilderness so untamed a man could lose himself in broad daylight only yards from his doorstep. My father remembers how good that spaghetti tasted. He remembers a time when all that mattered to any of them was the sure strength of their arms and the direction a tree might fall.

By the time I was ready to start school, Uncle Clyde had established a more permanent camp just off the main road between Pierce and Headquarters. It was across from a pole yard, a large landing where thousands of peeled poles rose in decks stacked fifty feet high. We called our new home Pole Camp, and once again we circled and leveled the trailers, but this time they were more fixed. Uncle Clyde and Aunt Daisy built themselves a frame house and painted it green. The men erected a large, two-story garage in which they could work on machinery in the coldest weather. Some of the smaller shacks were pushed together; ours, two trailers connected to form a

T, had an indoor toilet. We were close enough to town to have electricity. One day, Uncle Clyde ran a wire from trailer to trailer and into each of the long wooden boxes he had hung on our walls. The first time our new telephone rang, I held the black, bell-shaped receiver away from my ear, startled to hear my father's bodiless voice.

The shortest trailers, just large enough to accommodate a bunk, stove and wash pan, went to the itinerant sawyers who hired on for the season. Each in his turn was called "Swede," and when Aunt Daisy sent me to fetch them for dinner, the answer came from the doorway left open to air the smoke of their pipes and tightly rolled cigarettes: "Yah, um comin!" Their rounded consonants and opened vowels were a song to me, but I never worked up the courage to top the steps and pass into their secret lives: always dark, even the single square window curtained with a towel, the smell of woodsmoke and boot grease and that particular odor of old bachelors alone with their woolen underwear—sometimes, the whiskey on their breath, the heavy sharp scent of it as they came to the door, pulling up their suspenders, rubbing their teeth with rough knuckles.

My uncles each married women with children and soon brought their new families into our circle. Suddenly, my mother was rich in female companionship—women her own age to share her days with, other mothers struggling with the demands of young children. Suddenly I had cousins. My bed was no longer my own but a place where boys jumped with their dirty shoes and girls squabbled over my dolls. Aunts and uncles gathered close in our kitchen for long weekend games of pinochle and Monopoly, smoke from their cigarettes filling the air to a barroom haze.

• • •

In winter, after the rains when temperatures dropped far below zero and the heavy freeze set in, the loggers could continue their cutting, shoveling snow from around the trees' base, moving equipment across the icy clearings with the help of studded tires and chains. But for the pole-makers, winter meant no work: when the slim and fragile poles began snapping like toothpicks in the crackling cold, we would pack what we could into the trunk of our car, resting our feet on boxes and paper bags, and be suddenly gone from the woods to Lewiston, where my father and uncles would work swing shift at the mill or pump gas at the Texaco until the weather moderated.

The road leading from Pierce to Lewiston is narrow and winding, descending from the Weippe Prairie (pronounced "Wee-ipe") to the Clearwater River in a series of steep and pitching curves. The last fifty miles is river road, the part of Highway 12 now referred to as the Clearwater Canyon Scenic Byway. The entire trip took less than three hours—across flat farmland nestled between stands of timber; past Fraser Park (named after David Fraser, the man supposedly murdered by the Chinese), complete with a rough baseball diamond, a single set of warped pine bleachers and a galvanized-pipe swing set; down the grade with its switchback turns so tight the trucks with their long loads of poles took both lanes at the curves; across the bridge at Greer and past Orofino with its doctors and tiny airport said to be cursed so that all owners died in fiery crashes while trying to maneuver their single-engine planes between the highway and parallel water; alongside the widening Clearwater to its confluence with the Snake at the mouth of Hells Canyon—out of the absolute blackness of nights in the forest into a city of twenty-four-hour markets and cars lined up at the intersections ten deep.

As the years of our travel passed, Greg, four years younger, would listen intently as I read to him from the Children's Library of Classics our parents had purchased with the set of encyclopedias we hauled with us from one place to the next. Arabian Nights, Robinson Crusoe, King Arthur, Robin Hood, Treasure Island, Swiss Family Robinson—the worlds I fantasized were lush with exotic flowers, full of giant pythons and man-eating natives, populated by gossamer fairies, men and women who conversed in words I had never heard spoken, words I mispronounce to this day because their sounds existed only in my mind's ear: *joust, vizier, yeoman.*

The books kept me anchored—not in the real world, but in worlds I carried with me, stacked neatly in a cardboard box I balanced on my knees as the heavy car leaned into the curves of the road. I marked the miles reciting lines from Tennyson's "The Idylls of the King":

> *"My good blade carves the casques of men,*
> *My tough lance thrusteth sure,*
> *My strength is as the strength of ten,*
> *Because my heart is pure."*

The sentiment echoed that of the children's hymns we sang when my grandmother took us to Sunday school: *Onward Christian soldiers, marching as to war* . . . Reading the tales of Arthur, I mooned over the mystery of the Silent Maid, whose throat was as white and round as the cup of a lily and who waited silently for the arrival of Perceval. I thought that if I could not be a queen I might be the Maid, who "prayed and fasted till the sun/Shone and the wind blew through her."

My fantasies of feminine loyalty and sacrifice would be interrupted by my brother's yell that he could see the mill as we came into Lewiston. Its towering smokestacks belched out sulfuric steam, and the fog rising from the giant settling ponds shrouded the river and road in a foul mist. The lights seemed blinding, so bright they swallowed the stars and left nothing secret. Sometimes I'd move my box to the center of the seat and sink down to the floorboard, where I covered my head with my coat and made a night for myself: through the seams, pinpricks of light shone through and I imagined constellations of my own naming: *Avalon, Galahad, the Holy Grail.*

One winter there was no travel. Instead of heading to Lewiston, we remained circled at the edge of the meadow, where elk grazed, herds of a hundred or more filling the evening air with high-pitched whistles and barks. The men had decided to wait out the cold. They pooled their dole, and for a short time we were rich in food: canned fruit filled the cupboards; bags of beans slouched in the corners of the rooms like woozy children. The single refrigerator we all shared burgeoned with carrots and cartons of Camels, so that the air wafting from the opened Frigidaire carried the mixed incense of sweet earth and tobacco.

My father and uncles filled their deer and elk tags, and then those bought in their wives' names. Night after night they came through the door, a haunch or back strap thrown over their shoulders, or the full body of a yearling, lean and tender. The women worked at the counter and table spread with butcher paper, trimming and boning. Whatever meat was left after the steaks and roasts were cut was fed into the hand-cranked grinder and mixed with pepper and sage for sausage.

Snow drifted against the windows, filtering the winter light to charcoal. The circle became a wheel with shoveled spokes leading from its center to each trailer door. As the days grew shorter the snow deepened until the pathways became corridors rising several feet above our heads.

My mother rose early enough to pack my lunch and send me off to catch the bus, but my father often slept past noon. On weekends, I watched them linger over their coffee before beginning their daily chores. While my father split and stacked another day's firewood, my mother prepared her share of the communal meal—mixing flour and shortening into pie dough, filling the shells with syrupy fruit, or sorting the beans as bacon browned in the bottom of the soup pot.

Those winter afternoons, the aunts and cousins arrived first, bringing with them the smells of woodsmoke and freshly baked bread. By the time the men had gathered in, slapping their hats against their knees, the snow on their backs already melting, the plates were laid out and the bread cut. The other children and I ate where we wanted—on the couch or cross-legged on the floor—and no one cared that we coaxed out thick wedges of pie with our fingers. Miraculously set free of baths and bedtime, we whispered secrets, shielded from our parents' view by a makeshift tepee of wool blankets. As long as we kept our quarrels to ourselves and minded the general rules of the household, we were blissfully ignored.

While the women cleared and washed the dishes, the men leaned back in their chairs, sucking on toothpicks. After the dishes were done and another pot of coffee put on to perk, the adults scooted their chairs closer around the table and began their game of poker or pinochle that would last long into the night. The snow and below-zero temperatures meant little more to them than inches and degrees: no matter how bad the blizzard, no matter how low the thermometer dropped, we were safe in the circle, with enough food and fuel to keep us for weeks, the gift of land to sustain us—wood to burn, package after package of frozen venison, spring water cold and plentiful running pure beneath a crystalline crust of ice.

Uncle Clyde had known what Idaho offered to people made poor by Oklahoma dust, and we were blessed to be there. What went on in the rest of the world—whatever wars raged in the jungles of foreign countries, whatever prices rose and fell—could not affect us. Our days were made of ourselves. There was little to pull us outside that circle.

I realize now that my mother and aunts were some of the first women to reside in the camps. Before, without the machinery needed to punch through roads, the men left their families at home. Only men manned the cookstoves and loaders, made the coffee and skidded the poles. The closest women were town whores, who hung from upstairs windows and called sweet things to the loggers in their cleated boots, wages heavy in their pockets.

During the mid-fifties and early sixties, logging equipment became more advanced and efficient, capable of reaching into the deepest pockets of virgin timber. New roads crosshatched the mountainsides, and existing roads were improved to allow easier passage of the machinery. With the improvement in access, most of the camps were abandoned altogether, and those that remained served only as temporary shelter for the loggers, who arrived in town late Friday evening, spent weekends with family, and left hours before dawn Monday morning to begin the week's work. Pole Camp was a compromise, close enough for the men to make their daily commutes, but isolated enough to make us believe the wilderness still touched us.

Like my mother, my aunts were beautiful women. Dorothy, Ronnie's wife, had deep auburn hair, which she combed into an elegant chignon before breakfast. She was from Tennessee, and she carried herself with all the elegance of a horsewoman born to Southern aristocracy. I shivered at the pure beauty of her town clothes—matching high heels and purses, emerald greens, black patent leathers—and the way words dripped off her tongue, slow as winter syrup.

Aunt Bev was only slightly less displaced in the winter snow and spring mud than Aunt Dorothy. Born in Texas, she mixed her own Southern drawl with that of her new Oklahoma relatives, who teased her, as border-sharers often do, about her home state allegiances. She was barely five feet tall and even when pregnant never moved the scale above a hundred pounds. (Her husband, Roland, stood over six feet, as do all the Barnes brothers.) She reminded me of my Barbie dolls —a tiny waist and blond hair looped and pinned in a fashionable twist. She was the only woman I knew who wore false eyelashes, and she taught her sisters-in-law how to mend a torn nail with cigarette papers and clear polish. My strongest memory of her is shooing me and my cousins out the door and locking it behind us, ensuring that her newly mopped floors would remain spotless until her husband got home. I see her standing on the threshold in a summer top and tight knit pants, broom clutched in one hand, the other hand cocked on her hip, enchanting in her blue eyeshadow and pink lipstick.

Other than my father, Uncle Barry, the youngest brother, remained the longest. He brought to the woods a woman from Colorado named Mary, and with her came Lezlie, a little girl with startling white hair and green eyes. I was a year older than she was, and the relationship we established in our shared yard became less that of cousins than sisters, with all its inherent jealous rages and intimacies.

Mary had the high cheekbones of her Indian mother. She came without pretense, equally at home in the trees as on the sage and cinnamon plains of Colorado. Her beauty was enhanced only a little by makeup and polish: large brown eyes and dark lashes gave her an exotic appearance even when she fluttered at the door in her soot-streaked bathrobe, and no matter how long the winter, her face and arms seemed bronzed.

She, too, left a life less than fortunate. The women in her family had run their men off, sometimes with the help of a gun, and her first marriage had lasted less than a year. She entered into our family with the bravado of a woman used to making her own way, and her spontaneity and the childlike pleasure she took in games and holidays often lent a carnival-like atmosphere to our get-togethers.

Each morning, the wives rose first to make their husbands' breakfast, then stood at the door to see the men drive off into the pre-dawn light. They waved, hollering their day's plans to each other across the yard before turning back to wake the older children for school. After the dishes had been done, the laundry hung to dry or sprinkled and rolled to be ironed later, my mother would take the cap off the tea kettle and whistle from the door, then wait for the long, high-pitched reply to echo across the meadow.

What time they did not spend baking or sewing they filled with wishing: mail-order catalogs cluttered the table. I often came home from school to find one of the women perched primly in a child's high chair while another cut her hair, Sears models for inspiration, or one of the aunts straight-backed as a Buddha, clothespins numbing her earlobes, waiting for another to sterilize the darning needle over a kitchen match. I couldn't bear to watch the needle punched through to its backing of raw potato or cork, and hid in my room, covering my head with a blanket.

During the high-altitude heat of summer, we loaded the

car with iced tea and root beer, sandwiches and fried pies, and drove to the creek. While my cousins and I waded the shallow current, hunting periwinkles and crawdads, our mothers lounged on old sheets, their bathing suit straps undone, draping their shoulders.

They seemed glamorous and distant then, leaned back on their elbows, one knee slightly raised, not at all like the same women we saw scooping up their husbands' piled work clothes, mixing batter for breakfast, still wearing long johns and flannel to fend off the night's lingering chill. On the banks and small pebbled beaches of the Musselshell they smoked and talked quietly, calling us in when we ventured too far, threatening early naps and spankings when we quarreled. I would look up from my pool of tadpoles and see them perfectly composed against the sheets' white backdrop, smooth legs positioned to flatter, as though the world might be watching, judging their flat stomachs and ruby nails.

Often I forget how young my mother and aunts were, barely into their twenties. Their men coming home must have meant everything, and to welcome them with golden shoulders and sun-tinted hair was an offering: *Even here, in the deep forests of Idaho, in the wilderness, I can give you what you desire, what you love the most.*

The men returned each evening to find them tanned, glowing, arranging children and pork chops with equal ease. They must have wondered what kept them there—women any man might long for. Certainly, my father and uncles were jealous of their wives' attention. I imagine that when the itinerant buckers and sawyers visited our camp, the women kept busy in the kitchen. All knew the few things that could fill a man's gut when the isolation and deep-woods silence set his teeth to chattering for something he could almost taste, like the sweet whisper of last night's whiskey: more whiskey came easy from the town taverns, but not the shoulder of a woman, bared for his mouth and no other.

Eventually, the isolation and lack of even minimal luxuries such as indoor toilets and hot running water took their toll. By 1966 my aunts and cousins were gone, settled into city homes with yards and draped windows. My father must have felt the circle tighten, at its center my mother—the one who stayed, who never asked for more, who had been raised to believe each kindness shown her a gift, every grace mercurial as moonlight.

CHAPTER FOUR

With the family gone, my parents were left to find for themselves what comfort and communion resided in the wilderness. The circle was broken. Even the land seemed to have
lost its balance. I half-listened to men talk of helicopters and
shutdowns, of a new machine with clipperlike jaws that could
do the work of twenty good sawyers—snipping off trees at the
base, mowing them down like ripe wheat. The adults shook
their heads, perhaps foreseeing what I could not: the stores
closing, the town deserted.

The forest must have seemed to them, as it did to me,
inexhaustible. I knew no one who had flown above the trees to
see the clearcuts scabbing the land like mange. There would
always be more timber on the next ridge, another stand of
cedar over the rise. It was like picking huckleberries, like find-

ing a good patch, fruit as big as your thumb and everywhere. You strip one bush, surrounded by others just as lush, and you find yourself panicking to get them all; though they stretch as far as you can see, you want them all.

Some of the loggers packed up and took jobs at the pulp and paper mill in Lewiston, sorting green lumber, checking plywood for warp, initialing case after case of toilet paper. Others remained, hitting the bars before staggering home still sticky with pitch, forgetting to kiss their waiting wives. The wives forgot to fear for their husbands when the wind rose, and feigned sleep when rough hands touched their hips.

My father dug in, determined to stay. He had seen how the dispossessed could turn to liquor and how liquor could in turn possess the soul, as had my mother. Perhaps because it was she who felt the impending isolation most keenly, she was the first to turn to fundamentalism. I'm sure that the presence of the Pentecostal preacher and his wife who had married my parents was a comfort in the absence of family. She began attending services, relating to her husband the words of joy and faith—the promised sustenance the Bible offered.

The Bible and its teachings were not unfamiliar to my father. His mother's roots were Baptist. The songs she had sung for them spoke of life's hard road and Heaven's sure peace, and I'm certain that Hell was made real by her readings from the Scripture. Still, I can only guess at what drew my normally shy father to the small group of Pentecostal worshipers who gathered several times a week to praise God in loud voices and denounce the ways of the world. Was he intrigued by the unequivocal dictates of the religion? Given his life—the seemingly haphazard set of circumstances and catastrophes that had beset his family—the sterile reasoning of an all-knowing God negated the need to question. What comfort it must have seemed for a man and his family come to the wilderness, escaping whatever demons that had threatened to destroy them. What he believes is that it was the Spirit that spoke to him, that it was my mother's faith and prayers that led him to pick up the Bible she had left on the table and begin reading the words that would change and direct his life.

And so my life is divided by this line: before the church, and after. In the photographs taken those first years when she played with her husband and his brothers like a child set loose from school, my mother is startlingly beautiful. More often than not, she wears a pair of my father's jeans, a man's shirt and cast-off logging boots. She poses on a stump, tall and slender, or rides the boom of a loader, looking playful and brave, game for anything. Her lips are colored red or deep pink to match her nails, and her hair is short, wisping at her neck and temples. She reminds me of Ingrid Bergman in *For Whom the Bell Tolls,* and, like her, my mother's bobbed hair gives her a boyish prettiness, making her seem even more feminine and vulnerable.

I don't remember the moment my mother pulled the golden hoops from her ears, collected her carefully chosen tubes of lipstick, gathered her swimsuit and open-necked blouses and pushed them all into the drawers' dark corners. Nor do I remember the moment my father began to believe that angels and devils walked among us, in the groves of cedar and stands of tamarack, that their voices could be heard above the saw's loud litany. What I know is that our lives shifted. Where before we had thrown our suitcases and boxes into the car and left one home for another on a day's notice, we could now make no move, no matter how small, without careful consideration and prayer. Three times a day we prayed over meals. When my father left for work, we prayed for his safety; when he arrived home that evening, we prayed in thanks. If the car developed a rattle, we prayed as my father leaned into the tangle of wires and hoses, asking God to give him the knowledge to fix it, or for God to fix it Himself, knowing, as He must, how little money we had to spend.

My father's authoritative presence became absolute, my mother's desire to please him even greater. In the teachings of the church, a man's duty is to be the physical and spiritual protector of his wife and children. The woman is to be chaste and modest, subservient to her husband's guidance, lest the mar of her sex tempt her to stray into the ways of the world.

My mother grew her hair long until it hung in satin ringlets, which she backcombed and pinned into a shapeless mass. Her cheeks and lips remained clear, no trace of the paint a ruined woman might wear. Plain, wide-cut skirts brushed her legs mid-calf. Only the tiniest holes scarred the lobes of her ears.

It is this mother I remember most, cloaked and colorless, her virtues defined by what she covered and erased rather than by what she presented to the world. She could not be aware of her own beauty, lest others become aware of it too. Because her husband was the hammer and she the nail, she built a house of acquiescence, allowing herself only the reward of steadfastness, holding the walls together with silent compliance. Because a quiet woman was a treasure, she seldom spoke except to offer and agree. It was as though my mother had disappeared, as though the doctor had once again come with his ether.

We lived for a while in one or the other of the identical houses built by Potlatch Forests Incorporated on the outskirts of Pierce—a development called Whispering Pines. The rent was often more than our budget allowed, but my mother had learned early the worth of hard work. She took the most abused houses, the ones left filthy and broken by previous residents, because no one else wanted them and the owners would lower the rent. Then she would barter a month's payment for fixing up the place, scrubbing and painting, trimming shrubs gone wild, planting colorful, even rows of marigolds. One house was littered with straw, the floor covered with the leavings of dogs and goats that had been allowed the run of the home. She shoveled and bleached until her back ached and her hands were blistered. No one would have guessed the tidy rooms trimmed in calico curtains were once a stable.

It was my first real neighborhood, a place where children gathered at the end of the block to play hopscotch, a place where my brother and I could set up a lemonade stand and depend on a customer an hour. It was also the first place where I saw clearly how different the world was outside our extended family. The couple next door filled the evenings with screams and curses; even the voice of Jim Reeves singing his heart out on our old stereo couldn't compete with the noise. I never asked why the man and woman were screaming, nor why the woman often appeared at our door, bruised and bleeding. My mother would lay her on our couch, call to me to bring her a cold rag, then shush me from the room. I'd lean against my bedroom door, straining to hear their muffled conversation: the woman's voice high and hysterical, my mother's sometimes soothing, sometimes stern. Before she left, I knew the woman would bow with my mother in prayer.

I never knew what reasoning passed between the two women, but I cannot imagine my mother counseled her to leave her husband. Even my grandmother once told me that sometimes when a woman got to thinking too much of herself, got a "smart mouth," she needed to be "shaped up," "put in her place." And while the church never condoned abuse, I always understood that it was the woman who was responsible for her husband's actions toward her. I wondered what it was our neighbor had done to deserve her beating.

The last year we lived in Whispering Pines seems a golden time in memory. I had a best friend, Glenda, who believed that her dolls came alive at night to keep her company and that her mother's washing machine groaned when it worked: *I don't WANT to wash, I don't WANT to wash.* I saw nothing strange in this and chose to think that whatever spirits possessed toys and appliances must be friendly. Glenda and I listened to her older brother's music, jiggling our larynxes to mimic the quivering voices of Tommy James and The Shondells singing "Crimson and Clover." I watched with fascination as her mother melted wax in an aluminum pan and then applied it to her upper lip, waiting a specified number of minutes before ripping the mustache from her face.

That year, I had one of the few conversations about sex I would have with my mother, when she asked me if I knew about menstruation. I said yes, my best friend Glenda had told me, which was true, and my mother seemed satisfied. Glenda prayed for the day she would "get her little friend," as her mother put it, and kept a pink-belted pad in her top drawer just in case. Every time I went to her house, we'd get out the Kotex and consider its mysteries. When finally it was I and not Glenda first beset by the ritual bleeding, she was mute with envy. I would have gladly given her my status. I didn't tell her that when the rusty stain appeared on my panties, I thought I was dying and locked myself in the bathroom to await my fate. Finally, after much cajoling, I let my mother in and explained my condition. Her shoulders slumped and a look of pity and regret showed on her face. "Oh, honey," she said. "You've started your period."

She brought in her purple box of Kotex and handed me an elastic belt like the one Glenda kept in her drawer, then left me to work out the mechanics of attaching the pad to the two hooks, which I finally managed to do in a haphazard fashion. I hated it already, hated the attention and concern and the look on my mother's face that said I was now doomed to my life as a woman. I hated to think that I would be strapped and uncomfortable for a week each month, and that someone might notice the bulging pad or discover me in the bathroom at recess, struggling to bandage and bind myself and staunch the betraying flow of blood.

Then the cramping started, and for one day each month I lay doubled up in the school's sickroom, pleading constipation or food poisoning but determined to never admit that the ache I felt somehow stemmed from the weakness of my gender. I had never felt anything that hurt so badly. It began in my thighs and rose in spasms to my pelvis, where it settled into a constant dizzying pain. My mother had explained that this would happen—it was part of what we must expect to endure as women.

One such day the principal, concerned by my pallor and the fact that I was lying on the cot with my knees drawn tight to my chest, called my mother to come and take me home. But my mother had gone to Orofino to buy groceries, so he called a neighbor, who swooped me into her car and led me into Kimball's Drug to be inspected by the white-frocked pharmacist. Dr. Kimball was no physician but we respected his college education. The nearest medical attention was a hard hour's drive in good weather, and anything that required less than surgery could be attended to by our one local nurse or the pharmacist. Most of the men's wounds they treated themselves, and the women's maladies, usually "female problems," Dr. Kimball might remedy with laxatives and vitamins.

He asked me a few questions, pushed at my abdomen, then pressed my nails to check the color. I didn't say a word, but he must have known. Undoubtedly, I wasn't the first tight-lipped Pierce girl to be ushered into his presence, suffering from the same condition. (I would read one day in the paper that the pharmacist's wife had reported him missing. The search that was launched covered three counties—everyone suspected foul play—and when they did discover him, not dead or even lost but simply hiding out, safe and supplied with enough food and clothing to last a while, the townspeople were stunned, the sheriff furious. How could the man on whom everyone depended suddenly disappear into the woods, leaving his family and community in torment? The county sent him a bill for thousands of dollars, and though he resumed his place behind the apothecary's counter, he never again held the trust of the people. I wondered what affliction he suffered from—what had driven him into the wilderness— but knew without question what words would be spoken of him from the pulpit the next Sunday, his a lesson we all might learn from: *Physician, heal thyself*).

Dr. Kimball suggested rest and that I be kept warm, and I spent the rest of the afternoon at the neighbor's house beneath a pile of blankets, nearly happy to be there since she had a TV and I could watch a *real* doctor at work—the dreamy Dr. Kildare, not at all like our bespectacled, sterile-smelling practitioner with hands white and dry as cornstarch. I didn't think I'd mind Richard Chamberlain prodding my insides, knowledgeable as to the intimacies of my sex.

That winter the snow fell for days on end and only by

constant shoveling could we guarantee our escape from the house. My brother and I charged ten dollars to scoop the heavy snow from the nearby roofs. Soon the berms and piles covered the windows, and we could step from the peak of our own house and sink neck-deep into star-shot whiteness.

Uncles, aunts and cousins came back to visit for Thanksgiving, piling into our small house with sleeping bags and pillows. But no one was prepared for the sudden drop in temperature to 40 degrees below zero. We were even less prepared for the electricity to go out. We woke Thanksgiving morning to rooms frosted in ice and our breath falling into crystals. Potlatch, in a fit of misplaced modernizing, had equipped each residence with baseboard heaters, and only my father's boss down the road, Max, had a fireplace. To his house we went, our large extended family snuggling close with his around the inadequate fire.

Whatever prayers were offered for heat failed to bring the desired results, and we must have finally decided that our being brought so intimately together had divine purpose. That purpose became clear when the woman of the house, Sandra, doubled over in pain.

While her husband and my father remained with the children, my mother and Uncle Roland, not so far gone to California that he couldn't maneuver through an Idaho snowstorm, drove Sandra to the drugstore, where Dr. Kimball promptly and accurately diagnosed appendicitis. The forty-mile trip to the hospital in Orofino seemed impossible given the weather, but there was little choice.

They made their way across the white expanse of the Weippe Prairie, along roads closed by blowing drifts. Max had a short-wave radio in his basement, allowing those left behind to communicate with the four-wheel drive, at least until it reached the icy switchback curves of Greer Grade. Whenever Sandra raised up from the backseat to say with hope in her voice that the pain had stopped, my mother and uncle glanced at each other and then away. They knew that while the pain continued she'd be okay, but once the appendix ruptured, the relief from pain was temporary: peritonitis would set in.

My uncle had seen it before, when they lived in Oklahoma. The youngest brother, Barry, had been diagnosed too late and lay for weeks on his hospital deathbed, brought back to life, they believed, by nothing more than their mother's prayers and constant presence even after the doctors had told her to go home, they couldn't save the boy.

This night they made it in time. Sandra was immediately admitted to surgery, and after making sure the operation had gone well and she was resting comfortably, my mother and uncle found their way back to their families, who were done up like Eskimos and eating whatever food could be found not frozen.

I was happy in that place, bundled against the cold, surrounded by people I knew and loved. My cousins and I made a game of it, serving Kool-Aid milkshakes and congealing cereal. Even after the electricity came back on and we returned to our own house, we bumped and huddled against one another for the remembered pleasure of closeness.

The warm spring days passed quickly. My brother and I played with the other children from morning until night, stopping only to heed our mothers beckoning us to lunch or dinner. Weekends, we built forts in the woods behind our yards and pretended the muddy gouges left by bulldozers were pits of quicksand. We walked the two miles to town grouped tight as a clutch of chicks, the dimes and quarters we'd earned selling lemonade sweaty in our palms. Back home we'd come with bags of penny candy, racing one another up the hills, balancing on the logs that bridged the gullies, made brave by our independence and wealth of treats.

But our time left in that place was short. Even as my brother and I filled our days with childhood adventures, something was at work in my father. It was nothing that Dr. Kimball or a hard day's labor in the woods could heal or fix, and I'm not sure that even now I understand it. For most of his life, as a sinner and a Christian, my father had felt the workings of otherworldly things through dreams and intimations. His conversion to fundamentalism made him even more aware of the division between the forces of good and evil, and he had come to understand that dreams could be visions, that a sudden and overwhelming sense of darkness and despair could be the presence of Satan himself. In that tract house on the hill, in a place that represented the realization of modest ambition for a man striving to feed and shelter his family—to provide for them a safe and simple life—my father saw a demon.

It is a story I've heard told only twice but remember with a child's sense of horror, how he woke chilled by the sudden false movement of air, damp as wind across rotting snow. He turned his face slowly toward the bedroom door, the stench of decay filling his nostrils, and saw the dark body and hollow face. It offered no word or sound, peering from its place at the threshold as though gauging my father's wariness, sucking from his night breath the secrets of his soul.

He had never felt such fear, such abject, mute helplessness. He could not scream or move his hand to touch his wife's shoulder so that she might bear witness to the specter. Even the simple rote of exorcism—*In the name of the Father, the Son and the Holy Ghost, I command you to leave*—was more than he could utter. For a long moment the demon held its place, then vanished. My mother woke to the bed rattling, my father violently trembling. In the next room, I felt the house shudder, the mountain possessed by wind. I heard my father's whispering. I thought, *prayer.* I snuggled deeper beneath my covers, nothing in this world to fear.

One afternoon in early fall, my mother picked Greg and me up at school before we could board the bus. Her eyes were red and she pinched her nose with a handkerchief. I peered intently out my window, fearing what she was going to say. She patted my hand.

"I've got some bad news, sweetie."

I waited, my breath coming out shallow and quick. Greg was already crying in the backseat.

"Uncle Ed was killed today."

I nodded without looking at her, not sure how I was supposed to respond now that I knew it was not my father, only a great-uncle I hardly knew—Aunt Edith's husband, the red-haired Swede whose hands had built the bomb shelter in one day. He was known as an expert sawyer, a shy and gentle man comfortable only in the presence of timber. He had been struck by a felled tree, his shinbones driven through the soles of his boots and into the ground like marking stakes.

I felt around for grief or sadness to match my mother's, but all that came to me was a sense of something gone from the world. My mother took us to the Headquarters Cafe for ice cream, and I swirled the cone with my tongue, considering how easily death came: my friend Anita Kachelmier's dad had died at this very counter, strangled on a piece of steak, still wearing his boots and red suspenders.

It was God's will for Uncle Ed to die, just as it was God's will for us to move from our house in town to Dogpatch and begin making payments to his widow. I knew I would miss my neighborhood friends, and I cried when we pulled away and I saw Glenda waving from her bedroom window. But my parents had said we would *own* our new home, and something in the word sounded permanent to me, settled.

When we drove down the driveway and into the hollow, Aunt Edith was waiting. She showed us through the narrow house and led me to my bedroom, with its curtain for a door. The room had once belonged to her son Larry, but he had left home years before. Now it was empty except for a doll, rigid in high heels, her feet glued to a platform. She wore an odd little hat, round and pointed, and her eyes were the shape of almonds. When Aunt Edith handed her to me, I could hardly believe my luck. "Is she Chinese?" I asked, smoothing the silk tunic over her white leggings. "No," she said. "Larry brought her back from Vietnam, but I can't imagine what I'd do with her now." She looked around the room sadly, then lifted the curtain and disappeared.

I sat down on the bare floor and contemplated my new possession. Her hair was thick and black, parted and gathered into two braids. Painted red lips, breasts high and pointy, waist narrower than her hips by half—she was beautiful. I brought her to my nose. Even her smell was exotic—spice mixed with the smoke of Aunt Edith's cigarettes.

I took her to show my mother, who was quietly crying as my aunt's car bumped up the driveway for the last time. I did not think then to consider how my mother saw in the older woman the shape her own future might take. What would be left to the widow of a logger whose house squatted on borrowed land and existed only by the favor of the company? The choices were few: find another man to marry, or leave. But I was too young to see these things and took off with my brother to explore the outhouse and meadow, leaving my doll to my mother, who cradled it gently, as though it held all the hope and fragility of her life.

We arranged our few pieces of furniture, unpacked our boxes of books and clothes, and I began to believe that we'd be there always: nestled in the draw, protected from wind, a few distant neighbors, a school-bus stop at the top of our road.

My father worked so close we could hear the thrum of machinery, the saws catch and whine, the trees crack, the dull echo of their falling. When the other men began their talk of new equipment and less land, my father leaned harder into his cut, feeling in his arms the strength of pine and muscle, the familiar ache in his back. He was blessed by wood, blessed by God to be there with his wife and children safe in the draw with the woods all around where, unless you had been there, you would guess no house existed, no people lived.

Between Dogpatch and Pierce lies Cardiff Spur, a cluster of faded trailers and creosote-stained shacks named after a saw-mill operator. One of those shacks was the parsonage, which shared a large open space between the road and Trail Creek with the Cardiff Spur Mission, the Pentecostal church my parents had chosen for us to attend. Our first meetings were around a potbelly stove, scooted so close the preacher was made to circle behind us, calling on us to confess our latest sin.

The men who attended were loggers and mill hands, men who blended easily with the small population of the area. On Sundays, they wore freshly pressed shirts, suitcoats and trousers; other days, they were distinguished only by their profession: black boots and stagged pants cut to mid-calf, out of the way of saws and snags. The women who attended our church, however, with their long skirts, plain faces and coiled hair were easily identified as holy-rollers. I became aware of the fact that I, as a girl approaching adolescence, was being dressed accordingly—no shorts, short-sleeved blouses, blush or pierced ears—only when we made our visits to Lewiston, where Nan would shorten my dresses and trim my hair, clucking all the while about never having seen such nonsense. She believed I could be a beauty queen: how was that to happen if people's only notice of me was the simple curiousness of a girl dressed like a dowager?

I signed the church's youth pledge and carried a white waxy card listing the regulations governing my behavior. I promised never to dance, drink, smoke or swear. I would not go to movie theaters, frequent bowling alleys, swim with the opposite sex or dance except under the Spirit. The hem of my dresses would measure two inches below my knees, and I would refrain from wearing pants. I would wear no jewelry, makeup or other adornment that might draw attention to my physical self and cause another to lust after me in an unholy way. I would pray daily, fast frequently and believe always in the Lord as my Savior. I embraced these commandments, thrilled to have in my new purse a card bearing the large script of my signed name. When I made my commitment public, my parents and the other adults beamed with approval and prayed with hands on my shoulders that I forever follow the path of righteousness and turn not from the hard road onto the wider path of wickedness leading only to Hell.

I don't remember the name of our first preacher at Cardiff, thumping his Bible behind my head, taking great leaps around the room, agile beyond his years. He is a presence, a bellowing exhortation. Nor do I remember the day he left, the Sunday our new pastor, Brother Lang, took his place at the podium.

Joseph Lang was short and stocky, ruddy complected, with

thick black hair that glistened like patent leather. His wife, Mona, was shorter still, burdened with enormous breasts that she shrugged and shifted into balance. She sat ramrod straight at the piano, hair the color of granite brushing the bench behind her. Their children were all ahead of me in school— Sarah, the eldest, then the two boys, Matthew and Luke.

They seemed always happy, singing separately or as a family, teasing with affection, catching us up in their enthusiasm for God. We often gathered at the parsonage for long hours of music: Brother Lang on his banjo, my father strumming along on the guitar my mother had bought him for Christmas—a Gibson arch-top f-hole—playing the simple chords he had learned as a boy. Brother Lang was originally from Texas and knew many of the bluegrass songs my parents loved, and when not playing gospel they filled the small room with the loud and vibrant twang of country.

Perhaps my father saw in Brother Lang the man he might become—a preacher, a husband whose family followed the path he laid out without question. My mother found in Sister Lang something her own life had never offered: a role model of Christian womanhood. And I found the same in Sarah, nearly a woman herself but willing to treat me with kindness, teaching me the art of modest behavior: keep your legs together, your skirt pulled over the caps of your knees; don't chew gum; run the water when you use the bathroom to mask the noise. Her long blond hair and virtuous demeanor brought her the attention of an eighteen-year-old boy from downriver, a trapper and wilderness guide, red-headed and easily embarrassed. At sixteen her parents believed her more than ready to marry, and before the year was out she and her new husband, Terry, had taken up matrimonial residence in her upstairs bedroom.

But there was one stipulation to their union: Terry could

marry their daughter, but he must agree to never take her away from the family. Brother and Sister Lang believed that Sarah and Matthew had a singing ministry to fulfill, a calling that might bring them recognition and success in the process of spreading the Gospel. At some point during each service, Matthew and Sarah would take the stage. Matthew strummed his twelve-string and sang with his eyes closed while Sarah crossed her hands in front of her and focused on something just above the heads of the congregation. If Terry were to separate the family, their dreams would die.

At fifteen Matthew was impish and quiet. He loved hunting nearly as much as Bible study, and his mature approach to both impressed everyone. He delivered the Sunday sermon when his father was away, unmoving behind the podium, attempting only occasional and solemn glances at his attentive audience. His brother, Luke, a year younger, had high cheekbones touched by his father's coloring, full lips, startling blue eyes, a James Dean swagger. Cocky and intelligent, less serious than Matthew, he sometimes gave me the gift of his gaze, and I found myself shuffling the awkward corners of my elbows into a more presentable picture.

Along with my desire for his attention came an awareness of the failings of my eleven-year-old body—the skinny legs and ridiculously large feet, the heavy glasses that constantly slid down my nose. In his presence I jumbled my words and tripped for no reason. His smug grin humiliated me, and I came to realize that my best self lay in stillness. When around him, I moved only when I had to and spoke only when addressed, answering in clipped phrases, but no matter how I held myself in, wrapping my arms about my waist, double-crossing my legs, something escaped to betray me: I stuttered out the wrong chapter and verse when asked to recite Scripture; my stomach growled in the quiet between prayers; sweat pooled in my palms and beneath my arms. Surely he and everyone else could see how imperfect I was.

Sometimes, after church, after the foyer had emptied and the adults had gone to the parsonage to drink coffee, he'd teach me the chords of a forbidden song—"Hey Jude" or "House of the Rising Sun"—and I'd plunk along on the old upright, filling the sanctuary with wanton rhythms. When he lowered his eyes and sang, I felt dizzy with a feeling I could no more identify than the taste of sugarcane. It was a tingling in my belly, a lightness in my bones. It felt like sin and I knew it.

What I did not know, could not foresee, none of us could, was how the church would cleave, how the congregation would be divided by the new preacher, this man of God come to the wilderness to save us. Then our numbers would grow, drawing converts from the camps and near towns until the pews filled with believers. The building itself would be torn down, a new one built. The old woodstove would be hauled across the creek and dumped; a new oil furnace would blow its warmth into the church. Our circle would once again tighten, drawn together by the Langs until our lives—theirs and the lives of my family—became meshed, inseparable. We rocked in the comfort of their ministry until those last few months when one died, another dreamed of demons so horrible he purged his body of food and trembled in his wife's arms to stand and sing God's praises and another locked himself in an earthen cell with only a few jugs of water and a Bible, praying for a sign, deliverance for us all.

Tuesday night, Pathlighters. Wednesday night, prayer meeting. Thursday, men's Bible study, women's Aglow. Sunday school, church, choir practice, evening service. In between we gathered informally, sharing dreams and Scripture, passing out tracts in town, witnessing to our few and patient neighbors. And every few months, *revival*.

The revivalist would arrive, bringing with him an air of excitement, the anticipation of a circus or carnival. We held meetings in our church, in the grange halls of other small towns or, most memorably, in huge tents set up in mown fields and vacant lots. If a creek were close by, we had full-immersion baptisms, sometimes so spontaneous the women had no time to don double slips beneath their dresses. When they surfaced, hands raised to heaven and speaking in tongues, translucent pink showed through the wet cloth. Their skirts floated up like lilies.

Meetings lasted for hours, every night, beginning with the opening prayer, a few answering amens, then singing. As our voices rose, people began to clap, then sway, palms raised to the ceiling. When the missionary took the podium, we were primed for his outpouring of God-given wisdom and spiritual insight. By the time the sermon ended, the pitch of our praise had built to the point of drowning out his closing words, and he called on us to confess and be reborn in loud outbursts that sounded more like commands than entreaties. Finally, the entire congregation shouted and stomped, those gifted in tongues adding their heavenly language to the booming chorus.

Each preacher was different. One might holler and wave his arms; another pounded the pulpit with his Bible until the spine broke and pages flew. The missionary from down south danced in the aisles, twirling with his arms outstretched, head thrown back, heels clicking the wooden floor in the measured beat of flamenco. The first man to prophesy my future was a grandfatherly missionary with hair the color of new dimes, who sold us beautiful wooden boxes carved by the natives of

Haiti. In our second week of revival, two people had been healed: one of an ulcer, the other of a slow-knitting rib, cracked when his saw kicked off a limb and knocked him flat. It was this preacher who called me out one night after the sermon, after Sister Baxter had prophesied in tongues and Sister Johnson had interpreted God's message, a message of warning lest Satan rally his army, jealous of our praise. Several women had fallen under the Spirit and lay on the floor weeping—others less stunned draped the women's legs with lap cloths to ensure modesty.

He found me, head bowed, a little sleepy, muttering my prayers and unprepared for his attention. The voices quieted as he called me to the altar. I stepped away from my seat and made my way toward the front, weaving through the prostrated bodies. His eyes were serious and piercing, as though there were something I was hiding, as though he could read in my face what had roused in him the need to clasp my head between his sweaty palms and drive me to my knees.

I felt no fear. I felt the roughness of his hands and the eyes of the church upon me, but I believed in this man of the Lord. I had seen him heal the Paxson boy, seen the short leg lengthen in the preacher's cupped hand. What wound or fault he might find in me I could not discern, but I waited calmly to be free of it, to be made newly whole.

"What is your name, child?"

"Kim," I whispered.

"Sister Kim, God has brought us here together tonight for a very special reason. Do you know what that is?" He let his gaze sweep the room. "Sister Kim walks among you with a gift. Sister Kim, do you know what that gift is?"

I heard the voices behind me: "Yes, Lord!" "Thank you, Jesus!" I thought I heard my mother crying. I shook my head, filled with a growing curiosity as though a stranger were about to read my palm, uncover a family secret. I steadied myself against the weight of his hands.

"You, my daughter, have the gift of healing. You are a healer!" Behind me the praise grew louder. The room felt suddenly hot and I wished for an open door, a window letting in the cool night air. His hands were heavier than my legs could stand and I fell, sweat trickling down my sides.

Sister Lang pounded out chords on the upright. I don't remember the hymn or what other hands came to bless me. I only remember my knees on the cold wood floor and wondering what my father thought then, what would be expected of me in the days to come. I wondered if Luke had witnessed my anointing. I wondered what part of him I might touch.

The next Sunday I sat at the table of Brother and Sister Baxter. They ran cattle outside of Weippe, an even smaller town than Pierce, twenty miles southwest. There were others there my age, children still wobbly in their manners at the table's far end, eating silently while the adults pondered the day's sermon and praised the wife's fried chicken. If there was a lull in the conversation, if the discussion had turned to the past week's revival, I don't recall. I only know I felt a sudden pain, as though a nail were being driven into my ear. I whimpered and my fork clattered to my plate.

I had never had an ear infection, had never felt the kind of pain I now felt, both throbbing and sharp. I remembered the missionary's words, and with absolute certainty stood up and announced, "Someone here has an earache."

Looking from one unperceiving face to another, I pressed my hand to the right side of my head.

"Someone's ear hurts."

I stood with my neck bent to ease the pressure. At the other end of the table a woman let out a single sob. It was Sister Baxter.

I moved from my child's place and walked to her chair. She bowed her head, softly crying, and I placed my hand on her right ear. I could feel the heat there, the drumming pain. Others joined me, clasping my shoulders, touching my back.

"Dear Lord, our sister has a need. She needs you, Jesus." My words were met with a chorus of *amens* and *hallelujahs*. I drew a breath. My eleven-year-old awkwardness was gone. The words flowed.

"We ask that you take this pain from her. Heal her, Lord! In God's name we pray."

The chorus grew loud and encompassing, until the body I touched and the hands touching me melded. I floated in a swell of sound, a humming of breath and blood.

"You will be healed!" I demanded it, surprised by the volume of my voice. The woman shuddered and groaned. The heat from her ear spread from my fingers into my arm and shoulder—my neck and face flushed with it. I opened my eyes and found myself in that room, the chicken half-eaten, gravy scumming the plates. The woman shivered in my hands.

Later, I played with the other children in the barn. The woman's one daughter and I hid from the boys in the stubble, giggling with pleasure at their blindness. We rooted tadpoles from the shallows and stabbed them onto rusty hooks. The creek held catfish and we bobbed for them in the manure-silted water. Each one we pulled from the muddy stream seemed a miracle, so different from the blazing trout I caught in the clear runoff of Reeds Creek. I held their sleek black bodies in my hands, smoothing the spiny backs, careful of their poison.

We trapped the big green frogs that huddled beneath the overhanging grass, and while the girls swaddled them in the hems of their skirts the boys got a hammer from the barn and made little crosses of split barnwood. Holding the struggling frogs by their tiny wrists and ankles, we drove small nails through each webbed foot, then studied them for a while. Their white bellies spasmed, their mouths opened and closed. They looked like rotund little men with their legs stretched straight. Someone suggested making miniature crowns of nettles but no one wanted to be stung.

We planted them in the muddy creek bottom, three frogs hanging above the water, arranged to mimic the painting we had seen of the crosses on Golgotha: Christ, the largest frog, in the middle, the two thieves on either side. Something about the symmetry of the martyred frogs seemed targetlike and the boys ran to the house and came back with their BB guns. Bulls-eye was the belly, and we all took turns until the frogs sagged on their crosses and we lost interest in the game.

That night, after evening service, Sister Baxter slipped into bed beside her already sleeping husband. When she woke the next morning her pillow was sticky with pus. The fever was gone. Whether it would have been so had I not touched her, I don't know. I can explain the progress of illness and infection but not that moment when her pain took hold of me as though it were my own affliction.

She testified at church that a miracle had been wrought, and only then did I feel the weight of expectation fall upon me, heavy as the missionary's hands. My parents allowed me to walk in front of them. The other children began to resent

the way the adults nodded whenever I spoke. The attention
made me aware of how seriously everyone looked upon my
gift, yet I wasn't sure I could do it again. If I failed to discern
an illness, or if I prayed for someone to be healed and nothing
happened, would it mean I had sinned, that I was unworthy?

And then there was Luke. How did he fit into the maze
my life was becoming? Somewhere between a child's innocent
cruelty and her coming initiation into the world. When I
thought of Luke's hands, how they touched me accidentally or
on purpose but always in a way I remembered for days, I was
filled with more emotion than I had ever experienced cruci-
fying frogs or healing the sick.

Many Sunday afternoons my family spent at the parsonage. While the women made stew or fried venison dusted
with flour, Matthew, Luke and I hunched together on the
narrow stairway leading upstairs, sharing the dirty jokes we
had heard at school, guessing what went on in the bed of their
sister.

It was always dark there, and we spoke in whispers. The
closeness of our bodies took my breath away. When Luke's
leg rested against mine I could no longer hear what was being
said. When he put his hand on my knee, the sweet shock
traveled to the bone and began a fire that spread its warmth to
my crotch, a feeling so pleasurable I shuddered with the sure
sin of it.

When we returned to the company of our parents, I could
still feel the heat of his hand. Even if I could not articulate
what I was feeling, I understood that what we were doing fell
into the category of sin called "petting"—touching between
young men and women that brought on our elders' direst
warnings. I burned with shame to have given myself so easily
to his caress. I prayed for forgiveness, for strength, for whatever temptation this was to leave me. But even in sleep I

remembered his palm pressed against bare skin beneath the hem of my skirt.

The more I tried to forget the pleasure of being close to Luke, the more I longed for it. This was a symptom of Satan's influence I recognized: the greatest sin was desire for anything other than God. Desire for money, whiskey, the touch of another without the marriage blessing—any possession or wordly place—was lust and must be controlled, purged and destroyed.

I saw that something had begun its slow possession. How could I be both healer and sinner? How could I close my eyes in prayer when all I could see was the face of the preacher's son? I was lost, no language to describe how I savored this sin, no one to prophesy my salvation or damnation. I huddled beneath the covers of my bed, hearing the wind rise, the pinecones tacking the ground. Surely God would cause a tree to fall, send it crashing through the roof. I imagined Luke's kiss, then the slide of his hand between my legs. The night held still. I could dream of no more.

Enlightenment came via my teacher, Mrs. Nichols, a young and beautiful woman who sang opera and demanded that we sing with her, her high soprano voice rattling the windows in their panes. She seemed especially fond of Handel's *Messiah*, and we belted out *hallelujahs* no matter the season. Blond beehived hair, red nails that clicked like beetles against our chairs—we could hardly believe she lived in our town. As eccentric as she was, there were still some things she would not tolerate in her charges: a clumsily held pencil (she would sneak up behind us, jerk the pencil from our hand, rap us sharply on the head, then slide it back into our quickly corrected grasp), a messy desk and, oddly enough, given her own propensity for adornment, pierced ears. She held to her own kind of fundamentalism, a code that dictated her expectations of our demeanor.

We sat one drowsy afternoon, warmed by the popping steam heaters working to keep at bay the below-freezing temperatures. (Even in winter the girls were forbidden to wear anything but dresses, except during the periods of bitterest cold, when, with a special dispensation announced by the principal, we were allowed to don pants under our skirts. My church's rules governing modesty seemed little displaced.) We nodded over our Idaho history books, which were hopelessly outdated, with no sympathy for what stood in the way of Manifest Destiny. Lewis and Clark were nothing short of rustic gods adorned in their buckskin and high leather boots. I tried to focus on the illustration of Sacajawea pointing toward the west with a sweeping, grand gesture, as though she could see every bend and bog that lay ahead. She was beautiful— slim and burnished atop her rocky pinnacle—and the aura radiating out from behind them left no doubt that the three were ushering in a golden era.

We did our best to stay awake, knowing that at any given moment our teacher's displeasure could take new and startling forms. When she stopped at the desk next to mine, I closed my eyes and flinched, the dates of gold discoveries and town settlements swirling through my head: history was a whirlpool, and I was hopeless in the face of chronological sequence. My mind worked in other ways. I could recite the story of Polly Bemis, the Chinese girl bought and lost in a game of poker. I could tell you the shade of her red dress, the way her hem swept across the rough-cut floor, how the room smelled of bacon grease and the sweat of men just come in from the mines, the light sifting through the warped logs like gold dust, falling across her arms as she went silently about her chores.

I had already worked my way to the part in the story where the man who owns Polly loses the bet and she sees her life pass into the hands of another, when I heard Mrs. Nichols's voice rise. She was standing over Julie, whose eyes had widened in fear.

"Stand up!" Julie stood. The teacher's movements were swift and I thought for a moment she had cuffed Julie along the sides of her head. Julie gasped and covered her ears, and it was then I saw the small gold hoops Mrs. Nichols held in her palm.

Perhaps, like the crimson hue of Polly's skirt, I have only imagined the blood that pearled and dropped from Julie's torn lobes. Mrs. Nichols took her by the shoulders and marched her out of the room, and none of us dared even look up. We never doubted the teacher would win, that her rule—"No pierced ears in my classroom"—as well as her actions would be supported. We knew the laws that governed us, and few were prepared to face the kinds of punishments meted out for disobedience.

I also knew that there was some exciting stigma attached to having holes punched in one's ears, and that it had something to do with men and women and what I was coming to recognize as sex. Nan once told me only ruined women pierced their ears, and from that I gleaned some vague sense of what "ruined" might mean: a woman no man would want to marry. Why, then, had my father wed my mother when *she* had pierced ears? Even the fact that her ears were pierced intrigued me: what had she been like before she was the woman whose back I knew so well, having studied its shift and set as she worked over pie dough or biscuit mix?

Another classmate had pulled me aside one recess and guided me behind the huge shed that covered the playground equipment and protected us from the wind and snow. There, she whispered that her older brother often crawled into her bed at night and rubbed himself against her, and that once he had stuck *it* in. I listened mesmerized but could not imagine the mechanics of such an act, much less the motive.

"Why does he do that?" I asked.

"Because," she said, "he loves me."

"Does it hurt?"

"Sometimes. But he gives me a quarter when it does." She pulled a fistful of penny candy from her pocket and giggled. I contemplated the sticky remains of suckers and malted milk balls but took nothing. Something wasn't right about it, and after that I avoided her on the swings and slide, watching as she took other classmates behind the shed. Some came in wiping chocolate from their mouths, but all of them ran when back in the familiar domain of children, leaving her alone with her pocket of sweets.

After the incident with Julie's ears, we watched Mrs. Nichols even more closely, hoping to give ourselves enough time to bolt should she move on us, although we doubted we'd have the courage to make even the smallest gesture of escape. She seemed more withdrawn, given to staring thoughtfully out the window with her lovely hands crossed behind her, her fingers entwined, her nails clicking.

It was during one of these pensive moments when she turned suddenly toward us. "You think you know things," she said. "You don't." We were startled into rapt attention. "You are animals, and like all animals your bodies know only these two things: pleasure and pain."

The best we could do was to let her go and maybe she would forget we were there, waiting for our lessons. Out of the corner of my eye I saw Brian's hand shoot up. He was the class nosepicker, and I groaned inwardly at his foolishness.

"Mrs. Nichols, what about itches?"

She studied him intently for a moment, then walked slowly to the side of his desk. "Itches," she echoed flatly. "Itches are *slow* pain. Each and every feeling you have is the *man-i-fe-sta-tion* of pleasure or pain." She turned her back on us and once again focused her attention on the air outside the window.

Wasn't what I felt when I thought of Luke a kind of pain? I ached to be with him, yet suffered no less in his presence than I did in his absence. Sometimes I thought pleasure inseparable from pain and wondered if I'd ever know when one became the other. It all seemed a riddle to me, a world in which things were not as they appeared, as though our emotions were reflected back on us, reversed, warped. What gave me worldly pleasure was the very thing that caused me spiritual pain.

But what did I know of suffering, of the makeup of souls? I must not think that the teachers of the mind such as Mrs. Nichols might have insight into the ways of the Lord. I opened my Bible to Corinthians, to the words of Paul: "When I was a child, I spake as a child, I understood as a child: but when I became a man, I put away childish things. For now we see through the glass darkly; but then face to face: now I know in part; but then shall I know even as also I am known."

It had been three years since my mother stood at the kitchen window, pointing up and out into the haze of August sky.

"How many, Kim? How many birds on the wire?"

I looked from her to the square of light and back. The clues lay in the words—*bird, wire*—just as they did in my father's riddles: If a plane crashes on the border between the U.S. and Canada, where do they bury the survivors? If a rooster lays an egg on the peak of a roof, which way will the egg roll? Kits, cats, sacks and wives, how many were going to St. Ives?

I could no more find the true meaning in my mother's question than I could see the birds and wire. The distance from the window to the table where I sat, nose rubbing the pages of my reading book, was no more than ten feet, but even that distance would have been enough to fade her features to an airbrushed silhouette.

Some weeks afterward, I sat in the optometrist's office, surrounded by cases of heavy frames, trying on pair after pair. I could not see myself in the mirror the assistant held out for me: the dark plastic lines faded into the peachy canvas of my face, which I obediently studied for a weighty minute before reaching for the next pair. Days later, when the doctor slid them over my ears, the glasses settled onto my nose with surprising heaviness. Even more startling was my mother's face peering into my own, so close I could see gray flecks in her pale blue eyes. Behind her, the doctor and assistant leaned toward me as though I had just been given the power of speech and were about to utter my first word.

What had I seen before? The birds on the wire I had imagined as leaves on a branch; now, when I saw them from the window, I could count their feathers, watch the small beaks preen for dust, see them tense for flight before rising into the air and disappearing. I described for my mother the colors of grass, the movement of shadows, the ever-changing shade of my aunt's hair.

The language of vision had always been with me—pale, clear, bright, deep—but my sense of the words had been tactile, palpable, something I felt rather than saw. I remember the smell of smoke, the auroral glow of my father's cigarette as we drove the dark road to town or back to camp. The trees and river flew by, miles I knew by heart but could not describe any differently in daylight than at night, although I never doubted their existence any more than I doubted the presence of angels, whose wings I imagined the cloudiest white, softly downed without quills or striation, large enough to carry me aloft in huge breathy beats.

In the parsonage stairway I came to believe the absence of light a blessing. I prayed for the counterfeit night and the sound of Luke's voice husky with desire. I prayed we not be found out, knowing God's grace covered a multitude of transgressions, knowing my wickedness lay in the very prayer I offered—the prayer of a sinner jealous of her sin.

It was Luke I thought of one Sunday night as I waited for my parents to finish their good-byes. Brother Lang's sermon had been a long one, and everyone seemed ready to file from the pews and head home. No one had a special need or pressing confession to present to the congregation—not even Sister Paxson, a large, dark woman given to fits of lumbago, who normally went forward to have her swollen knees anointed with the thick green olive oil kept pushed to the back of the lectern. People had already begun pulling on their coats and shaking hands with their neighbors when Brother Lang stepped from the stage and clapped his hands together.

"Our work here tonight is not done," he announced loudly. Everyone stopped still, eyes widening with sudden interest. "There is one among us who has a weakness, a need." He released one of his hands and held it out, fingers together, pointed at me like a hatchet. "Sister Kim, will you come forward?"

My parents looked from Brother Lang to me, then shuffled back to let me pass, their hands lifted in prayer, palms up, as if to catch rain. Those who had left their seats, thinking the evening's worship closed, settled back into their rows.

What was it I needed? My throat wasn't sore. The pain in my shins had stopped, healed by the woman revivalist in Orofino who told me I lacked calcium, pressed her thumbs into my temples until my head pounded, then released me with her encouragement to drink more milk. As I walked down the aisle, mentally checking my stomach for pain, the balance of my shoulders and hips, I passed Luke. He sat in the front, leaned casually into the pew's hard corner. Even the backs of his ears were beautiful.

Brother Lang grasped my shoulders, then gently pivoted me to the congregation. I looked out over the room, into the upturned faces and moving mouths of God's people. Luke, only a few feet away, met my eyes with such intensity I felt suddenly paralyzed. He was seeing something in me no one else could see, something that threaded through the soles of my feet and into my leg bones like the ancient canes of berries, piercing my bowels and lungs, twining its tendrils around my throat so that I labored to breathe. The intimacy of his vision was not holy. The way his mouth, lips slightly parted, drew me in with all the air in the room made me reel. The hands gripped my shoulders tighter. I felt each finger and thumb press into my flesh—I counted them under my breath, eyes closed.

"Sister Kim," the voice spoke to the back of my head, "how long have you been burdened with poor sight?"

I opened my eyes slowly, blinking for a moment to force the room into focus. My mother stood with her hands clasped in front of her breasts.

I thought back to that August afternoon, to the birds on

the wire. How old had I been? That girl was another lifetime ago. Was I eight?

"At least three years," I whispered.

"These glasses are a heavy burden. The Lord can heal these eyes, and will," Brother Lang turned me back to face him, "if you will only have faith."

I looked into his own eyes, so dark the pupil and iris bled together. Like the eyes of an animal, I thought.

Until that moment, I had seldom considered my vision. The glasses were a part of me, an extension of my body. Because of them I could see my way from one room to another without holding to the walls and shuffling my feet. Now, their presence seemed less a gift than a flaw, a mark of weakness.

I felt a sudden growing shame, the same shame I felt at the new roundness of my breasts, the hair in hidden places. I lowered my head. I remembered my hand cupping Sister Baxter's fevered ear. The image reviled me. How foolish to believe that I held in my power the gift to discern the infirmity of another: I could not even see the reflection of my own face in the mirror without the grotesque magnification of glass.

"Sister Kim. Do you have faith?"

I nodded slowly.

"Do you believe God can heal your eyes?"

I nodded again. I had never before been afraid of prayer. Many times I had felt the laying-on of hands. Now the preacher's fingers seemed locked, digging into the soft pockets of flesh between my neck and shoulders.

I did not want to be there, my ears filled with moans and high singing building into the staccato rhythm of tongues. I did not want others to see my disgrace: my pride had blinded me to the blemishes of my own body. In believing that I, a silly, stammering girl, could work miracles, I had drawn attention to myself. My spiritual vision had clouded to match my eyesight. I thought of Luke, the cloistered stairway. Had I really believed God could not see through such blackness?

I waited, eyes closed, for the touch of pungent oil, Brother Lang's finger sliding twice across my forehead in the shape of a cross. Instead, I felt my glasses lifted from my face. I opened my eyes to see the blur of his hand tucking the dark frames into the pocket of his white shirt.

I lost my balance and grabbed for his arm. He steadied me, then pressed his thumbs against my eyelids. The prayers rose higher, a loud thrum of joined voices, yet each voice distinct and recognizable: Brother Story's *b*'s and *p*'s popped from his lips in little explosions; his wife's language was a monotone string of *m*'s, *ah*'s and long *e*'s, sustained, it seemed, without her ever having to take a breath. The combined chant surrounded me like the amplified murmurings of bees.

"Hear us now, Jesus. We come to Thee to ask that these eyes be *healed. Heal* these eyes, Dear Lord, so that our sister might see clearly all you have created."

He made short, sharp jerks with his hands. I strained with the effort to keep rigid.

"She knows, Lord, that if she has enough faith, if she will only believe, *she will be healed!*"

Others were shouting now. Their feet stomped the wooden floor as they called on the Spirit, *Jesus. Sweet Jesus.*

Then the hands pulled away, the voices quieted, and I opened my eyes.

"Sister Kim, how many fingers am I holding up?"

I blinked, my vision still dark with the print of his thumbs. His hand floated so close I could see the half-circle of his wedding band.

"Three," I answered. Somewhere behind me, Sister Johnson called out, "Praise the Lord!"

"Can you see your parents?" The hand was at my arm, turning me once again to the room. I looked to where I left my family. Browns and blues washed together as though I were looking through water. I peered harder. Sister Johnson twirled in the aisle—I recognized her high-pitched voice, the characteristic trilling of her glossolalia. But I could not see my mother and father, only the arms raised to heaven, undulating like meadow grass. I shook my head. No one seemed to notice. The room vibrated with the loud praise of men and women given over to the Spirit. Sister Lang pounded out a hymn on the upright, and I knew the meeting would last long into the night.

"You must believe and you will be healed. Go home tonight and pray for faith to accept this truth." Brother Lang released me, and I felt my way up the aisle until my father caught my wrist.

Three days passed before I regained my sight. Three days of not seeing the blackboard, of being unable to find the swings at recess. I told my teachers and friends my glasses were broken and let them lead me like a pet dog. I clutched my mother's sleeve when we walked to and from the car, and even though I had never needed it before, I began to leave a light on at bedtime: If I woke, I could not see beyond the lamp's dim silhouette. I was no longer a child secure in my parents' bed, their closeness giving boundaries to my nighttime world.

Did my mother feel her own faith waiver, watching from the window as I stumbled up the driveway to catch the bus, holding to my brother's coattail, clutching the books I could not read? Did she long to take from that preacher the glasses he had pocketed and lay them beside my bed as I slept? I'd wake and find them there, my prayers answered, the prayers of a child wandering scared, lost in the waters, waiting for a hand to reach from the bank and pull her to safety.

I imagine my mother kissing my eyes when she believed I was deep into dreams, as I now kiss the fluttering and delicate lids of my own children. I hear her whispering, *believe*. I open my eyes and see her disappear into a rectangle of light.

At the next Wednesday night prayer meeting, Brother Lang slipped the glasses into my hand, as though he himself were embarrassed by my failure. I waited until the singing began before I put them on and reached for the hymnal, thrilled to see the black letters distinct against white pages. It seemed miracle enough. With the book held straight out before me, I began to sing.

Later, in the stairway, air damp with close breathing, Luke reached to slide the glasses from my face. I caught his hand.

"You're so much prettier," he whispered.

I folded the hard frames in my palm and clasped them tightly. I closed my eyes and waited in darkness for his kiss.

CHAPTER FIVE

The company town of Headquarters, just over the hill from the hollow at Dogpatch, consisted of two groups of houses separated by the railroad tracks and large shop buildings belonging to Potlatch. The small dwellings south of the tracks housed company workers—those who felled, hauled, scaled and processed the timber. North of the tracks, behind the Headquarters store, a wooden stairway led up to the Circle, where the road threaded between the shop buildings and store before looping back on itself at the top of the hill.

The Circle was where the supervisors lived—men who, by skill or inheritance, held positions above the other workers. The homes facing one another across the Circle were larger and better appointed than most I had seen. Real grass rather than wild clover and timothy grew to the doors of the houses.

The children who departed the Circle to catch the school bus, taking the wooden steps two at a time, wore store-bought clothes. The boys had cartoon lunch pails; the older girls shimmered in nylons and red leather shoes.

Lola Johnson and her husband, Pete, lived in the Circle. They had attended Cardiff Spur Mission for years, and they themselves were active missionaries: whale baleen and ivory decorated their walls and shelves. Their house, with its second story and separate dining room, seemed enormous, populated by four boys and one girl, Cynthia, whose room I longed to lounge in and never leave—pink everything, ruffles everywhere, wallpaper with the tiniest rosebuds I had ever seen. Even the sun slanting in through her dormer window, filtered through lace, softened to a delicate and powdery light.

Before the Langs came to Cardiff and my parents began spending more and more evenings at their table, we had spent a great deal of time with the Johnsons: late-night sledding parties, taffy pulls, dinners of exotic dishes Lola had learned to cook from one native tribe or another. Cumin and curry wafted from her kitchen, and I thought I had never inhaled anything so foreign and rich, as though a hole had been dug in the earth, releasing secret and mysterious smells.

I remember their easy laughter and their patience with me when I asked to set to ticking the only metronome I had seen in my life. I remember afternoons when my mother and Lola drank coffee at our kitchen table, leaning into their whispered conversation with the intensity of message bearers. And I remember my mother, many months later, standing at the sink, crying as she read the letter Lola had sent—an explanation maybe, perhaps a plea for my mother's intervention, but nothing I can imagine now as a confession.

From the beginning, Lola had voiced her disapproval of the Langs' ministry, casting one of the few votes against their bid for pastorship. After their arrival she continued to play the organ during service as she had always done, but now Sister Lang had a place at the piano, playing with modest composure the unembellished chords she had taught herself. Lola, a teacher of music, made the organ an instrument of exuberant praise.

I see now how she brought judgment upon herself. She prayed louder than most men, twirling in the aisle until the long fall of her auburn hair loosened from its bun and flowed around her shoulders. Sister Lang said once she had seen her at revival dance out of the sanctuary and into the foyer. "I peeked around the corner," she told us, "and there she was, smoothing her hair and checking her teeth. Then here she came back out, singing and swaying. She thinks she's got us all fooled, but she ain't fooling nobody." I remembered all the times I had heard Lola sing in the Spirit and prophesy in tongues. Even in shapeless skirts and high-necked blouses, there was something unfettered about her, something beautiful. Maybe it was this that caused Brother Lang to dream.

I sat one night in the parsonage kitchen with my parents, listening transfixed as he told of his vision: a chipmunk with eyes like obsidian rode his shoulders, whispering in his ear an evil seduction. He said that each time he reached to pull the harmless animal from his neck, it would turn into a lion. In fear, he would release his hold, and the demon would resume its original form.

He mimicked the motions, grabbing the air behind him as though dragging the thing from his neck, his eyes widening in surprised horror as he described the lion's foul breath and glistening fangs. We felt its weight on our own shoulders as he hunched in his chair, breathed out our own relieved sighs when the monster metamorphosed back into its small squirrel body.

Finally, he straightened and opened the Bible he held in his lap, one finger marking the chosen passage:

"He that heareth you heareth me; and he that despiseth you despiseth me; and he that despiseth me despiseth him that sent me." And the seventy returned again with joy, saying, "Lord, even the devils are subject unto us through thy name." And he said unto them, "I beheld Satan as lightning fall from heaven. Behold, I give unto you power to tread on serpents and scorpions, and over all the power of the enemy: and nothing shall by any means hurt you. Notwithstanding in this rejoice not, that the spirits are subject unto you; but rather rejoice, because your names are written in heaven."

Brother Lang said that God had revealed to him the dream and its meaning: the monster was Lola, full of deceit and cunning, revealing her true nature when threatened—she was predatory, destroying the church with false witness. To drive her from our midst would require great prayer and sacrifice: only the purest spirit could hope to face such a demon without losing his own soul to Satan.

The Devil walked among us cloaked in good deeds, a devil who could quote Scripture and pray in the tongues of angels. Wasn't Satan, after all, once an angel Himself? Brother Lang said we must purge ourselves in order to see the enemy's true form. He said he would take the burden upon himself so that God might enlighten us all. The next Sunday, he would begin his fast, forty days and forty nights, following the example set by Christ to purify his body before crucifixion.

Each of us had fasted for shorter periods but none could remember when a leader or member had taken on such a trial. When he asked that we gather around him to pray for strength, for God to accept his sacrifice, we reached out our hands, humbled by his willingness to suffer such pain on our behalf.

Over the next few weeks, we watched Brother Lang take on the carriage of an old man. His wide, ruddy face yellowed and shrank; the skin of his forehead tightened across his skull. The belt cinching his waist became riddled with newly punched holes, and his suitcoat hung from the bones of his shoulders as though still on its hanger. We held our breath as his sons helped him from his chair to the podium, where he tottered drunkenly, lisping out God's promise of retribution.

As we lifted our voices in prayer, I opened my eyes just enough to see the faces of those around me, and I knew they were wondering, Who? Who walks among us disguised as one of God's own? I dared not look at Lola, who lifted her voice highest of all, calling on Jesus to open our eyes so that we might see the true nature of the devils who deceived us.

Perhaps Lola knew all along that the preacher's words were directed at her. As the knowledge of his intent spread, the church divided, a few believing their pastor's words less Gospel than the rantings of a jealous man, but most caught up in the fever of his convictions. He stood before us, willing to die in his quest for truth, while Lola continued to dance, whirling from pew to pew, singing out God's praises.

Finally, the family was shunned. Cynthia and her brothers, whose eyes no one could meet, filed that last time from the church, following the march of their mother, their father, a tall, handsome man, who rose last, wanting more than anything to fight it out, to grab the skinny man from his shoes and shake him till his bones rattled. No one turned to meet his challenge, offering only their bowed heads in compensation. Brother Lang sat weak and smug, shriveled to a hard, leathery knot.

I think of that letter my mother held in her damp hands as she leaned against the counter, letting the hot water run and drain until steam rose from the scalded dishes. It was written by a woman who, like herself, had been given the command to serve and obey. And like her, even covered and unadorned, the woman was lovely.

Did my mother wonder why Lola did not give in, why she did not submit and allow whatever possessed her to be exorcised, cast out by the elders, by the preacher whose hands trembled to touch her? What secrets had they whispered across the table while we went about our play, children oblivious to our mothers' lives, their desires, their unnamed temptations?

This was my mother's lesson, and my own, a lesson I have not yet unlearned: be still, be invisible. Do not draw attention to yourself, for in doing so you become a target. I would learn that unholy men will rape you. Men of God will leave their meditations and good wives to lust after you. Satan himself will see you flashing, drawn like a fish to a vulgar lure, and take your soul for his own. Even then, before I knew what awaited me in the world outside our circle, I felt the threat that I as a woman was to myself and those around me. We were weak, unpredictable, no more capable of controlling our whims and desires than Eve, whose very nature caused the fall of Man, was able to control her gross appetite.

I became determined to deny myself any pleasure. I fasted for days to rid my soul of whatever evil I carried inside me, even those evils of which I was unaware. I stayed with the adults in the kitchen after service, avoiding Luke's eyes, praying into my hot cocoa when I saw him disappear toward the stairs. Women, I knew, were responsible for every temptation. If Luke sinned, if he touched my knee or brushed his arm against my breast, judgment would fall on me.

• • •

I loved the time I spent with Sister Lang and Sarah, perhaps believing that my kinship with women would be what would save me. I imitated their modest gestures, combed my hair and curled it just as they did, sat next to them at the table and filed my nails into blunt rectangles instead of the smooth ovals my mother preferred. Often, they took me to town with them —into Pierce with its sidewalks and American flag flapping above the new post office. They'd let me stop at the library, window-shop at Kimball's Drug, buy me a cone at the Confectionery. The Confectionery seemed a rarity: soda fountain, booths and tables, a jukebox against the back wall, around which the high school kids congregated afternoons and weekends. Sometimes we lingered long enough over phosphates for me to catch a chorus of "Cherry Hill Park" or Elvis's deep voice lamenting, *If there's one thing that she don't need it's another little child and a mouth to feed in the ghetto.* I had never heard of a ghetto and could not imagine any mother mourning the birth of her baby, but I understood it was all very tragic. The songs left me feeling touched by something outside, real: there were places where people led lives of ongoing drama and magnificent despair while I raced the boys at recess for the one unbroken swing.

During one outing, while Sarah shopped for material at Durant's, Sister Lang called me to a display against the wall.

"You don't have any nylons, do you?"

I shook my head, feeling both childish for having to say no and excited by her interest. She held up a pair of tights the color of sand, nearly opaque.

"I bet your mother won't care."

I looked doubtful. She might not care but my father would, and she would not risk his disapproval.

Sister Lang placed them on the counter with her other purchases. I had never received such a gift, a gift made even more special by its provocative and conspiratorial nature; girls wore kneesocks because their legs had little value beyond simple locomotion, unlike the legs of women, whose shape and composure elicited considerable attention—why else were they so careful to wear their skirts covering their knees? It was permissible for a woman to show a certain portion of her body —the shins—as long as she did so with modesty. Too much revealed led men to imagine more.

Sister Lang's instigation meant she saw me as more than a child, and I clutched the small package to my chest as we drove home. I could not wait for Sunday, for Luke to see me in this new way. I hoped my father wouldn't notice, although he seldom missed scrutinizing my dress and demeanor. Still, there was my mother, whom Sister Lang had made to seem different somehow, on my side. I felt how the circle could split like the cells we studied in school—a line through the middle like a stricture between the women and the men—and I felt newly joined to the lives of my mother, Sister Lang and Sarah. There was some power they had that I sensed more than understood.

It confused me, seeing them without their husbands and still able to find their way in the world, making decisions as though the men did not exist. I thought of the night when Brother Lang had pulled his wife onto his lap and she whispered something in his ear that made him blush and squirm. Then, when she rose laughing, he watched her walk into the kitchen as though no one else in that room existed. What had she said to him? Whatever it was, it took him a moment to come back to his Bible, which had slipped between his knee and the chair cushion.

• • •

When I got home, I locked myself in the bathroom, stripped off my kneesocks and pulled the silky tights over my pointed toes and up over my thighs. I bunched my dress at my waist and turned in front of the mirror, trying to make familiar the body in the glass. From the hips down, I looked like a woman, but above the gathered material I seemed still a child. My hair hung limp and stringy. My glasses slipped down my nose so that to look through them I cocked my head back, letting my mouth slack open. I dropped my dress and began brushing my hair furiously. One hundred strokes, day and night, Sarah said. Mayonnaise wash and vinegar rinse to make it shine. Someone knocked.

"Kim, what are you doing in there? Come on out, now. Greg needs someone to play with."

I scowled at my mother through the door. I waited until I heard her step back into the kitchen, then gently pulled off the nylons, one leg at a time. The hair on my shins lifted with static. I had asked to be allowed to shave my legs, but my father said no. "Maybe when you're thirteen," my mother had said. She knew the boys at school teased me about the dark down. At least the nylons were heavy enough to hide the hair until my father gave his permission for it to be removed.

I stepped into the kitchen, where my brother waited. "Wanna go outside, Sis?"

I looked from him to my mother. No, I didn't want to go outside. I wanted to stay in and wash my hair in eggs and honey, rub lemons on my knees to erase the rough skin, just like it said in *Ladies' Home Journal*. My mother dipped her head toward the door. "Go out for a little while, just until dinner. I'll call you when it's ready."

Outside, the late afternoon air made me wish I'd pulled on pants beneath my dress. Ice on the eaves glistened, catching the last sparks of sun. I refused to talk to Greg and began trudging in circles, kicking aside moss and pine needles, scuffing lines into the damp ground. I took my time, working my feet close, until the letters looked perfect, joined by a cursive flourish—"LL+KB." Greg watched from a distance. There was something different about me he wasn't sure of, something secret. Instead of a playmate I'd become an adversary. When he edged toward me, I shuffled and kicked through the lines before he could see what I'd written.

He looked at me curiously. Had he done something wrong? Was I angry? All those years in the camps and moving from one house to another, he and I had shared everything— baths, beds, toys, the child's heartache that followed being scolded and spanked. Now, I wanted to share nothing with him. Even his eagerness for my company disgusted me.

"Why don't you leave me alone? Why are you always bugging me?" I gave the letters a final sideways kick and started for the house. Greg hesitated, then followed, wiping his eyes. I felt a twinge of guilt but could not bring myself to offer him anything other than indifference.

More and more, I wanted to be with the women, doing the things that gained them praise and proud glances from their husbands. My mother was an experienced seamstress, and I watched in fascination as she cut and pinned the onion-skin paper to the fabric she had chosen for a new dress. The illustrations on the front of the Simplicity patterns showed several young models, hips cocked and hair flowing. I knew my mother always bought extra material to lengthen the hem, but as I studied the girls I longed to be like them, in whatever place it was they existed. They shaved their legs and floated little capsules of scented oil in their bathwater. They had more than one pair of shoes. They looked happy and not too sinful.

The cold coming on brought my family and the Langs together even more. The parsonage was always warm, seasoned by years of woodsmoke and the heavy smells of simple cooking: meats roasted and fried, potatoes and onions and bacon grease.

The gut smell of green hides that Sarah's husband brought home seemed as much a part of the parsonage as the brewing aroma of coffee. Off the kitchen, the enclosed porch housed Terry's cache, the tools of his trade: skunk scent (to mask his own human odor), Borax to cure the hides, waterproof boots and cold-weather garb, and the traps hung according to size— the small rodent and weasel traps with their lightly hinged jaws; the larger ones for cats and coyotes, possibly bear. Rods and reels, creels, his bow and sharp arrows, targets he would tack to a tree and aim at, as though he needed practice: at the center of each one, a fist-sized pattern of holes.

As much as I anticipated my times with the women, I thrilled to be with Terry on the porch or out past the creek. The attention he paid me was that of an older brother, and even though I knew that what he did with guns and hides was men's business, I found the intricacies of stretching hides and target practice much more compelling than baking the perfect pie.

Terry knew the secrets of the woods. Once he caught a young red-tailed hawk from its nest and brought it to the parsonage, believing he could train it like a falcon. It glared at us from its perch above the curing pelts. Sunday morning service found it screeching its hunger while Brother Lang raised his voice, competing for the congregation's attention, until Terry sneaked out and shot a squirrel to satisfy the bird, demanding as any god.

His expert sense of the woods and the ways of animals drew Terry the respect and recognition of his peers—other men who, like him, loved their lives in the woods. He could exist for weeks in the wilderness with nothing other than his knife to live by, mimicking the magpie's chortle, bellying down to the water to drink like a cat. When strange men came into town, wearing their stiff new hats and pressed pants, flipping their wallets open at the cafe long enough for Gladys or Holly to take note of the sheaf of bills, it was Terry's name that got passed to them: he was the one who could find them the elk they wanted, who could lead them to the bear raking grubs from the spongy wood, taking on her winter's fat.

One winter, a group of these men paid Terry well to track a bear to her den, where they aimed and shot the sow to death with their precisely honed arrows. When they pulled her from her cave, Terry discovered the cub.

He would never have done it had he known, he said. He brought the young boar to the parsonage and made it a bed behind the stove, holding it when it cried in its little human voice, rocking it like it belonged. I loved to cradle the cub and feed it its bottle. It grunted and mewled, docile until something set it off—the bottle gone empty, its plaything snagged beneath a chair leg. Within a few weeks we were jumping atop the furniture to evade its rampages and sharp teeth: Sister Lang's calves were mottled with punctures and bruises, and I can still see the small white scars where the cub sunk his sharp incisors into my shoulder.

Eventually, Terry sold the cub to a man who ran a tourist trap farther east on Highway 12. We heard later that the bear had bitten someone and been shipped off to a zoo in California. I wondered if it remembered us as it snuffled in its bedding for warmth, looking with its small eyes into the sea of faces.

Terry showed me how to slide the knife between hide and muscle, how to make the short, delicate cuts that separated the sticky tissue. I'd watch him work the body of a coyote from its skin in one easy piece, leaving the pink carcass glistening in its shimmering caul.

Once, while walking his trapline, Terry discovered the tracks of two bobcats, a mated pair thickly furred from the autumn's early cold, its promise of hard winter. He set a single trap near the water, baited it with rabbit or squirrel and waited.

I remember him describing the female's high-pitched yowling as he let her struggle against the teeth embedded to bone, knowing her howls would bring the male, and then he would have them both. Terry made plans for the money two good pelts would bring: the truck needed tires, or he might buy Sarah a new coat. He'd buy more traps to make more money, to keep doing what he loved—walking the woods, conversing with the owl and hawk, pounding the stakes down through the metal rings.

I knew this was his trade, his job: he was a trapper, a careful tracker, a good shot, one of the best around. Things like this happened, and we all knew it was best to stay tough, to not let the agonized screams of an animal get in the way of practical sense. He shot the male first—an easy target as it turned to him, ears flattened, teeth bared, protecting its mate—and then he killed the female. After the bodies were skinned, the pelts scraped and Boraxed, Luke built a fire in the back yard, hung a large black kettle above it and dropped the still-meaty heads of the cats into the boiling water. We stood close to the cauldron for warmth, watching the eyes bubble up, gelatinous as poached eggs at first and then hollow. We stomped our feet and drank hot chocolate as the night lengthened and the moon rose. I watched the skulls roil, clicking against each other, a sound I still remember when fall nights come and the acrid smoke of field-burning fills the air.

What ancient ritual were we observing? What drew us together around that fire and kept us there, fueling the coals with more wood long after the skulls had sloughed off their flesh and shone white as shell beneath the moon? Was it some racial memory that drove us to celebrate the hunt? The hides, cured and sold, would serve to sustain our tribe. The skulls themselves would become icons: bleached and polished, each anchored a corner of the preacher's desk, where he studied his Scripture for the next week's sermon.

I leaned one evening into the arm of the Langs' sofa, lulled by music and fire. Luke sat on the floor across from me, forcing square after square of wadding through the barrel of his rifle until the cotton emerged clean, gleaming with oil.

The parsonage was so warm I felt bundled, protected from the wind whipping the pines and swirling the year's first snow into sugared drifts, rattling the windows in their crumbling panes. In the kitchen, my mother, Sister Lang and Sarah diced carrots and potatoes while last year's venison browned in a big cast-iron frying pan.

I could hear my father and Terry laughing on the porch. The one vice my father had never been able to give up was his cigarettes, and when he stepped outside to smoke, one or the other of the men often went with him, taking, I think, a kind of vicarious pleasure in this small weakness. Brother Lang sat in his chair with his Bible, underlining passages for next Sunday's sermon. Closest to the stove sat Matthew, chair leaned back against the wall, softly singing and strumming his guitar. I knew the words to the song he sang, but there was something comforting in his single voice. I drifted in and out of near-sleep, thinking of Matthew and Mary, his girlfriend from downriver. It must be for her he sang, I thought, even though the words were for God.

Mary was darkly beautiful, with long, straight hair parted down the middle and pushed behind her ears. When she visited our church, she and Matthew sat in the back pew and held hands in a quiet and modest way. They planned to marry the following year, with their parents' blessings. They would be sixteen.

I wanted to be to Luke what Mary was to Matthew. Their love seemed rooted in something pure. I knew they never groped in the dark stairway. Mary would not have allowed it, would not have invited such a possibility. She had a wonderful full smile, but she kept her head bowed a great deal of the time. Her legs were always firmly together. I wanted to carry Luke's Bible the way Mary carried Matthew's, wear his jacket over my shoulders when the weather suddenly turned. I wished Luke would carve for me, as Matthew had for Mary, a wooden heart engraved with the numbers "1-4-3," which meant "I love you." If I could come and live in the parsonage forever, nestled beneath the slanting roof with Luke as my husband, I would be happy.

The snow promised easy hunting. My father and Luke picked up their own guitars and joined Matthew. Brother Lang followed with his banjo, and soon the room filled with louder music. The women came in from the kitchen, wiping their hands on their aprons, and we sang late into the night, some gospel, some country, the words all about love and God and husbands leaving and women who wouldn't do right.

I watched Luke's fingers grip and strum, fascinated by their rhythm and his concentration. The last song, he and Matthew played together. Matthew unwrapped his harmonica from its buckskin pouch, something he seldom did, and began to breathe out the slow notes of a melody I did not recognize. Everyone sat still to hear Matthew finish the last chorus, eyes closed, still leaned back in his chair as though he existed alone in that room with his music. We all knew he was in love, and even the adults, perhaps remembering their own first stirrings, allowed him the sweetness of his misery.

My father did not join the hunt the next day. Perhaps he was working. Perhaps he had no desire to share even with Brother Lang and Terry the solitude of the forest. I'm not sure when they left the parsonage, but I imagined them bundled in the truck, leaving narrow black lines in the snow. I thought we might find them that way, if we had to, follow the twin trails down the road to Bertha Hill, where their footprints would lead into the woods.

I longed to go with them, to walk the ridges and smell the musk of rutting elk. But women did not often carry rifles into the mountains. There was one year my mother disappeared into the forest behind our shack, the fall after my father hurt his back. She pulled on his jeans, wool shirt and red cap, then set off into the grove of cedar as though she were intimate with the habits of deer, the rifle slung across her shoulder. She returned within an hour, dragging by one hind hoof a fawn the color of caramel. The tender meat lasted only a few weeks, long enough to keep us fed until my father's compensation check came, but the memory of the deer's smallness in her hand never left her, and she never again raised a rifle to her cheek.

This had been many years before, and still the need to hunt outweighed any number of things. Each year, I felt the pride of seeing the men off: the ritual of early mornings and frost; thermoses of sweet hot tea; the orange hats, wool and gleaming rifles. My father and uncles never took more than they needed, never hunted for size and racks, preferring a fat young cow elk to a swollen-necked bull. The Langs needed lockers full of venison and elk to last the long winter; the men needed to feel the balance of steel and polished wood in their hands, the mastery of lead and powder. The boys needed to learn from their elders the ways of the woods and how to take their place as providers.

Early that evening, Brother Lang called my father from the cafe at Headquarters. Could he meet them there? Matthew had gotten separated and they were having trouble finding him. He was probably already waiting on the road at the base of the butte, but they might need to split up, do some circling.

They called my father because they believed if anyone could find Matthew, it would be him. I imagine my father with the heavy black telephone in his hand, moving slowly to light a cigarette, his motions already weighted with the knowing, that sense he had when things had already fallen into their fated place.

My mother must have taken my brother and me to the parsonage to wait with Sarah and Sister Lang. I remember night coming on, the light fading in degrees, like a drape being pulled against any vision we had of ever seeing Matthew again. I remember the stillness, the house so silent, words all we had to bid against the dark.

How long before we heard the doors slam, the men tramping onto the porch? When Brother Lang stepped in, he was pale and sweaty. He looked to me and then Greg, as though in our eyes he might find what he was searching for.

Sister Lang stood facing him, her eyes taking in the slump of his shoulders, the set of his mouth. Cold pushed in behind them, filling the room with the smell of woodsmoke.

"What is it, Joseph?" she asked. Then louder, *"What is it?"*

"We can't find him."

"What do you mean, can't find him?" Sister Lang stepped toward her husband, but when he reached to touch her arm, she brushed his hand away.

"You've got to go back. He'll die out there."

"No one's going to die, Mona. Matthew's smart. He knows what to do." He let his voice drop and rested his hands on her shoulders. "We must have faith."

"How could you leave him? Go back! Go back!" She lunged, slapping his coat, his arms, his chest.

I felt my brother crowding against my side. My mother had run outside to meet my father. The moon cast long, narrow shadows across the snow, and through the window I could see my parents facing each other beneath the burned-out floodlight. They looked young to me then, maybe sixteen or seventeen, as though they were on a date and taking as long as they could before being called in for the night.

They set up search camp at the base of the mountain—townspeople and every available adult from our church. The women brought casseroles and coffee. The men napped in their pickups between sweeps. The nights' cold blanketed the trees with a thin layer of crystalline ice. Ravens sat like little priests in the blown-out crowns of yellow pine.

My brother and I were left with Sister Ward. We sat in the

strange living room, watching TV and eating popcorn, focused on the blue square of flickering light, while she puttered in her kitchen, muffling every move as though the uninterrupted noise of the soundtrack were all that kept us tamed and content. I let myself exist in that room with studied attention. I did not think of my parents on the mountain, nor of Luke with his father and Terry calling Matthew's name. I didn't ask when anyone would be back. I sat beside Greg, cross-legged on the floor for hours, he as silent as I, watching Frankie Avalon and Annette Funicello in bathing suits dance by the light of a beach fire.

They found him three days later, his neck wedged in the fork of a downed tree. Some believed he had been chasing an elk and slipped; he was unconscious immediately from the pressure against his jugular, the sheriff said, unable to free himself, the limbs holding his face to the sky as though he had simply fallen asleep tracing the movement of stars.

Greg and I had been shuffled to the house of Sister Ward's daughter, and when she told us they'd found Matthew and that he was dead, I ran to the bathroom and locked the door. I sat on the rim of the tub, trying to focus on the linoleum's intricate geometry. I heard my brother crying, and then a gentle knock.

"Kim, are you all right?"

"Yes."

There was silence and then the woman's voice comforting Greg. I knew I should go to him. I should be crying too. I picked at my knees, the scrapes from a playground fall nearly healed. I said "dead dead dead" over and over again until I didn't know the word anymore and it was just a sound in my mouth.

. . .

Days later, when Brother Lang opened Matthew's Bible, left on the chair by the woodstove, he found passages underlined in red, all seemingly prophetic of Matthew's death. He'd been so quiet the night before, playing his harmonica more plaintively than we'd ever heard. Had he known he was going to die?

Even though we believed God's will had been done and all things work together for the good, that last winter held little comfort for any of us. Brother Lang continued preaching, approaching the podium with the same halting gait as when he had fasted. Their ministry was broken; without Matthew, their dreams of a brother-and-sister singing success could never be realized. I wonder now why it seemed they never considered Luke as part of the mission. Maybe it was because he seemed to lack the seriousness of the calling that Matthew had possessed. I wondered if they wished it had been Luke they'd found dusted white with snow.

In town, when women offered their opinions, clicking their tongues over the tragedy of such a wonderful young man so soon gone, my mother lowered her eyes and closed her ears, knowing that Matthew's death was no accident but an act of God's will. When men at the lunch counter wondered out loud why anyone would let a fifteen-year-old kid trail off alone, my brother and I glared at their wool-covered backs. "Found him stiff as a board, no matches, no nothin'." "Aren't from around here, are they?" I burned with anger at their smug ignorance. I wanted to believe that something had led Matthew into that wilderness, that he had known and accepted his fate with brave resignation, but I wasn't sure that God should warn you like that, then make you go anyway.

• • •

It had been dusk when they pulled off the road and began their hunt, crossing into a forest they knew little of. It is this my father cannot understand—why men intimate with the ways of the woods would go against a code they understood held the balance between life and death. Matthew's death has remained a mystery—a freak accident, we call it now. Still, my father shakes his head when we speak of it. "There comes a time in the evening," he says, "when you should never go into unknown country."

Our life with the Langs was never the same after that. The laughter quieted to an occasional weak chuckle. Sister Lang barely acknowledged my presence, and Sarah's face seemed permanently altered, drawn into rigid lines. It seemed to me that both women blamed their husbands for Matthew's death, and when Sarah looked at Terry I saw in her face not love but something closer to hate.

I missed the parsonage, the warm room and dark stairway. I missed the late evenings of music and laughter. Now there was this thing that separated us each from the other, as though the pain we all felt would only be intensified by our sharing it. My parents were silent. My brother and I kept to our books. The winter passed into my memory as bitterly cold, more night than day. We drifted through the stillest air, tethered to our tables by threads of hunger, to our beds by their small promise of warmth.

I watched Sister Lang's face, motionless as the moon, Luke forever beside her, his hand at her elbow. I watched Sarah turn from the husband she believed should have known better than to let Matthew go off alone, who should have called him in before it was too late. Wasn't he, after all, the one the hunters from California called to lead them to the dens of sleeping bears? How could he track a sow gone weeks to her bed and be unable to find a boy lost only hours in new snow?

My father I saw brace himself to take on whatever pain another could not bear. He never questioned out loud, never asked how or why, but eased the grief of others onto his own shoulders. He spoke slowly, smiled just enough to make us all believe God's will was still sweet, his ways mysterious.

What was it, then, that brewed in my father that winter if not the battle he waged with his own will? He wanted every cell of his existence to submit to God's order. He wanted to be tested and consumed by the Spirit, to hear the voice of Christ Himself call from him some sacrifice. Perhaps he saw in the movement of seasons something unfolding, threatening his guarded circle, his family, his life. The demon he had seen at the bedroom door the year before still cast its shadow across his soul, and as winter deepened and the cold shut down logging, he studied his Bible late into the night. I fell asleep to the murmur of his prayers.

CHAPTER SIX

Grass sprouted from the cratered snow. The creek flooded its narrow banks and spread into the meadow. Spring came late to our hollow, the trees grown close as ribs around us. During high summer, we would welcome the dense shading, but the blossoming of April and May was lost to late frosts. Mornings, my brother and I ran to catch the sun long before the bus made its way to our stop, happy to sit at the side of the road, where the asphalt radiated warmth and robins trilled.

Most loggers found the layoff of spring thaw a time to mend the shingles loosened by winter winds or putter beneath the mud-crusted engine of a favored pickup. My father did neither. My mother, Greg and I stood in the yard, a small gathering of silent well-wishers watching him walk toward the bomb shelter, lift the latch and step in. The door seemed to shut of its own accord, darkening his face an inch at a time until all that remained of my father's presence was the lingering smoke of his final cigarette.

He was embarking upon a quest, like Jesus in the wilderness, or like Sir Galahad, I thought. He intended to remain in the bunker for forty days and forty nights, fasting and praying. He wanted to be wholly taken, to be tested and purified, perhaps to understand the meaning of the demon's visit. He would hold his own body hostage until it became both sacrifice and ransom, until God offered in return for his suffering a vision.

My mother stood wiping her hands again and again in the damp folds of her apron. "Now," she said, an affirmation of something about to begin or end. She turned and walked back into the kitchen, leaving my brother and me to wonder at the two closed doors: our father behind one, a man driven to acts of abstinence and conquest; our mother behind the other, working over the counter her incantations that made dough rise and egg whites stiffen into perfect peaks.

For a moment I felt orphaned, shut off from either world. My mother was not the same, could not be the same, with my father gone. His absence both diminished and enhanced her presence, and I wasn't sure how things would be between us. Her usual threats of discipline—*I'll tell your father if you don't . . . You better not let your dad see you doing . . . We'll talk about it when your father gets home*—were suddenly worthless: she would not dare break his solitude. With this realization came a sense of my mother's vulnerability and my own responsibility to shelter her, to take on my role as eldest child. The romance of it all thrilled me; already I had transformed my parents into gallant lovers, my father a knight striding off to do business with dragons (how fitting that even though he went by Neil, his given name was Arthur!), my mother, the fair and faithful wife left to keep the homefires burning.

"Now," I said to my brother and turned him toward the house, where we were needed.

I stole glimpses of the shelter those first few hours, imagining my father kneeling by the single cot, or stretched out on the floor, face down, suppliant before the Spirit. I never saw his shadow pass the small window. Not even his prayers escaped the earth-bermed walls. It was as though he had been swallowed into the hillside, gone to die or win the battle with hellish things. I offered my own prayers for his journey as I dusted and swept, mimicking the quiet diligence of my mother, who seemed to have shut herself away in her own body, her weapons of defense a mop and sponge. Instead of watching the shelter like a wife might watch the sea for sign of her sailor, my mother filled her hours with intense cleaning and organizing. The pained longing I had imagined she might feel—the sighs, the lingering contemplation of her husband's chair—instead took the form of determined orderliness. Guinevere was a drudge.

My mother's emotions were no doubt closer to fear and concern than any kind of chivalric nonsense, and like many women, she quelled her tremors of anxiety by controlling what she could: the state of her household. The intended length of my father's isolation must have seemed infinite. Since her marriage at age sixteen, the longest she had been separated from her husband was for a week when she took my brother and me by train to visit relatives in Oklahoma. Certainly, if a bear were to ramble into the yard or a fire break out, my father would be only feet away, able to rescue us if needed. But it was the nights she feared, not because of wild animals or even demons, but because it was then she had to lay down her weapons and be still. It was then that she felt the doubts and the guilt that accompanied them, wondering at the makeup of this man who had brought her into the wilderness.

She remembered Brother Lang's fast, how weak and brittle he'd become, and she could not imagine her husband's body wasted, his broad chest and strong legs gone to bone. She believed in his need to do this thing. She believed in divine inspiration. Yet the voice of the world still reached her, in that gray sea of near sleep: *He's abandoned you in the middle of nowhere. He thinks he sees demons. He's obsessed, dangerous, mad.* The voice was sometimes one she recognized, come from the past to haunt her. What would her grandmother think, her mother? She could see their eyes narrow, their mouths tighten, their judgment settle heavy and unspoken. Even some of the church people were sure to view such conspicuous self-denial as suspect, and she steeled herself to ignore their looks of pity, the wagging of heads when they thought her back was turned. Perhaps, too, she feared for the sake of me and my brother. Our school friends might find out, taunt us, deny us a place on the merry-go-round, throw rocks at our backs as we walked from the bus. Already we were set apart by our dress and our daily prayer over sack lunches.

These fears raised yet another fear: that Satan was weakening her in order to reach my father. If she were not strong enough to resist such trivial concerns as gossip and peer exile, she would fail in her role as helpmate. She remembered the words of Christ—"O thou of little faith, wherefore didst thou doubt?" She prayed that the vision would come soon.

• • •

On the third day of my father's seclusion, a Saturday, a white Ford station wagon bumped down the narrow road to our house, Uncle Barry grinning behind the wheel. My cousins sat in back, holding strawberry sodas and Planters peanuts. Aunt Mary grasped the dashboard with one hand and the door handle with the other. "Surprise," they yelled as they crawled from the mud-spattered car. "Surprise!"

My mother stood still in the doorway as my cousins handed me and Greg a soda. Their mouths were circled in red.

"You didn't call that you were coming." My mother looked from them to the shelter and back.

"Where's Neil? Tell him his little brother's here. He ain't working, is he?"

I sipped the warm pop. Greg had already run across the bridge with our cousins, who thought the outhouse was a castle.

"Barry, Neil's not here. He's searching for the Spirit."

Mary stood fanning herself by the car. She got carsick a lot. Barry, who had no religion at all, stared at my mother as though it were she who had lost her mind.

"What do you mean? Where is he?"

My mother wiped her hands on her apron and nodded toward the shelter. I kept my eyes on the car and wondered if my father could hear us.

"He's set himself off, Barry, so God will speak to him. He'll stay in there forty days and forty nights if he has to." My mother's voice was steady, and I took my cue from her, straightening my shoulders and bringing my gaze up to meet my uncle's. He looked from one of us to the other, then ran his fingers hard through his hair.

"Well, for Christ's sake!" He turned several small circles, as though trying to get his bearings, then stopped and glared at the bunker. X-ray vision, I thought. He wants to be like Superman.

"Lezlie! Chad! Get in the car." His bellow echoed through the hollow, and my cousins came running, something in his voice that made them think trouble. Aunt Mary was already in. I don't remember that she had said a word. She was watching my mother.

The station wagon left a cloud of gray smoke that settled around the house and shelter. I tasted the sweet pop, savoring its syrup, then thought of my father and his sacrifice. I stepped to where the bridge crossed the spring and emptied the bottle into the pure rush of water.

My mother wrapped her hands in the dishtowel she carried and pressed the cool cloth to her lips, then looked at me. "Go find your brother. He didn't come down."

She took my empty bottle and went into the kitchen. I hesitated for a moment, studying the shelter, then walked up the path to the outhouse. My brother was inside, reading a Superman comic.

"Mom wants you," I said, and watched him rise, still reading, and disappear down the trail.

I stepped behind the outhouse to the tree where weeks before I had carved a heart around the initials "KB" and "LL," a secret promise to Luke that as the tree grew, so would our love. But the letters and heart were gone, the bark stripped and weeping. *No, no! Why would anyone do this?* I shook my head, trying to hold back the tears and rush of heat I felt rising in my chest. Greg did it! Greg and my stupid cousins.

I ran across the bridge to the house, slamming through the door. My brother sat at the table, the comic in one hand, a peanut butter sandwich in the other. I looked from him to my mother, then burst into sobs, unable to think of any word that would convey to them the depth of my pain.

My mother followed me to my room, where I threw myself on my bed and buried my face in the pillow.

"It's okay, Sister. You don't have to feel bad. Uncle Barry just doesn't understand."

"It's not that." I turned my face toward her, let her pull the strands of hair from the corners of my mouth.

"Well, what is it, honey? What's wrong?"

"I don't know," I said. "It's just not that."

She patted me on the back, then walked quietly from the room. I lay for a long time, feeling sick with betrayal and confusion. Why couldn't things just be normal? Why was everything all wrong?

After a while, I rose and tiptoed out the door. I gave the shelter a wide berth, circling behind it, into the deeper woods. I didn't feel like carving another heart. Instead, I took one of the trails that connected the old skidroads and walked aimlessly, not caring where it took me, until I stumbled into the clearing where Gerty Buck's house sat, older than ours, never painted, the cedar shingle siding weathered to black. I stopped, surprised. Gerty's son, Ned, knelt only a few feet from me, polishing his motorcycle.

"Hi," he said.

"Hi." He was older than I was but not much taller. His sandy hair, unlike Luke's, was cut short and uneven, and his eyes were an unremarkable green. He smiled at me, and I found myself moving toward him and the bike. It seemed natural, the way I ran my hand over the black leather seat and along the shiny gas tank. I felt a little thrill knowing he was watching.

"Want to take a ride?" he asked. I looked past him to his

house, where I knew his mother sat, knitting an endless sup-
ply of pillow covers and afghans, which she sold at the community bazaars. Mr. Buck had died years before, crushed
when his bulldozer rolled.

"Come on. Let's just go to the tracks and back."

He was already on, gunning the engine. I straddled the
seat behind him, hesitating only a moment before circling his
waist with my arms. He smelled like the forest, like pine and
woodsmoke.

We started down the road, then turned onto a wide trail. I
leaned out just a little, just enough to see where we were
headed, just enough to catch the wind in my hair.

When we reached the track, he turned the bike and
headed back to his house.

"Can you take me home?" I hollered, hoping he could hear
me over the roar.

He turned his head and nodded. A few minutes later, we
emerged from the woods into my yard. I hoped someone
would see me, seated on a rumbling bike behind a boy who
seemed happy to have me huddled against him.

My mother came to the door, curious at first, but when
she saw Ned and his motorcycle and me on back, windblown
and flush with freedom, her mouth settled into a tight line. I
was pleased.

We chatted for awhile, the three of us, my mother asking
after his, Ned innocent and polite as pie. When my brother
came to stare big-eyed at the cherry-red Honda, I felt a surge
of pride. This was much better than gouging a lopsided heart
into a dumb tree.

No, Greg could not go for a ride. My mother seemed as
concerned about my brother's lust for the machine as she did
about the possibility of mine for Ned. When Ned said it was
time he got back, we watched him speed up the road, popping

the clutch just enough to raise the front tire. Greg was mesmerized. "Geez!" he said, and then looked sheepishly at my mother, who scowled. "Geez" was just another way of saying "Jesus," and it was a sin to take the Lord's name in vain.

"Don't you have chores?" my mother asked, directing her gaze at me. I nodded and headed for the house, nearly ecstatic. I wondered if my father would find out. Surely he had heard the noise. Still, he would be gone for days, maybe weeks. Already, it almost seemed as though he had never existed.

When I woke the next morning and walked into the kitchen, I was stunned to see him there, eating breakfast at his usual place. My mother cushioned her steps and warned me with her eyes to stay quiet. Had God spoken already? If so, why was everyone so silent, so glum? I sat at the table and ate my cereal, taking in the subtle signs: my father's studied attention to his food, my mother's tentative movements. Something had happened. Maybe God had told him something horrible, that he was going to die or that someone else was. Maybe some evil had been revealed. I thought of Lola, but she was already gone. Who else could it be?

I didn't ask these questions out loud, and no one in my family ever again mentioned my father's quest. Only recently did I learn why he abandoned his vigil and rejoined us at the table: his brother had threatened to have him committed.

I imagine the struggle he faced: continue with what he believed a good and sacred task, or risk losing everything—his job, his home, perhaps even his family. I do not think he cared that people might label him crazy, but his responsibilities as a husband and father were also sacred. I'm sure he prayed before leaving the shelter, at first asking God why this obstacle had been placed in his path, and then understanding that he must not question, that his brother's interference must in and of itself be part of the trial. God must have other plans, another way for my father to prove his spiritual commitment.

Perhaps for him there could be another form of sacrifice. What was it my father loved the most? He could survive without food, could live for long periods divorced from those in the world he cherished. As much as he loved my mother, he knew that his love for God was greater and that if called upon to do so, he would not hesitate to leave her. My brother and I belonged not to him but to God, and if asked he would certainly do as Abraham had to his own child: place us upon the rock and raise a dagger above our breasts.

What was left? What was he most jealous of? What I know is that the wilderness has always seemed my father's greatest love. The woods had saved him, had provided a home for his family, had brought him to the church and to God. To separate the land from the Spirit might prove the ultimate sacrifice.

He heard it in the voice that came to him one night, woke him into a light so bright he had to shield his eyes. This time, there was no demon, no chill air, only the light and the voice that might have been a dream except for the light and the way the words rang in his inner ear for hours afterward, saying, *Go. Go now.*

My father's decision was made: we would leave the woods. I don't remember being told or how I took the news, but it was spring and everything seemed new and reasonable. Besides, Luke and his family were leaving too, first for the cherry orchards of Washington and Oregon to work the harvests, just as they did each year. They would not come back. They'd find another church in another town where they could start over and leave Cardiff Spur and its memories behind.

Before then, there would be a baptism. By May, the month I turned twelve, the age when children were believed to be mentally and spiritually mature enough to determine the destinies of their own souls, the ice along Reeds Creek had thinned and collapsed. In a small eddy not far from our house, the congregation gathered to witness the total immersion of several members. After asking my parents' permission, I added my name to the list of those to be baptized.

The newly warm air, the birds chittering in the greening trees, the smell of the meadow opening into tiny flowers, all added to the dreamlike feel of the day. I stood with my parents, savoring the sun on my shoulders, shivering in my crisp white dress and bare feet.

I felt it was expected of me, given my age, but I also remember thinking that everything was changing, that this ritual would be a fitting symbolic end to my life in the woods and my relationship with the people of the church, whom we would be leaving behind. And it would also mark the end of my childhood, both spiritually and, I thought with a shiver of expectation, physically. It was a rite of passage, and I was painfully aware of my nipples already rigid from the cold air. My prayers were forgotten as I considered how I would survive the embarrassment of having my wet dress cling to my chest, the shape of my breasts exposed for all to see in that moment before I could cover myself.

When Brother Lang called my name, I passed my glasses to my mother, then took the hand of my father, who gave me like a bride to the preacher. He stood waist deep in the frigid pool, solid as a stump against the slow current. I shuddered in the runoff of mountain snow, my eyes already closed.

"Sister Kim, I baptize you in the name of the Father, the Son and the Holy Ghost." I felt his arm low at my back, and then his hand against my forehead. We dipped like dancers. The current caught my feet just as the water closed over my face, then I was lifted up and helped to the bank. My mother wrapped me in a blanket and cradled me against her warm shoulder. It all happened so quickly I didn't have time to worry about modesty. I blinked in the light. It was beautiful, the way the trees and sky looked without my glasses, like a watercolor painting. The dome of blue blended seamlessly to green, then back to the lighter blue of water. Figures moved before me, dark against the sun.

This is the way it's supposed to be, I thought. Like spring, everything reborn, everything whole. I closed my eyes and listened. *Hallelujah*s rose and I knew someone else was going under.

There is something about that moment when I stepped from the water into my mother's arms that I want to hold on to. The sun's warmth, my father's steadying hand, the familiar voices praising God from whom all blessings flowed, and in every new leaf and birdsong a promise of everlasting life. Yet there are times when I remember myself silent, an observer, reflecting the ecstasy of others just as the water mirrored the sun. I could mimic their prayers, sway with them in my pew. Was I doing only what was expected of me, acting the role I knew would gain approval and praise?

Sometimes I think I never felt anything, only imagined the pure joy of absolute faith. There are times when I remember the peace that filled me at the end of hours at the altar, hoarse from calling on the Lord, exhausted and nearly incoherent. I felt emptied, purified by my physical weakness. Often, these were the times when I could feel the new language rise in my throat, feel the rhythm of the words suddenly come to me as I began to speak in the tongues of angels—a gift that each of us quested for, a gift that never came to some.

My glossolalia was guttural, the hard sounds low and deep

in my throat. I felt I could speak it for days, my eyes closed, sustained and mesmerized by this thing that controlled my body and my soul.

That day at the creek, when the water closed over me and then parted, I felt the magic of the ritual. I could never deny the rapturous exhilaration of being renewed, knowing I had pleased both my people and my god. Stepping from the water into the warmth of my mother's arms, feeling my father lay his hand on my head as he had done when I was young—I felt in that moment wholly loved.

I knew Luke stood nearby, but without my glasses he was only a blur. The pleasure I dreamed of with him could never be this pure. Yet when I thought of the way he might wrap the blanket around me and hold me against his chest, I felt both lightheaded and weighted in my heart. Why did every moment have to be compromised this way? What was wrong with me that I couldn't deny my flesh, that I so easily slipped into the carnal even as the hallowed water dripped from my body?

The ride home was short, around the meadow and down the rutted driveway. My father lit the stove just for me while I changed. My mother melted Crisco and salted the chicken. Greg, not yet old enough to truly commit himself, fell asleep on the couch. In a few days we would leave our house for good and drive the winding road to Lewiston. I began clearing my shelves and dresser, filling boxes marked in big black letters, "KIM'S ROOM" and "BOOKS."

It didn't seem real that I might never see my room again. After years of seasonal moving, nothing seemed ever to be left wholly behind: we always came back to the fragrant smell of pine, to the creeks, to the town where every building, fence and driveway was familiar and expected.

Still flush from the cold water and the attention of my

elders, intent on doing a good job of packing to show how responsible I had become, I never thought I'd miss the trees or the narrow spring. I wish I had looked one last time to the mountains that had folded us in and kept us for so long, for when I think of them now my mind's eye cannot see past the clearing: everything beyond comes up dark, impenetrable, as though the world itself fell away beyond the perimeter of my vision.

There is a photograph of me taken on my twelfth birthday, in which I stand posed against the snow berming the bomb shelter, squinting into the newly warm sun. My hair is long and straight, nearly to my waist. My kneesocks reach to the hem of my homemade dress, the only concession to style a pattern of muted orange and yellow rings against the brown background, a print that I remember thinking was almost psychedelic (a word I hissed in a whisper between my lips when no one was listening), something the hippies in San Francisco might wear.

I had seen hippies only on Nan's TV, and their wondrous hair, bright colors and dangling beads amazed me. Even so, I could hardly connect them to the monsters the townspeople spoke of over coffee at the cafe. If we weren't careful to run them off the minute they set their sandaled feet inside the village, they said, the hippies would poison our water tower with LSD. The results would be disastrous: normally decent men, women and children running naked through the streets of Pierce, murdering their neighbors, throwing themselves from the hotel's balcony, addicted until death to the mind-altering drug. The entire population of our community would be destroyed, the wiser ones said, shaking their heads in grim contemplation.

I could hardly imagine the carnage. I pictured the burly Mr. Butler with his ax, running bare-chested after his neighbor Mrs. Ball, her enormous breasts flopping loose in front of her. I wasn't sure what the "orgy" was that I heard spoken of as a result of this behavior, but it must be something close to "ogre," and certainly Mr. Butler and Mrs. Ball barreling down Main Street naked fit that bill.

My last gift from the Langs would help guard against such evil. It was the blue Bible I had seen at the Christian Gift Center in Lewiston, my name embossed in silver on the cover. Inside they had written, "To a *very* lovely girl by the Rev. & Mrs. Joseph Lang May 1970." It was the most important thing I could carry with me into my new life, they said. I hugged it to my chest, loving the smell that rose from its cover of morocco leather.

I can't look at that photograph with its promise of hot July days without remembering the summer before, the last summer we spent in the woods, when we had gathered at the parsonage, piled into several cars and gone deep into the forest to where the North Fork ran the color of jade. Matthew was alive then, and while he, Terry and Luke dove from the jutting boulders and swam the strong current from one side of the wide river to the other, the women arranged potato salad and lunch meat on paper plates, shaded by cedar and pine. It was a celebration of summer, of friendship, and the prayers we offered over our dinner echoed through the trees.

It would be the last time any of us would ever see the river free, and that, finally, is why we had come—to see it once more before the giant slab of concrete already rising miles downstream blocked the flow and sent the river back on itself, flooding the land.

I could not know what the dam would mean to my life any more than I could have foreseen Matthew's death, my father's demon or the physical and spiritual upheaval of the next two years. The cycle of the river would be broken. Salmon would die by the thousands, snouts abraded to bone from their attempts to break through the barrier. As I folded my clothes into the cardboard boxes, I knew things would change, that our move to Lewiston would mean a new house, new people. But I had moved many times as a child and had come to believe that even in strange homes and new schools, some things would always remain constant: the love of my parents, the circle of our family and my belief in God.

When we drove that last time from the house in the hollow, I didn't look back. We crossed the river at Greer, down to Orofino, where my father pulled onto the shoulder of the road. At first I could not see it, so large it seemed another mountain—but then the sheerness of it, the steep, smooth expanse. Dworshak Dam braced itself between the canyon walls. I had never seen anything man-made so immense, and I stood still, letting my eyes adjust to the vision of something foreign in a familiar landscape.

Even now, when I drive the few miles east to Orofino, the dam catches me by surprise, looming up from the river, towering over the small town below. It flooded my place of memory, my place of birth. As the dam rose, so did the walls that severed my ties to my family, my god, the land. Sometimes, trying to find my way back, I want to go at the concrete and steel with my fists, beat it until the real water flows and I, like the salmon, am raw to the bone. That last summer, the syringa just beginning to spray its heavy sweetness into the air, I hung my head out the window to watch the dam disappear, then turned to the road ahead, the wind in my face.

CHAPTER SEVEN

I trace the road from the dam west to Lewiston, where the mill spews its poison, where, in winter, the Nez Perce once gathered their families close along the joining banks of the Clearwater and Snake rivers. The town itself is not large—thirty thousand, another ten thousand in the sister city of Clarkston, Washington, connected by two short bridges spanning the Snake. But for me, coming out of the woods, the place seemed never to stop, to sleep. Even at night the traffic continued, the stores stayed open and people went on about their business as though they had no home to go to.

We stayed with Nan for the first few weeks, and my memories of that time are heavy with nostalgia, sweet as the lilacs that grew in a hedge outside her door. Early summer in Lewiston couldn't be more idyllic: crocus and daffodils begin their bloom in March, and by May the valley is rich in color. Morning winds clear the air. People rise at dawn to vie with their neighbor for earliest garden, bragging in June of two-pound tomatoes and knee-high corn.

I luxuriated in the warm weather, burrowing my bare feet into the ground we turned to plant potatoes. I loved my grandmother's house, the worn chair where we cuddled together to watch her soap operas; the kitchen, where something was always baking or boiling; her bedroom, where I slept curled against her back, wearing my Grandfather Edmonson's T-shirts.

My step-grandfather had been killed the summer before, the summer I turned eleven. Nan had been waiting for him to come home from his sales rounds when she saw on the evening news that he had been hit by a drunk driver while crossing the street. She sat stunned, watching the police mark the distance between one scuffed Romeo slipper and the pool of blood.

When I was told, I felt numb and far away, not just out of grief for my grandfather, whom I would miss, but also out of grief for Nan. Why was she given so much to bear? It didn't seem fair that she should lose her mother, then her first husband and father, and now this other husband who had once embodied the promise of a new life.

Even now, I wonder at my grandmother's fortitude. Once, a few months after her open-heart surgery and a year before she died at seventy-three of heart failure, I asked her how she had stood it. She told me, "You just go on, Sister. There's not much choice." I looked at the still-red scar splitting her chest, her face drawn with the effort to breathe. Yet in her eyes I could see the spark, that will to survive.

Those nights as a child when I lay in my grandmother's bed, comforted by her soft presence, I felt little nostalgia for the woods, or even Luke. Instead, I thought of the faces of young men I had seen on Nan's TV: Bobby Sherman, David Cassidy, others with pearly grins and hair brushing their shoulders. Nan gave me money to buy the teen magazines that held their pictures, then gave me half the wall space in her room to hang the glossy centerfolds.

I don't know what my parents thought of this. I'm sure they were not pleased, but what could they say? Nan still held sway as the family matriarch and harrumphed mightily at the stodgy teachings of our church. She trimmed my hair, painted my nails, asked me to stay up late to watch Dean Martin and the Gold Diggers. I leaned into her shoulder, eyes down, imagining her staring my father cold in the eye, daring him to challenge her. I was thrilled to feel some nick in my father's omnipotence, but I know now that she was only slightly less intimidated by his sternness than I was, and that he often demurred to her as much out of amusement as authority.

During the course of those long summer days in Lewiston, I became more and more aware of the changes in my body. The hair on my legs and under my arms had set in with earnest. Now could I shave? Absolutely not. My mother passed on the answer from my father, then looked at me sympathetically. She knew that dark hair sprouted above my kneesocks, but she would never consider compromising my father's authority.

Ronnie, my father's eldest brother, lived with Nan then. He and Dorothy had divorced, and he played guitar with his own country-western band, traveling around the Northwest, wildly popular with the locals. He was a tall, handsome man, blue eyes and black hair, and his voice held just enough edge to make the women wonder what he had suffered in love. He'd come home late, and I often woke to hear him humming in the bathroom. The next morning, I could still smell the sharpness of his aftershave mixed with the bar smells of stale cigarettes and whiskey. I breathed it in, wondering at the way it moved me, as though what I inhaled were attached to some memory.

I found my uncle's razor in the medicine cabinet. I picked it up, considered its edge bristly with whiskers, then carefully replaced it next to the can of shaving cream. The next morning, Sunday, I told my parents I didn't feel well, then watched them pull from the driveway, headed for church. Nan was in the potato patch, a mason jar of gasoline in her hand. Normally I would have run to help her. I liked pulling the striped beetles from the leaves and dropping them into the amber liquid, not because of the killing but because of the good it did: less bugs, more spuds. I was drawn to these kinds of easy efficiencies.

This day I had something else in mind. I went into the bathroom and locked the door, then opened the cabinet. The razor lay as I had left it. I memorized its angle on the shelf, the direction it pointed. I didn't think Uncle Ronnie, who wouldn't be out of bed for hours, would notice if I were careful.

I filled the tub with hot water, undressed and stepped into the steaming water. I had read in one of my magazines to soak for a few minutes to allow the hairs to plump and rise. While I waited, I studied the razor: black handle, a broad triangular head, the blade a long ribbon of steel that could be rolled forward with the twist of a dial to expose a fresh edge. I turned the little plastic knob until the old blade and whiskers disappeared, then lifted my left arm.

The hair had curled and tightened in the water. I pressed the blade above the dark mass and drew it downward. It didn't come off as easily as I'd thought it would: a clump fell into the water, but scattered patches of hair remained, and even where

I had shaved looked dark and prickly. I tried again, this time pressing harder and adjusting the angle of the blade. After several strokes, I paused to admire the scraped and bleeding skin, thrilled to have the ugly hair gone.

I shaved underneath my right arm, an even more awkward task, then emptied the tub and ran fresh water. Dark, telltale hairs stuck to the sides and I wiped them up with toilet paper. I listened for Nan, less afraid of what she would think of my shaving than the fact I was using my uncle's razor without asking. How many times had I heard my father and uncles and other men complain about their wives using their razors, returning them dulled, somehow tainted?

Beginning at one ankle, I made several passes upward to my knee. The blade seemed slow and sticky, catching every few inches, nicking me until little rivulets of blood ran down my leg. I checked the razor and saw it was clogged with hair. This was taking longer than I had thought it would. My armpits burned.

I twisted the dial, but nothing happened. I twisted harder. The plastic snapped and fell into the water. The narrow blade, curled inside like the keyed band of a coffee can, sprang out into a yard of glinting metal.

Fear set in. My punishment for disobedience had begun before I could even finish my sin. Hands shaking, I gathered the pieces from the water. Everything was there. Nothing looked truly broken. Maybe I could get it back together and no one would know. Laying the plastic parts along the edge of the tub, I saw that the first thing I had to do was re-coil the blade. After that, it would be easy.

I picked up the long strip and began straightening it. Suddenly, blood was pouring from my hands. I dropped the blade and held up my palms. Along one thumb ran a gaping, inch-long cut.

I grabbed a towel, then put it back: blood would stain the cloth. Pulling the plug, I held my hand over the drain, watching the darker liquid join the clear, then swirl and disappear.

How could I hide this? My parents would be enraged, not only at my rebellion but at my disrespect for my uncle's possessions and my grandmother's house. The bleeding from the cut slowed, and I ran more water, splashing it over my shoulders and along the sides of the tub. Holding my thumb over the toilet I dried myself with one hand, then rummaged through the linens until I found a frayed rag. I wrapped it around my thumb, swept the destroyed razor into the garbage and covered it with tissue.

Nan was in the kitchen, drinking iced tea, fanning herself with her apron. I entered the room slowly, head down.

She turned to where I stood, seeing first my stricken face and then the blood-soaked rag.

"Oh, Sister, what have you done?"

She pushed herself from her chair and pulled me to the sink. When the rag was undone, she let out a sigh of relief: the appendage was still attached. She clicked her tongue at the thumb as though it and not I were responsible for the fear she had felt.

I began to confess, to tell her how I planned it all. I had lied to her and my parents, then stolen my uncle's razor, and now it was broken. She held my hand beneath cold water, then dried it gently with her good tea towel. I flinched when she poured half a bottle of iodine into the wound. She studied it thoughtfully, then cut several strips of white tape, which she crossed back and forth across the cut.

"Will I have to have stitches?" This possibility worried me. I had cut my leg several years before, and I had never forgotten the sting of the numbing needle.

Nan shook her head; I couldn't tell if that meant she didn't know or simply no. She was muttering to herself, louder and louder, building up to something.

". . . should've let you do it months ago." I could tell now that she wasn't mad at me, but she was still angry. "All this foolishness. Never seen the like." She began pulling pots from the stove drawer, canned corn and shortening from the cupboard, banging them onto the counter.

"Mom and Dad will be mad. And Uncle Ronnie."

"Don't you worry about them. This is between you and me. Next time you want to shave your legs, you tell me and I'll let you use my Lady Norelco."

"But I'm not supposed to . . ."

"I don't know what they're thinking." She set the cast-iron skillet down hard on the burner and lobbed in a big spoonful of Crisco. "Big girl like you, already having her monthly. They should know you need to do these things."

Whenever my grandmother talked to me like this, I felt both pleased and sickened. I didn't like attention being brought to my body and its changes, yet she seemed to understand something my parents did not. As she cut up the chicken and dusted it in flour, I felt my fear subside. I didn't know what I'd tell my parents or my uncle, but Nan would protect me.

More and more, I was beginning to sense how different my family was. I watched the commercials on Nan's television, intrigued by the laughing, nearly naked teenagers running across the beach with their ice-cold Pepsis, and I slowly came to understand that I could be like them if . . . If what? My parents would never allow me to buy a bikini, much less mingle with boys on a beach while wearing one. But those young men and women seemed so happy, and there was nothing detectably dark in their pleasure. I saw the girls' long, smooth legs and perfect hair. Was it a sin that I wanted to be like them?

Compared with the other girls my age, I felt childish and dowdy. Compared with what I saw on TV, my family lived in the Dark Ages. Without the Langs, especially Luke, to validate my adherence to the laws of dress and behavior, I felt isolated. Even my grandmother (my *grandmother*!) thought us ignorant and old-fashioned.

I studied my body in the big bathroom mirror, sucked in my stomach and threw my shoulders back to enhance the jut of my breasts. I let my hair fall across one eye and pouted seductively at my own image. Not bad. Digging through Nan's toiletries I found a cake of Maybelline and a tiny red brush. I moistened the bristles and worked up a suitable goo, which I combed onto my lashes. Up close, the mascara looked "gommed on," as my mother would say—balled up and flaking—but if I stood back against the wall, my eyes took on a shadowed glamour. I dipped into a compact of oily rouge and rubbed it high on my cheeks, then made a kiss of my lips and circled them in Parisian Red.

What I saw in the mirror thrilled me: color, contrast, a face that might draw the attention of young men like the ones whose faces adorned my wall. I looked like a ruined woman. Even the sound of it was delicious.

I studied myself long and hard, memorizing that other I could become with a few strokes of paint, before scrubbing my face raw with hot water and soap. I would keep my twin safe, keep her existence a secret. I dried my skin and caught a reflection of my plain self. The washing had pinkened my cheeks; my lips still held a taint of red.

• • •

By the end of the summer we'd moved into our new home. It was not far from downtown and belonged to a retired doctor, who had graciously lowered the rent when my mother offered to do extra upkeep. It was enormous, a white stucco bungalow with a hacienda-style porch and a red tile roof. For the first time in my life, I both heard the word "breakfast nook" and saw one, and it was ours. Off the utility room was a greenhouse with heated growing beds; grapevines covered its roof like ivy.

The backyard grew thick with exotic ferns and roses. In one corner, beneath the overhanging limbs of a weeping birch, a pond held goldfish the size of large trout. A miniature cement bridge crossed over, and on the other side was my favorite spot: a small patio and bench, surrounded by lush green plants. It was a hiding place, cool and sheltered, and I'd lie on my stomach, watching the carp flash in the dappled light, silver and orange, white and black—a combination of colors I had never imagined in a fish that size.

We moved our few pieces of furniture into the house, and still our voices echoed off the walls. Above the fireplace, a huge gilt-edged mirror reflected the emptiness. The dining room was sad, I thought, because we didn't own a real dinette, although there was a certain holiday flair to throwing a colorful sheet across the borrowed redwood picnic table and setting places for the family beneath the sparkling crystal chandelier.

There was no place for a television. My father thought it better to read, and our faith held that Satan's influence had manifested itself via the auspices of ABC, NBC and CBS. On any given night one could witness the decay of Christian civilization on Channel 3: uncensored *hell*s and *damn*s, women wantonly exposing their midriffs and cleavage, couples engaged in passionate kissing. And the music! Young people gyrating on the stage of *American Bandstand,* flailing about as though possessed.

This is how it would happen, just as it had at Sodom and Gomorrah, just as it had at the fall of Rome: all the sins of the flesh, the drinking and gluttony and adultery, the unnatural couplings, the orgies, the idolatry, everything was coming to pass just as the Bible predicted. Soon, very soon, we believed, Christ would return. Weren't we already seeing the final preparations, the crime and disregard for God's law, the wars and famines, earthquakes and persecution of the chosen people?

We awaited the Rapture, longed for it, prayed for it, several times a day looked to the sky to be the first to see the clouds separate, the golden light shine through, Christ descend with his army of angels. "Please, God," we prayed, "come now and deliver us from this world of despair, this den of evil, fly us to Heaven to live forever in the light of your love."

We were prepared, ready to enter our new bodies, to hear our names called, to receive our rewards. We would leave the nonbelievers behind to face the Tribulation—that time when the Antichrist would make himself known (even now, we believed, he may be alive, biding his time, eating and drinking with mortal ease), when every man, woman and child must be branded or tattooed on the wrist or forehead with 666—the Mark of the Beast. The Seven Seals would be opened, false prophets perform wondrous signs and miracles, and for seven years those yet willing to denounce Satan would be tormented and tortured beyond seeming human endurance. Even the Jews would turn to Christ, and for doing so would incur the greatest outpouring of Satan's wrath.

Until that time, true Christians must gird their loins with abstinence from worldly things, lest they too become mesmerized by the profane offerings of Satan bent on increasing his army, determined to take as many as he could with him in his final fall into the fires of hell. Each day presented new trials and temptations—lies to tell, money to covet, bodies to lust after. To be free of all desire was to be free of potential sin.

Having left Luke's presence, I thought I might exist in a state blessed by moral continence. I was twelve, and I had no idea what the world might yet lay on the table before me; I never imagined that what might tempt me was not desire for wine or food, money or sex, but desire for something even more insidious: some sense of myself as a girl becoming a woman, coming to age in a landscape empty of anything that might define her worth except as a good daughter and future wife.

These were my horizons: to remain virtuous, to marry a modest man, to provide him with a clean house and an attractive body, to bear his children and raise them accordingly. To want anything else was an act of selfishness and betrayal of my predetermined role—mutiny, pure and simple. Such women, I was made to understand, those who neglected their husbands and families, who pursued their own interests outside the circle of kin and church, were doomed by their weak nature to be sucked down. You could find them in any bar, hiking their skirts, leaving thick smears of lipstick on their whiskey glasses. If as I came into womanhood I should choose to make such a bed, I would most certainly lie in it eternally damned.

I settled into my basement room, larger than many of the shacks we had lived in. I lay in bed that first night, gauging the darkness against the city's sounds skipping closer, then more distant, like the radio shows my father used to tune in, ear to the Zenith's speaker, catching the music and strange voices that drifted to us in the hollow from up and down the Pacific Coast. But the new sounds seemed even more foreign —sirens, tires screeching, the continual hum of cars on their way to or from destinations I could not imagine.

I found I couldn't sleep with the noise and turned on the small transistor radio my cousins had given me for my birthday. The hard-driving beat the church believed incited lust filled the room, and I lowered the volume and listened until the song ended. Then George Harrison was singing "My Sweet Lord." Beneath the covers I held the music to my ear, hearing the words repeated again and again: *I really want to see you, I really want to be with you but it takes so long my Lord* . . .

I was stunned. Was this worship or sacrilege? George was one of The Beatles and off limits to Christians, but this song seemed different. I remembered playing "Hey Jude" with Luke in the empty church, and I sensed in this song the same kind of spiritual melancholy. But hadn't one of The Beatles said they were more popular than Jesus? Maybe that had been John. Maybe George didn't believe it. There was nothing in the song that seemed evil, and George wasn't screeching like some drug-crazed fiend. But maybe this was part of the world's seduction: overt evil was easily discernible to the righteous; it was the backdoor variety you had to watch out for, that kind that made you rationalize, made you think you were safe.

I listened until the announcer broke in with his revving parlance, wishing I could hear the song again. Even though I liked my room and our new house, I felt lonely, a little lost. My parents slept in their room upstairs, and Greg had the room next to mine, but something about the largeness of the house and all the walls and carpet we could not fill or cover left me hollow. The music filled the space around me, and I found it comforting. As I listened, knowing that hours were passing only by what the voice told me, even the more raucous lyrics lost much of their ominousness. I liked the sound of the deejay's voice and the way he introduced the songs like old friends, as though there was nothing more natural in the world than to be alone in a glass booth, talking to a microphone in the middle of the night.

In a way, we were alike, he and I, alone in our rooms, conversing with the air. Kevin was his name, and sometimes he asked me questions as though I could answer. "How ya doin' tonight? Ready to *rock and roll*?"

I fell asleep listening to Kevin. When I woke the next morning the radio lay on my pillow, its battery drained. That weekend I dug through Nan's basement until I found the old electric radio I'd seen there and asked her if I could have it. It kept me company from that night on, and I fell asleep to the sounds of Smokey Robinson and Cher, Rod Stewart and The Cowsills. I'm not sure my parents knew how much the music had become a part of me, for if they had they might have taken the radio and destroyed it. Years later, it would be the thing I imagined they pointed to: *There. There is where the bad first started. Through the music of the world the evil entered her soul. That is how we almost lost her.*

We attended a different church each Sunday, trying to find the one that most closely resembled Cardiff Spur Mission, the one whose doctrine seemed most familiar. Some my father rejected because the minister was too soft on sin; others we did not return to because the pastor thought too much of himself and not enough of his flock. My father was absolutely set in his doctrine, much of which he had determined himself. If the board of elders allowed a divorced man to sit at its meeting table, the entire church was opening itself up to sin. Did the church embrace predestination? Healing? Glossolalia? Full-immersion baptism? What was the role of women? How did the preacher's wife comport herself? Was the youth pastor overly progressive, given more to gaining the young people's favor than directing them down the narrow path?

Somehow, my parents settled on what I believed to be the least likely: the Assembly of God. Fundamental, certainly, but I didn't see how this church could be any more different from the one we had left in Cardiff. The building itself was enormous: two double doors led into a foyer big enough to hold our former congregation; the sanctuary held hundreds. The choir wore purple robes, the preacher seldom lost himself in the throes of spiritual ecstasy, and the light shone through glass stained blue and green so that we all seemed to float in a landscape of water and grass.

The Assembly shared many of the same codes with the more rigid Pentecostals, but like city cousins shrugging off their country kin, the believers in the big church forsook many of the dress and behavior guidelines in favor of a more worldly existence: knees showed indelicately beneath the hems of dresses; rouge and light lipstick colored the women's faces. Others there my age peered at me from behind their parents' shoulders, taking in my long skirt and heavy glasses, and instead of feeling welcomed, once again part of a people who thought, acted and dressed as I did, I felt hopelessly outcast.

In Cardiff, we had been part of a community, a circle, joined with others who sang and prayed as we did. Even though our new fellow Christians spoke in tongues and professed to believe in miracles, they seemed less inclined to make a show of it all. My family bunched together at one end of a long and padded pew, holding tight to the belief that God could never approve of such giving in to the ways of the world. We sat straight-backed and lowered our voices, feeling compromised but somehow more civilized in moderation.

I could not imagine then and still am not sure why my father chose this church as our new place of worship, but we attended faithfully. He has said he found peace there. He faced head-on one of his greatest tribulations, his shyness, in order to praise God, and stood in front of the audience of hundreds to sing "Satisfied Mind" and "I'll Fly Away" and "Life Is Like a Mountain Railroad." I watched with nervous pride as he strummed his guitar on the big stage, his Wrangler slacks pressed to a fine shine, his Sunday boots—black eel skin —gleaming, his eyes closed.

I joined the choir, volunteered to pass out tracts. Slowly I began to make friends. I was reminded each week that the world outside loomed larger, the city a den for greed, malice and lechery. Anywhere that people gathered with no intent to call on Christ's name could only breed sin; every bar, movie house and dance floor became the foundation for another Sodom and Gomorrah.

How can I describe the sense of fear my parents must have felt? They knew how Satan worked, tempting by degrees—first in smaller things, tiny manifestations of earthly desires: earrings, a glint of vanity; lips outlined to draw carnal attention, only a prelude to complete seduction. Each day the paper told the stories of children hooked on heroin, riots against our country, rock bands whose satanic lyrics and vulgar gyrating sent entire audiences of young people into fits of shameless sex. Having left the woods, my parents found they had entered into a whole other kind of wilderness.

I felt I had entered another world. Each night I had my music. I started school at the local junior high, and from the teachers and books came a new kind of knowledge. In literature class we read stories of dragons and magic I had been taught to consider evil and demonic. In science we studied Darwin and evolution, and I was stunned by the gullibility of my fellow students, who seemed willing to believe our ancestors were monkeys (I could think only of Brother Lang years before, laughing: "My ancestors might have hung by their necks, but never by their tails"). History taught me something I had never considered: other civilizations had lived besides ours and those recorded in the Bible. Government, sociology, psychology—all things I knew to distrust, for the authority of man was weak and fallible, easily guided by Satan. Our authority came from God and the pulpit, and it could never be questioned.

Current events I had never been aware of announced themselves each morning in the newspaper's headlines. In 1970, when we first moved to Lewiston, I knew little of Vietnam, but I felt the waves it created as the conflict settled into the pooled American psyche. Even in Idaho, would-be hippies brandished their peace signs like silver crosses, and from our pulpit came the verdict: the peace sign was indeed a cross, but a cross broken by the forces of evil to resemble instead a witch's foot. Behind the movement to make-love-not-war lay the unbridled desire of people doomed to self-destruction, not by bombs and guns, but by uninhibited copulation and drug use. The evangelist from Kansas called for a record burning, and the church's teenagers lucky enough to own albums by The Beatles and Black Sabbath made a pyre in the parking lot, which the preacher saturated with gas and set afire, damning Satan back to His hell.

Something in the drama thrilled me. Anything that warranted such protest held incredible power, although I could not then articulate it as such. But the lives of those my elders feared—the rock stars, hippies, gang members, runaways—seemed to hold some spark, some power my own life did not.

Even while I prayed with the others for God to strike down the army of dissent rising from the ranks of the country's youth, I found myself secretly wondering what it would be like to be among them. I knew that rock and roll promoted it all—disrespect for authority, anti-patriotism, drugs, sex, Satanism. "Strawberry Fields Forever" played backward was The Lord's Prayer, and still I listened late into the night, unwilling to give up my radio.

Maybe it *was* the music. Maybe what I heard in the lyrics and the rhythm and the deejay's voice was what shook me, made me desire more of the world. I longed to be part of the group of girls at school who marched at half-time beneath the lights while their ruddy-faced parents applauded from the bleachers, but when I asked to try out for junior high drill team, my father said the skirts were too short. My brother was encouraged to participate in sports, but I could find nothing acceptable to fill my hours between school, church and sleep. *No* to the after-school dance, the movies, the swimming pool. The threat of assault from the outside world coupled with the laxity of the church's concern with modesty and strict moral behavior burdened my father with even greater responsibility. He drew his family tight. He would protect us, be the gate-keeper of our souls—his duty as a man.

My father became for me a wall of unreasonable denial, and I was unable to separate his distrust of the world from his distrust of me. He believed in absolute patriarchy and counte-nanced no questioning of his authority. His word was final. I chafed against his unwillingness to listen. I wanted only to assure him that I would be good—hadn't I always been?—that I would not do anything wrong or sinful. His night job as a truck driver, hauling wood chips from the forests he once loved to the mill at Lewiston to be made into paper and plywood, distanced my father even more. I saw little of him except on Sundays, when he drove us to church morning and evening and slept the hours between in his recliner.

My mother too seemed to me more and more unreasonable. One afternoon, we stood together at the sink, rinsing the dark blue grapes that grew thick over the greenhouse. We were making jam, and the sweet steam that filled the kitchen made my mouth water. My mother hummed at her work, and I felt happy to be there with her.

I didn't feel like this very often, this close and intimate with my mother. There were things I wanted to ask her—questions about boys and babies, about her life at my age, about why my breasts hurt at night. But I didn't know how to ask without embarrassing her or myself. Some things, she has always said, are better left unspoken.

Perhaps because of the warmth and the way she hummed, I gathered my courage. "Mom, do you ever use tampons?"

My mother stopped humming and without looking at me asked, "Why do you want to know?"

I told her I hated the pads and uncomfortable elastic belt that caught and pinched. I wanted to try tampons, which seemed much more modern and unobtrusive. My mother looked horrified.

"*You* can't use them, Kim. Virgins can't or they'll . . . well, they might make themselves not virgins anymore."

I had no idea what she was talking about. I knew what a virgin was: a girl who had never had sex with a boy. I was confused and irritated. The way the conversation had turned out was making me feel nasty, and I worked myself out of the room, finding comfort in my grotto beside the fish pond.

My cousin, Lezlie, had her own box of Tampax, and she was a year younger than I was. My uncle Barry had moved his family from the woods years earlier, and the tow-headed toddler was now a teenager with long dark hair and a coterie of cool friends who had shortened her name to Les. The next time I visited her house, I listened to her encouragement, then closed the bathroom door, alone with the thin cardboard tube. I studied the illustrations on the instruction sheet for a long time—the strange postures of the headless women and the simple blue drawings of their insides and orifices. When I emerged, Les looked at me expectantly. I grinned, feeling light and unburdened, triumphant and no less maidenly.

It was not sin I longed for but rather a sense of identity, purpose. Who was I? A nice girl from Pierce, straight-A student, obedient daughter of a logger, someone anyone could just as easily not see. And what did my future hold? I never imagined it, never saw beyond my rigid schedule of school and church, other than to dream of someday marrying Luke and going to live with the Langs. I wondered if I would ever get back to them.

I became more and more sensitive to the way the girls at school snickered behind their hands at my long dresses. The beige tights Sister Lang had bought me pilled and snagged until my mother threw them away and I was again reduced to wearing kneesocks. I envied the girls' smooth legs and dark lashes, the carefree way they bounced across the field in their miniskirts. I felt a strange longing for the older boys who gathered around them at the bus stop, and I realized it was the same kind of feeling I had had for Luke but somehow more generalized, like the tingling I had felt when studying my madeup face in my grandmother's mirror.

Instead of smiling at others in the halls between classes, I began to lower my eyes and shuffle close to the wall. When I was noticed, it was to be pointed out as some kind of freak—the girl who wore her skirts long and her stockings short, the one who cringed behind her heavy-framed glasses and never made trouble. My only haven lay in silence, in stillness, and I hid behind my books, folded in on myself until I sat at my desk like a pretzel, a knot of elbows and knees.

I walked home alone, usually behind Maria, a girl my age with full black hair and a chipped front tooth. She walked with Sam, her skinny blond boyfriend two years older, and they wrapped themselves together so tightly—his hand in her back jeans pocket, hers in his—I wondered at their ability to remain upright. Every other block they would stop, turn to each other and kiss deeply. I stopped then, too, maintaining my distance, embarrassed and entranced by their open intimacy.

Maria was my neighbor, and I watched from my porch as she and Sam disappeared into the old white house across the street. Sam emerged later, tucking in his shirt and smoothing his hair before loping on toward his own home. The light that shone from the second-floor window I decided was hers, and I watched each night for some movement to reveal to me more of her life.

She waited for me one day after school. Sam, a good foot-and-a-half taller, rested his arm across her shoulders. They both smoked Marlboros, and the cloud they exhaled filled the air around them so that they squinted to see.

"Kim?"

I clutched my books to my chest, fearing what she wanted from me or meant to do. She had never teased me about my dress or religion as the others had, but I couldn't imagine why else she would call to me.

"Want to walk home with us?"

I looked from her up to Sam, whose expression had not changed. He seemed focused on some point just above my head.

"You live by me, right?"

I nodded.

"Come on, then."

She turned and Sam pivoted with her. I followed several steps behind, still not sure what to make of this sudden and unexpected interest. Maria was not a cheerleader or drill team captain, and I seldom saw her with other girls. She often wore the same red skirt bunched at her waist to bring the hem higher, and her shoes were scuffed, the leather cracked.

We walked for several blocks, and then Maria stopped. "What are you, weird? Come on." She grabbed my wrist and pulled me to her side. "Want a smoke?" I looked at the red-and-white pack she snapped between us. A single cigarette jutted out past the rest, perfect.

"No." I kept my eyes down, afraid to see how ridiculous she must think me.

She shrugged and slid the pack back into Sam's shirt pocket. We walked the rest of the way home in silence, but when we got to my house, she smiled and said, "See ya," before guiding Sam like a Siamese twin through her own narrow door. That night in my bedroom I listened to the radio. I missed the Langs, Luke, the hollow. Nothing but the music seemed to fill the emptiness.

The next afternoon, while my father slept and my mother was at the store, I rifled the ashtrays for smokeable butts. I opened the window in the bathroom and broke each ground-out cigarette at its base, rolling the blackened tobacco from the other end. Fitted together, the inch-long segments produced a manageable whole.

It was as though I had practiced the movements all my life. I hardly felt dizzy, and as I sucked on the filter flattened by my father's teeth, I took in what I saw in the mirror: no stranger, but a girl defined by familiar movements, in visible control of the air that she breathed. The next afternoon, I took the cigarette Maria offered. I knew its smell, knew the motions. It was easy.

The next week, I asked if I could stay all night with Maria, lying to my parents for the first time: her father worked at the mill; her mother stayed home with the baby; she got good grades and didn't cuss. Nothing was true.

Once in her house I was stunned by the wreckage. Soiled diapers and cereal boxes were scattered across the floor. The dishes filling the sink and overflowing onto the counters were crusted with egg and ketchup. Flies rose and buzzed with our movement, then settled again onto the garbage swept to the room's corners. There was no furniture. Maria dipped her finger into a jar of commodity peanut butter and sucked at it noisily.

"Mom and the kids will be back soon. Let's go up."

I followed her past the bathroom, holding my breath against the smell. I had never seen anything so unkempt, so completely used and ignored. I thought my incredulous silence might embarrass Maria, so I hummed a little as we ascended the narrow stairs.

I was right. The light had come from her room. It must have been a grand house once, with second-floor balconies and gingerbread trim, but now the floors were buckled, the wallpaper stained and peeling. Her window was a set of French doors that led out into air. Nothing hung in her closet except a few tangled hangers. No dresser, no desk or table. An old skillet sprouted cigarette butts. Empty Coors cans lined the mopboard, and a huge bleeding heart covered one wall, pierced through with an arrow, "Sam loves Maria" scrawled beneath. She plopped belly down on a thin mattress stained with urine and blood. "I had a tooth pulled," she said, seeing my eyes fix on the dark blotches.

I sat on the floor, feeling the breeze against my face as we smoked and talked. She told me that she didn't remember her father, that they had moved from California with some jerk her mom was living with who left months ago, and she was glad he was gone because he beat them all and snuck in her room at night; her mother got welfare enough to keep them in food. She seemed old, resigned to her life, with none of the longing for a better house and family that I expected. I watched her pull the smoke deep into her lungs and hold it there, her eyes seeing something beyond the crowded houses and topped-off trees of our neighborhood. She came and went as she pleased, had a boyfriend who dogged her every step, drank beer and bought her own cigarettes, never hiding them from anyone. She painted hearts on her walls. She seemed less damned than I did.

I told her everything I knew and could—about the church, about Luke, about our reasons for coming to Lewiston. I told her I wanted to do things like the other kids, that I hated my long skirts and plain face. She nodded as I talked. Nothing seemed to surprise her. The room darkened and our breath took form before us, flying out into the cooling air and rising. I didn't think I could sleep there in the dirt and stink, but I did, waking only once to hear her mother banging the cupboards below, searching for the jar of peanut butter Maria had hidden on the ledge outside our room.

It happened slowly, the sense I came to have of myself as separate from my family and church. For a short period during the process, I believed I could exist as a Christian both inside and outside the world. But I was wrong, I realize now, not because it is impossible to live a moral life without setting oneself apart, but because I would not be allowed to do so.

The lines were drawn for me. I must be either the daughter subjugated to her father's will and the dictates of the church, or the harlot turned against God and family. There was a time when I believed the choice easy.

I lied more. Over the next several weeks, I spent long hours with Maria, standing in the rooms' shadows while she and her mother screamed, "You bitch! You whore!" It seemed like a television show—watching them pull each other's hair and throw shoes against the wall while the babies wailed in their filthy nightclothes. Horrified and fascinated, I could not tear myself away. I came home electrified, vibrating with a tension I could not speak of and would never betray. And I was a good actor. I knew if my parents became aware of Maria's true life, I would be forbidden to see her. I washed my hands and sprayed my hair with Final Net to rid myself of the smell of smoke, chewed extra sticks of Dentyne, sucked on Sen-Sens, their licorice bite almost painful on my tongue.

One fall afternoon, with my father's permission, Maria and I retraced our steps back to the school and found a place on the warped bleachers just as the sun settled cold and firm behind the Blue Mountains. I had never been to a football game before, and the cheers that rose as our team ran onto the field touched off a sense of unreality I could not shake for the remainder of the night. The band blared its wretched rendition of the fight song, competing with the announcer's voice crackling from the loudspeaker. But mostly it was the lights that made me feel as though I were floating in a brilliant bubble, suspended in the outlying darkness. The players in their red-and-white uniforms, the cheerleaders bouncing about in front of us, all legs and pompoms—I thought I would fall over from the sheer sensory shock of it.

We left early, not because I could no longer endure the

stimulation, but because I had a curfew: seven o'clock and not a minute later. Maria graciously walked me the few blocks home, leaving me at the door because even though unspoken, she knew I feared her performance in front of my parents.

The walk home had done little to alleviate my disoriented state. I sat on the couch, trying to explain to my concerned mother the effect of the lights and noise, how everything had swirled together and made me feel light-headed, giddy and nauseated. My mother felt my forehead, then pulled my lids up and studied my pupils.

"You go to bed. We'll talk more about this in the morning when your father gets home."

I felt my way down the stairwell, then fell into bed. I found the dial in the dark and tuned in KRLC. The game was still on, and I closed my eyes and imagined myself there, part of a world I might step into like Alice through her glass. I wasn't sure I was ready. I wasn't sure I could hold my own in such a place.

Finally, the decision would not be mine. My behavior after the game had set alarm bells ringing in the minds of my parents: disoriented, pale, breathless, describing what could easily be hallucinatory events. It must be drugs.

They sat across from me, asking their strange questions that held some hidden meaning, I thought. Their combined and studied attention made me sweat.

"Did you take anything?" my mother asked.

I knew by the way she emphasized *anything*—drew it out, loaded it with a small nod of her head—that she meant LSD or speed or marijuana or some other horrible substance our minister was always warning us about. The idea seemed ridiculous to me: where would I get it? Why would I take it? What made them think I would do such a thing?

I might have laughed had it not been for the seriousness of their focus on my face. They were looking for truth in my eyes. I tried to appear humble, a compatriot, not a rebel.

My father crossed his legs and stubbed out his cigarette. He was still in his oil-spattered pants and plaid western shirt with pearl snaps, having made this time between work and sleep to address my last night's state. My mother had spread a towel on the couch for him to sit on. I waited for whatever thought or question that was forming in his head to manifest itself into speech.

"When we were teenagers, your mother and I, sometimes we dropped aspirin into our Pepsi." He paused here, gauging my response. I was intrigued by his confession, but I had no idea of its significance. Aspirin and soda pop? Did it explode? Was it like Alka-Seltzer, then? Was it dangerous?

"Why?" I asked.

My father glanced at my mother, who sat with her head bowed. I sensed she was ashamed of this story, just as she was about much of the life that had been hers before my father.

"It made us high."

I considered this tidbit of information from such an un-likely source. Pepsi and aspirin. I tucked the formula away. Maria would be amazed.

"Did you and Maria do that?"

I shook my head. "We drank pop, but we didn't put *aspirin* in it."

My father uncrossed his legs and leaned forward. "Did anyone offer you anything? Offer to buy you candy?"

I'd been cautioned to death about this. No, no one.

"Where did you get the pop?"

"At the snack stand."

"Did the cups have lids?"

"No." What were they after now? I wondered.

"When did you start feeling funny?"

I thought back to the game, the lights and noise. "As soon as we got there."

"Is that when you got the Pepsi?" He leaned back, flicked his lighter.

They were trying to trick me. "Yes, but we didn't put anything in it, honest, Dad, we didn't . . . we didn't even know . . ."

My father held up his hand, his cigarette nestled deep between his fingers. "I'm not saying you did." He looked at my mother and forced a jet of smoke from between his teeth. "I think someone dropped something in her pop."

I didn't really think I'd been drugged by some pervert hoping to render me helpless or a pusher baiting his next junkie—I still believed my altered state came from being in such an altered environment—but it got me off the hook. We could all rest easier knowing the blame lay outside our circle.

There was a penalty nonetheless. From that time on, football games were off limits, as were any other events that might draw a secular crowd. Who knew what evil lurked in the bathrooms and beneath the bleachers? They would keep me safe; they would protect me from the world.

And so Maria and I felt we had reason to escape both our families: she, the chaos and filth of a home defined by poverty and abuse; I, the suffocating restrictions brought on by the actions of a world I could not control. We spent more and more time outside no matter the weather, mostly in the alleys that cut through our neighborhood.

Sam and Maria introduced me to others—people my age, thirteen, fourteen—whose parents cared little for their presence or absence. My parents cared, but the attention and acceptance I found with orphans seemed familiar and comforting: they appeared not to notice my foolish clothing; they thought the drill team girls were stupid. I concocted tales of afterschool prayer meetings to be with them, able to evade my father sleeping his daytime sleep and my mother, who against my father's wishes had taken a job as a checker at a local market to help with the bills.

School became escape, a place to be with my new friends. But more important than the knowledge I learned from books was the knowledge that came to me in the girls' bathroom between classes: how to apply eye shadow and mascara; how to exhale smoke through my nose; which boys carried rubbers in their wallets. By the time the bell rang for second period, I'd rolled my skirt to mid-thigh and thrust my bra to the bottom of my book bag.

Even behind my heavy glasses, the makeup provided by my friends made my eyes seem bigger, bluer. I no longer slunk from class to class but met each face in the hall with studied indifference. Tucked in the waistband of my skirt, the pack of Marlboros crinkled and scratched: I loved its feel there—a secret possession, a red-and-white undercover badge, my ticket into the alley, where the bad kids gathered each noon hour to slouch and curse with abandon.

Soon, even school became unbearable. Once inside, I dodged the teachers and ran for the alley, where my friends already waited. Some days we spent in collapsing garages or hunched in the corner of a darkened bowling alley, doing nothing more than smoking and laughing at the fools left behind. Other days we made our way downtown and across the railroad tracks to the Clearwater River. There, among the lush growth of snake grass, cottonwood and locust, we found sanctuary with bums. Their cardboard lean-tos held treasure: Sterno, cigarettes, sodden magazines whose pages unfolded into bare breasts and spread legs. Most of the hobos tolerated our visits, even welcomed our company. Others chased us with sticks and rocks, and it was their camps we returned to later, kicking the makeshift shacks to the ground, burning everything.

We called the shallow ponds and marshy backwater the slough, and even the name seemed wrought with adventure, a place that Huck and Tom might have frequented. Beyond the small islands ran the river's swiftest current. In winter, when ice made for us a bridge from one bank to the other, we crossed and felt the rush of water vibrating beneath our feet. In warmer weather, we hauled from the back of Mac's Cycle Shop huge Styrofoam packing crates and made rafts of them, which we floated from one back eddy to another. Larry was there then, and Brad and Sam, Shannon and LaDean, and Laredo. Once, when I slipped from the crate and came out soaked, Laredo built a roaring fire of driftwood while Larry peeled his white T-shirt from his skinny chest. "Here," he said, and grinned as I turned my back to remove my own wet blouse.

I still have that boy's shirt folded in some box marked MEMORABILIA. I had never been offered such a gift, and wearing it home that afternoon, feeling its cotton weave stretch across my breasts, knowing his own skin had rubbed just where mine did, gave me a sense of intimacy I had not felt since Luke. I still had it on when Maria called that evening to tell me Larry was dead.

He had taken the crate out alone, too far. Laredo watched from the bank as the current caught, then tipped the Styrofoam raft. Laredo always wore heavy, square-toed boots, and had he thought to kick them off before going in, he might have made it to Larry. He was a strong swimmer and fought the swift water until he was exhausted. The others pulled him from the river and watched the white rectangle disappear in the distance, believing they still might see a dark shape pull itself up and on.

I locked myself in my room and cried as I never cried for Uncle Ed or Grandpa or Matthew. I wrapped my arms around my chest and hugged the shirt I wore and rocked, believing in my young girl's way that all that was left of Larry remained with me, in the air between a layer of thin cotton and my own still-warm body. When my mother offered comfort, "Let's pray he is with the Lord," I jerked in disgust. Somehow this had to do with them, my parents and all the other adults who believed they owned their children's lives. Better to live with our own dramas and deaths than allow the intrusion of elders, who spewed their nursery-rhyme dictates for good girls and boys. I added grief to my resentment, shaping each emotion to the bitterness I tended like a growing ball of wax—each candle drip first hot, then cooling into a hard, unmalleable core.

I began sneaking from beneath the nose of my Sunday school teachers to join others like me—church kids who bucked and chafed at the bit of obedience. We met at the corner Chevron station and bunched together in the women's room, sharing our Marlboros and cursing the air blue. I no longer cared that my parents might smell the evidence on my breath or in my hair. Let them. I had found my company.

Weekday afternoons, my friends and I met at the house of one whose parents were working and whose older brother, Scott, scored ominous amounts of bennies and beauties, cross-tops and windowpane. I was often the one who volunteered to "baby-sit," to remain straight and responsible.

I went there one day to be with Danny, a lovely boy with dark blue eyes and black hair. I wore the scar of his initials on the back of my hand, made by rubbing away the skin with the tip of an eraser, down to oozing flesh. I don't know what he ingested that afternoon, what combination of chemicals re-worked the circuits of his brain or what had gone into the making of the street drugs he took, but I watched in horror as he contorted on Scott's bed.

I thought I loved him then, holding him down while he screamed and writhed. He was *burning,* he said. Every move-ment of his body through air, no matter how slow or small, created friction, speed-of-light combustion, and even his breathing brought on the flames that consumed him. I cradled him in my arms, rocking slightly, but this too was agony.

"Danny, listen. You're okay, you're in Scott's basement, in Lewiston. It's 1972. You're okay."

He moaned and opened his eyes wide. I could see the fear there, the vision he could not escape. "Slap him," someone said. "Slap him hard." I raised my hand but could not do it and thought for a moment to pray. "God, he's dying!" I cried. "Help him, help him!" Someone pulled me into the next room, gave me a cigarette already lit.

"We've got to call the ambulance," I pleaded. "He'll die!"

"We call the hospital, we'll all get nailed. He'll be okay. Scott knows what to do. Stay cool."

I looked around me in the dim light of the basement, at the friends who stood hunched and pale, holding on to what-ever remnant remained of their own reality. Just then Danny let out a long and piercing howl. We stood for a moment, looked into one another's stricken faces, then I bolted for the stairs. I ran from that house into the street, not caring who followed me, running for home.

In dreams that night I heard his scream again and again, felt it vibrate in my chest, echo off the walls of my room. I thought of possession and exorcism, remembered how vio-lently his body had twisted, the fear in his eyes. The next day at school they told me Scott had tied Danny to the bed, put ice behind his neck and a gag in his mouth. Could a priest have done more?

In the outside world I had a compatriot: my cousin Les, the one who had shared the open sky and dark outhouses of camp life, who fought daily the same battle I did—against a father who seemed bent on breaking her will to his.

Large green eyes, brown hair falling straight and thick past her waist, highlighted with shades of platinum—the color it had been the first time I met her, when we were two and three. Small-boned like her mother, with the same honeyed skin and high cheekbones, she possessed the kind of exotic appearance that made the town girls look bleached and caused the farm boys to imagine spice on their tongues.

I envied the ease with which she applied her makeup, perched on the bathroom sink, coating each of her long lashes with triple layers of Max Factor. I envied her perfect white teeth, her collection of miniskirts that hung to just below where her long hair brushed her bottom. Mostly, I envied her way with boys. The phone rang from the time she got home from school until the suitors either lost their nerve or were forced to give up the receiver. My uncle Barry, now a construction contractor who worked long, out-of-town hours, intercepted what calls he could. The threat in his self-made voice would have deterred most grown men, but that was what was so amazing about Les: boys would risk anything, it seemed, to gain her attention. I realized early on that part of Les's appeal lay in her careless regard for the boys' admiration. By shamelessly baiting then discarding her wooers like trash fish, she ensured their undying adulation.

Even the crosstown boys found their way to Les's basement window. I spent many summer nights with my cousin in her house, surrounded by pasture at the edge of town, and we were often awakened by the scattershot ping of gravel, or, if the window were open, her name hissed out in a loud whisper —"Les, Les!" She'd sometimes grant the boy the favor of her attention, but just as often she told him to get-the-hell-gone. He'd slink off, grumbling and aching but not long discouraged. He'd be back in a week or two, bringing along a friend for me: maybe if he could get the cousin occupied, Les would be more inclined to his affection.

There were times when Les, in a fit of ennui, would call the boy herself. Would he like to stop by her window, oh, say, around midnight? I marveled at the ease and polish of her banter, listening on the sidelines as she worked her thirteen-year-old magic, the crackle and spit of hormones nearly tangible over the telephone wire.

One such night, her chosen beau, Geoff, scratched at our window, shadowed by Mike, a tall, precociously hairy boy meant for me. We smoked in the garish glow of Les's blue-bulbed lamp, then split into pairs. Geoff pulled Les into the next room by her belt loops and she smiled at him, a smile that held all the promise in the world.

As Mike's fingers began their forays into the folds and beneath the buttons of my clothes, I listened half-jealously to the moans and pleading coming from the next room. I had witnessed the ritual of Les's courtship enough to understand its rhythms: stroke him, give him a little, intimate more, then pull away, make him pout, pout yourself, let him woo you back, act petulant, kiss him hard, suck his tongue into your mouth deep enough to empty the marrow from his bones—then stop. Sit up. Light a cigarette. You are, your actions must say, bored beyond belief.

Geoff was frantic, begging so unabashedly that my own

face reddened just hearing it. If not for fear that it might wake my aunt, I'd have turned up the stereo, let Black Sabbath drown it all out—the mewling boy, Mike's raspy breathing, the sense I had of being the ugly sister who could not work this miracle of seduction.

My initial hesitation had goaded Mike into a stronger state of insistence, the intensity of which frightened me. When I pulled away, he was angry, and then my weakness showed through: I could not stand to think he might be mad at me, might be driven by my pathetic inexperience and prudishness to reject me completely. I fumbled apologies, offered shallow kisses.

"What's the matter with you, anyway?" Mike rose from the couch, tucking in his Mr. Natural T-shirt. He smoothed his shoulder-length hair behind his ears. He was handsome enough, cool in our crowd and generous with his dope. Why didn't I feel for him, this boy who would eagerly waste himself in my arms, what I had felt for Luke, whose elbow brushing mine had been enough to fuel a week's dreams?

"I'm sorry," I said. I was embarrassed having led him on. I deserved his ridicule.

"You know what you are? You're a prick-tease, that's all." He hit the wall with his fist, a loud crack that drew silence from the rec room.

I wanted Les to be there with me, to tell me what to do, *how* to do it. Mike scuffed at the rug with his boot, huffing and cursing Geoff for having dragged him along, and for what? His noise brought the others into the room, Geoff sweaty and ruffled, Les as casual and composed as a diva.

"What's up?" she asked, already knowing her country cousin had screwed up a perfectly good time.

"She's a fucking prude." Mike grabbed his jacket and stepped out of the window, leaned back in long enough to say,

"I'm leaving," then took off down the road, the crunch of gravel beneath his boots echoing like gunfire.

Geoff glared. Les sidled to the couch, slid down next to me. "Mike's a dick," she said, yawning.

I looked at Geoff, standing in the middle of the room, senseless as a toad, stunned with disbelief that he had been pulled back from the brink of having it all by some hick girl who didn't know her shit from shinola. Les stared at him for a moment, blinked slowly. He'd been dismissed.

It would take me years to realize what Les already knew: the trick is not in making them *think* you don't care; the trick is in truly not caring. Exquisite disinterest drew a boy like a peacock to its mirrored reflection. Geoff would be there the next time she needed diversion, ignobly and perpetually hopeful, and I would work on perfecting my own emotional veneer; but the truth is, it's no trick, and this, too, I would learn: the shell you build, one layer at a time, is real. No one gets in, and you may never get out.

Family visitations allowed me long periods of time to spend with my cousin. When we couldn't scrape together or steal the change we needed to buy cigarettes, we snitched whole packs from our fathers' cartons, the daring it took to encroach on such territory thrilling us to the bones, outweighing the severe punishment such an act might bring. We slept in each other's beds, whispering late into the night our secret desires: to make love to a certain boy, to run away, to be on our own until we died, and to die young because we could not imagine growing old and dull.

We parted our hair down the middle and tucked it behind our ears in imitation of the girls we saw on TV. Perhaps because my family felt they must make some, hopefully harmless, concession to my desires, they allowed me to don jeans, and I wore my Levi 501's pulled low on my hips. Les snuck me makeup and taught me how to blow smoke through my nose. I was happy, lying in her bed long past midnight, listening to Norman Greenbaum sing "Spirit in the Sky": *Never been a sinner, never sinned, I've got a friend in Jesus*—I sang along, calloused to whatever blasphemous implications might have once made their impressions on me. I no longer believed myself saved. Whatever heaven existed was right here, lying awake next to my cousin, watching smoke rise in concentric hoops toward the ceiling. If I were doomed, then so be it. I could not live the life asked of me because it was hell. What difference did it make?

When Les spent nights with me, in my house near the town's center, we feigned unbelievable exhaustion in order to huddle together on my bed with the radio turned down low, closing our eyes to the luminescent glow of my black light and the images sprouting from velvet: a brilliant orange and yellow peace sign; a woman with butterfly eyes and blue seaweed hair. We mouthed the words to "American Pie," deep into gut-felt appreciation of the obscure lyrics—*Helter skelter in the summer swelter*—bringing ourselves to tears of pity with the drawn-out refrain—*singin' this'll be the day that I die.* The song became our incantation, seizing us with its bittersweet nostalgia for a past we were too young to remember.

Above my bed hung a poster of some inane early seventies icon—I forget exactly what or who now—but when my father had left for his nighttime work and my mother's incessant footsteps finally fell silent, we'd pull the tacks from the poster's corners and flip it over: there, Peter Fonda and Dennis Hopper rode their one remaining Harley, gloriously doomed, flipping off the world in perpetuity.

We'd bide our time, share a cigarette in the closet, then, when we believed that everyone else in the city slept but us, we'd pull ourselves from my bedroom window and run through the alleys as far as we could until we collapsed, breathless and laughing. Sometimes we made our way to Imperial Bowl, where the few customers left were more interested in their beer than their score and no one bothered to question our presence. Other nights we sat with our backs against a Dumpster, content to shiver in the cool air and smoke, free until the birds began their singing and the horizon colored.

We had other friends who found no need to skulk and hide, and their lives were a constant source of amazement and envy to us. One night we sneaked out and made our way across town to the house of Rick, a boy our age with golden hair that hung in a thick shock across his forehead, a boy who walked with his thumbs in his pockets, never deigning to remove the cigarette from his mouth, clinching it between his teeth with a sideways grin, a boy we both hoped to kiss, though I knew Les would have the better chance.

We tossed a handful of pebbles at his window, then scurried behind the rosebushes. He stepped onto the porch of the towering split-level (his parents had money) and waited. "Rick," we hissed. "Over here."

"What are you guys doing?" He stood silhouetted by the light escaping from inside. I pulled him down to us.

"Wanna go run around?" He was our age, maybe fourteen, but the smile that spread across his face showed nothing of the lure of truancy.

"Why don't you guys come in?"

I looked toward the door. "Aren't your parents home?"

"Yeah. So?"

"*So?* What do you mean, *so?*"

"They like to meet my friends."

Les and I looked at each other. This was beyond our imagination. What if they called our parents? What if they called the cops?

Instead they welcomed us with hot chocolate and little tuna sandwiches on brown bread cut into rectangles, stuck through with blue toothpicks. Rick's red-haired mother lounged with her drink on the rec room sofa, her sculptured feet drawn up bare beneath a brightly flowered caftan like the ones I'd seen on the Gabor sisters (my grandmother's Hungarian ideals—such lovely skin! such finely boned faces!).

The father settled into his chair, crossed his legs and smiled. "So—is it Kim? Kim, how's school going this year?"

I shot a look at Rick, who sat on the sofa next to his mother, leaned toward her as though the few inches separating them were too great a distance to be endured. "Fine," I answered, then bit into my sandwich. There was something besides mayo and pickles in the tuna—green olives, I decided, worrying the wad of bread across my tongue—pimento, and worst of all, onions. My mother never put onions in tuna. My father hated onions and pepper, odd ingredients of any kind. He tolerated one spice—salt and lots of it. My brother and I had grown up knowing only white: Wonder Bread, mayonnaise instead of mustard, mashed potatoes and cream gravy, white toast dunked in white-sugared oatmeal. I swallowed twice, trying to work the mouthful down my throat without chewing.

Les reached for another sandwich, holding it between her first finger and thumb. She looked like a lady having tea with her matron friends. I watched in admiration as she bit and chewed, bit and chewed, never minding the grit of onion. Her mother made things like goulash and enchiladas. She was used to this stuff.

"And Les, are you a classmate of Rick's?"

"No, sir. I go to Tammany." She dabbed at the corners of her mouth with a napkin and added, "It's an okay school, small enough to give the kids lots of time with the teachers."

What in the hell was she talking about? She hated Tammany, called it a pissy little place. The father nodded, pleased with her mature evaluation. He offered her another sandwich, which she demurely declined.

The chat continued between Les and the parents as though they were country club pals. I couldn't believe it. Not a word was said about the inappropriateness of the hour or why we found it necessary to throw rocks at their son's window. They beamed their pride upon him and seemed to miraculously approve of us, and what I realize now is that they were both stone drunk.

I felt like I had that night beneath the blinding lights of the football field—as though I had stumbled into another dimension. When it became clear to us that we were not going to entice Rick into the streets, we wiped our fingers on the little napkins, said our thanks and were ushered to the door by Rick's father, who waved to us as we darted down the alley. "You girls come back and visit us again anytime," he called, his words echoing off the darkened houses.

We found our way back home and had just crawled through my bedroom window when we heard the sound of my mother's footsteps at the stairs. By the time she eased open the door, we were buried to our necks in blankets, working with all our might to breathe in sleeplike fashion. I felt her gaze cover us, and then she was gone.

I wasn't sure what I would do about the mud clinging to

our shoes, smearing the sheets, but the near miss sent us into spasms of laughter. We hadn't gotten what we wanted from Rick—something more daring than canapés with his parents —but there was nothing we couldn't get away with. There would be other nights, and when we parted the next day we grinned with our secret and the promise of adventures ahead.

I think we craved destruction. Even with the awareness I have now of repression and its common, reactionary results, I'm not altogether sure what drove us to challenge our place in family, church and community. Rebellion is natural enough, as is the desire to establish independence, a sense of individuality. But that does not explain for me why my cousin and I embarked on such a dangerous journey. We drank ourselves into stupors —barely thirteen and wise to the ways of Annie Green Springs and Mad Dog 20/20. We craved nicotine with the earnestness of our fathers. One night my mother caught me in bed, puffing the last inch of an old Marlboro. Before she could switch on the light, I foolishly cupped the cigarette and stuck my hand beneath the covers. When she threw back the blankets and pried open my fingers, the fire had burned a black pit in my palm. "Well, Kim," she said, looking at me with disgust. "Is it that bad?"

Yes, I thought, it's that bad, and wallowed in the truth of it. I floated through my school days on bad marijuana highs, taking my paddlings with the nonchalance of a full-grown boy whenever the principal found me smoking in the bathroom. And even though I was whipped and grounded for my actions, I did not stop.

Les and I believed that as long as we had each other, we could endure—certainly we told each other so. Then one night when Les was spending the weekend we took too great a risk. We had a friend call, say she was baby-sitting and sick, and ask if we could take her place.

My mother smelled a rat. "Why doesn't she just call the parents?" She eyed us skeptically, sounding our depths for truth.

"She tried. She can't reach them. She's throwing up and everything. The baby keeps waking up and crying and she's too sick to rock him."

I'd pushed the right button. My mother could endure a number of things, but the thought of a baby squalling pathetically in its lonely crib was enough to sway her judgment.

She dropped us off at the house, where our friend peered from behind the drapes, hoping she wouldn't have to look ill should my mother appear at the door. By some luck, we were left to wave good-bye at the doorstep. We stayed long enough to drink a Coke, called all the kids we could think of who might know where we could find a party and took off into the night, leaving our envious friend to her fifty cents an hour.

The party was in a boxy apartment only blocks from my house, and the proximity made me nervous. Once in, my fears were obliterated by Jimi Hendrix riding the rails of his high-pitched guitar and the cloying smell of hashish. An American flag hung from the ceiling by its four corners, covering a single bare bulb.

I recognized some of the high school boys who often gave us rides home in their Cougars and Mustangs and Javelins with baby moon hubcaps. One presented us with a couple of Coors, then directed us to a bed where bodies were piled and writhing in various states of undress.

I sucked at the beer to quell the tremor of nervousness that threatened to rise and make me stupid. Wasn't this exactly what I wanted? I felt the hands of the boy next to me—Jerry? —pull at the band of my jeans, then slide my shirt upward. I looked for Les and saw her pinned against the wall, holding the lit end of a cigarette between herself and whomever it was grinding his hips against hers.

Jerry had worked his fingers beneath my bra but I felt nothing. Maybe it was the beer, or the densely rolled joints that kept making their way around. I pushed away from the bed, ignoring Jerry's slurred protests. I needed to get outside, to see the stars and get my bearings.

Les broke loose and followed me. We leaned against a hot-orange GTO and drank the rest of our beer, then the extras she had grabbed on her way out. There was little to say: we had made it to where we wanted to be, and maybe that was enough. We had only a few hours until my mother would expect us home from our baby-sitting. How could we make the best of it?

Our answer came from inside the car. A young man I recognized as a high school senior raised up from the seat and smoothed his mop of red hair. Evidently, he too had needed some air.

"Hey," he said. "Wanna go for a ride?" We scooted into the front seat, but before we could get away half the party had decided to go along. I found myself wedged onto the lap of yet another older boy, and then we were speeding down the street, fishtailing around corners, headed for the Gut.

The Gut is what we cruised, a mile or two of Main Street that made a circular track through town. I held my breath as we hit the lights red, doing sixty past the admiring eyes of others who sat on the hoods of their own cars in the empty lots. I'd be chicken if I screamed, and truth is I never felt the urge. Nothing seemed to scare me anymore—not speeding down the road through intersections nor the nearness of death such recklessness whispered; not the church and its damnation; not the grounding or the belt raised over me for my worst sins. At least I am free, I thought as the wind whipped in through the open windows and carried the smoke away. At least I am free.

But I was not free. When Les and I staggered home that night, sodden with spilled beer and stinking, my mother was waiting. She took one look and without a word pointed her finger toward my room. We fell onto my bed, holding to each other not out of fear but because the room was spinning. I was too drunk to wonder what my mother's thoughts were as she shuffled in her robe from one room to the other, waiting for my father to come home.

I have no doubt that Les feared her father even more than I did mine, so that when my parents the next day told her she must confess or they would call and tell the tale for her, she broke into sobs. I watched her from my window after her mother had come for her, and I felt I wanted to make some rescue, make a break for it and pull her away as I flew by. But what wings did I have? I was too young to drive. I didn't even have a bicycle. Only my legs could carry me, and looking across the expanse of familiar yards and alleys, I knew my chances in broad daylight were slim.

My father called me into the kitchen. I glared my disgust at him. I set my lips against my teeth and stared out the window behind his head, waiting to be ordered to my room and await my whipping. But they had another plan, one they believed might hurt me even more: Les and I would no longer be allowed to see each other.

I was stunned. How could they deny me my cousin? Did they really think they could keep us apart? I fretted over Les's situation: her family lived on the outskirts of town, on a small ranch. How would I know what her punishment had been? We could stand anything as long as we could make a story of it, as long as we could shape it for the ears of the other and

control its end. I imagined her going about her chores, bringing in the firewood, doing the dishes, graining the big stallion
named Smokey her father had bought for her when she asked
for a horse. God, I thought, let her be okay.

Several weeks later, I was handed an envelope. It was a
letter from Les. She had the oversized handwriting of a child,
and the few words she sent filled the entire page of ruled
notebook paper: She was fine. Her horse had cut his fetlock
on barbed wire. That was all. I tried to read between the lines,
to gain some sense of her daily life. Was she under the same
restrictions I was, barred from using the phone, unable to
leave the house except under supervision?

Perhaps my parents knew that given the opportunity I
would bolt like a branded calf from the chute. What punishment was left to them? They had whipped me, placed me
under virtual house arrest. I no longer feared their anger or
their limited power to inflict pain.

Together, Les and I had formed an inner circle of companionship based on kin and something else—our desire to
escape our fathers. We longed to be orphans, free to make our
own decisions, free to die if we chose, or survive by whatever
means available. And isn't that what we were doing—making
the only choice remaining to us? We could obey and survive.
We could utter the simple word *no* and be whipped, locked in,
denied our meals. Or we could run. I bided my time, comforted by the music I believed might save me, the loud and
constant beat drowning out the self-loathing I felt no matter
which part of my soul I listened to.

By the time I was fourteen, my mother and father hardly
recognized me. My grades dropped from *A*'s to *F*'s, and I was

labeled a truant. The child with whom they had shared their bed and its warmth, the girl they had dedicated to God, who had spoken in tongues and healed the sick, who had emerged from the waters reborn, now slouched past them, hissing out answers to their questions. When my father caught me in a lie, he whipped me, but I was stronger now and did not cry. I met his eyes, in my own the glint I hoped he knew meant *you cannot hurt me, you cannot touch any part of me.*

At school I met Patti, a gum-snapping girl with long brown hair and wire-rimmed glasses, who even at the age of fourteen seemed absolutely sure of her place in the world. She was everything I wanted to be: smart and tough, afraid of no one. She made her own rules, somehow free of parental constraint. She dreamed of going to San Francisco, and because I knew nothing of her life, I believed she longed not for escape but adventure. When, because of my parents' growing restraints I could no longer make my own small escapes, we made our plans to meet at the high school track, stay in her apartment, then hitchhike the next morning for California.

I lay in my bed for what I believed would be the last time, remembering all I had heard of Haight-Ashbury and flower children and free love. We could steal to eat if we had to. I'd been told that some girls let men have sex with them for money, and even though I had never made love to a boy in my life, I resigned myself to doing whatever I had to do in order to stay alive. I believed that no matter how foreign the town and its people, I would feel no less lost than I did at that moment, in my house with its waxed floors and scrubbed toilets, my parents in the next room, the walls solid between us.

• • •

It is here, in memory, that I shiver with shame: meeting Patti at the track after school, where we shared a cigarette, leaned against the blue mats piled for the high-jumpers' safe landing; the two of us alone where the ground dropped and flattened, forming a deep earthen bowl, alone because the wind blew cold and the sky threatened rain. Not this, but the sudden call of my name across the oval field.

I looked up to see my mother against the cloud-darkened horizon, her silhouette even darker, the tails of her coat flapping out like useless wings.

"Kim, please. Come home." Her voice echoed off the bleachers, ringing back metallic and hollow.

"Oh, shit." Patti stared at my mother's form jutting up from the depression's lip. I could hardly believe she had found us. I slid from the mats and ran for the far fence, Patti a step behind. The distance separating her from us was too great— she would never catch me, I knew, but I felt her breath at my neck, her voice still echoing: "Kim, don't do this. I love you."

We scrambled down the hill, bent low behind hedges, weaving our way through the glass-strewn alleys and familiar shortcuts, following the same route we took to reach the slough. The last time I saw my mother that day, she was leaning from the steering wheel across the seat, driving slowly by. She might have seen me, crouched behind two cans rank with moldering garbage, so closely did she pass: through the narrow slot between the cans I could see her eyes, puffed and red. I held my breath against the smell, against the belief that even the air in my lungs might give me away.

"Sweet," said Patti as the car continued on and disappeared up the road. She lit a Marlboro before passing it to me. I inhaled until my heart seemed to beat outside its bony cage, then pushed the smoke out in a noisy rush.

"Yeah," I said. "Sweet," and took the lead, my mother's

words a cadence I marched to—*Kim* come *back* I *love* you *Kim*
—lengthening my strides toward Patti's apartment.

That night, I lay on a dilapidated brown sofa, feeling with
my fingertips the cratered melts of cigarette burns. In the next
room, a metal bed thumped rhythmically against the wall. I
couldn't make out Patti's face in the streetlight's curtained
glow. She lay on her own sunken couch across the room; I
knew by her carefully controlled breathing that she was only
pretending to sleep.

I tried not to listen to her mother's guttural moans, the
man's slurred cussing. Each time the thumping stopped, I
hoped they had fallen asleep or passed out, but then the
springs would let out their rusty, pinched sounds, the man's
coarse voice demand some other thing.

Her mother had come home after Patti and I had packed
our single paper bag with the pepperoni sticks and cigarettes
we had stolen from the IGA. She brought with her a man
who fell heavily against the counter, change in his pockets
jangling. I'd listened to them mutter in the dark, then
watched their staggering shadows as they dragged the TV into
the bedroom, where it sputtered and snapped its bad recep-
tion, not loud enough to drown out the clacking of the
woman's rings against the headboard.

I closed my eyes against the noise, breathing through my
mouth so as not to smell the beer-damped cigarettes and
soured dishrags. Where am I? I thought. What am I doing
here? In the dark I could not look to Patti, could not see her
wise half-smile and find the courage I needed to feel nothing.
Shreds of my old self rose up like half-burnt pages from a fire
—images of my own home, my mother running the bleach-
whitened dishcloth across the counter, stove, table, humming
in her broken way a hymn of sacrifice. I gritted my teeth and
focused on morning, when we would catch our ride to Cali-

fornia and be gone for good, away from the family and town I
believed I despised with every bone in my fourteen-year-old
body.

The distance between that filthy apartment in Lewiston and
the house in the hollow could be counted in miles, in years,
but not in any way that might measure the void separating my
life before and my life after our move from the woods. Who
was that twelve-year-old girl in long dresses, peering from
behind her heavy-framed glasses, her smile true and uncom-
promised? And the girl on the sofa, still wearing her Levi's,
her sheer blouse, her makeup stolen from the local drugstore
—who was she, is she? I cannot connect the two except
through the telling of it, and even the story seems foreign,
false somehow, memory that is both mine and not mine, as
though the girls are simply characters I have invented. I can
manipulate them, work their arms and legs like the wooden
limbs of marionettes, make them laugh, hate, pray, believe in
anything, believe in nothing.

What I cannot do is imagine the girl I was at twelve becoming the girl I was at fourteen. I remember the emotions
vividly—at twelve, adolescent confusion tempered by the security of family, a sense of trust, openness, innocence, I guess.
By the time I was fourteen, I felt only anger, loathing, a need
to escape from the restrictions imposed by my parents and the
church. Even now it scares me to understand how easily a soul
may pass from one dimension of itself into another, as though
the boundaries separating what we are and what we might
become, given an infinite set of motivations and conditions,
are little more than the line between waking and sleep, between story, memory, dream.

The most frightening thing of all is that each of those girls is still with me, both vulnerable and bitter, believing and hardened against belief. I could become one or the other of them again, I think, and so steel myself to become neither. And if I had to, which would I choose—the near-child about to lose herself to spite and anger? or the near-woman already there, calloused to the pain in her mother's eyes, the grim discipline of her father, the prayers of the church, her own sense of guilt and sure damnation?

That morning, when I awoke in the apartment of my friend, her mother and the man were gone. I maneuvered my way through piles of dirty clothes, past the bed with its crumpled gray sheets and into the tiny bathroom. Ash floated in the toilet water. Hair and wadded Kleenex covered the floor. I gagged against the intimate odors of other bodies.

In the mirror, I saw my own smudged cheeks, my eyes darkened by yesterday's mascara and blue shadow. The face disgusted me. I splashed cold water in the sink, hardening myself, spitting out the metallic taste of last night's wine. I'm nothing but a whore, I thought. Just like her. But even as I searched for a clean corner of the towel to dry my hands on, I never considered another course. There was comfort in the fatalism of my vision. Like my father, I yearned for my life to be expressed in absolutes. I had made my decision. I could never go back.

Patti and I never made it to California. That morning, as I walked from the apartment's bathroom, I heard a hard knock. Patti jerked her head and I stepped backward into her mother's room.

Two women were speaking. I recognized my mother's voice and whirled to search the room for a place to hide. The single window, swollen from the shower's mist, wouldn't budge. If it had, I would have jumped without hesitation to the ground two stories below. Instead, I crawled into the narrow closet, pulling the door shut behind me. I squatted beneath smoke-scented dresses and scratchy coats, piling shoes and boxes around my legs.

The voices moved toward me. Stop them, Patti, I thought. Jesus, please stop them.

The door swung open. Hands parted the clothes. I peered into the face of my mother and her friend Sally, eight months pregnant. Patti stood chewing her thumbnail like a child. *I could run. I could fly past them and out and run and they'd never catch me.* I looked at Sally's bulging belly. *This isn't fair.*

"Look at you." My mother bent slightly toward me. I clutched my knees to my chest, nearly growling. My father appeared behind them, the shadow of his body blocking the light. "Come on, Kim. Let's go," he said, and though I had thought I'd make him drag me out, I rose and followed him past Patti and the sagging couches, through the greasy kitchen, down the stairs to the car. He did not look at me nor I at him as I slid into the backseat and rode the few miles home in silence.

There was little I felt then—not fear, or loathing, not even a need to escape. I was still in that closet, my knees drawn tight, my chin tucked. It was dark and quiet. If I just sat still and breathed carefully in and out, no one would see me, know I was there. I might even forget myself.

Again, shame. I'm to undress. My mother searches the bends of my knees and elbows for needle tracks. She leaves me, goes to her room, closes the door. My father comes, raises the back of his hand, says through his teeth, "Don't you ever do this to your mother again." I stare out the window. I am solid, I feel nothing. I wait for my door to close, then pull back the clean blankets and place my body between the whitest sheets. After a while, pots clatter in the kitchen. The washing machine hums. I sleep for a long time.

The next day, it is explained that I have become impossible. I understand that I have a choice: juvenile detention at St. Anthony, or summer spent living with the Langs outside of Spokane. I've heard what happens to new girls at the juvenile detention center—rape, broken broomsticks, razors. I choose the Langs. I have not seen them for over a year. I think I can keep my new self safe from them. I think they cannot hurt me.

CHAPTER EIGHT

The hills of the Palouse Prairie rose and fell outside my window like the deep swells of an emerald ocean. The land, only twenty miles north of Lewiston, seemed yet another kind of foreign—no trees, no water, only wheat and peas stretching off into the horizon. I leaned my head back against the seat and thought of all I had left behind: Patti, the slough, my hidden stash of makeup. One pack of cigarettes was tucked in my sock. I'd have to ration them carefully, not knowing how or when I'd get money to buy more.

What I'd been allowed to take was little: a suitcase full of clothing, and the blue leather Bible the Langs had given me two years before on my twelfth birthday. Whatever else I might need, the Langs and the Lord would provide.

I closed my eyes and imagined what Luke must look like.

Sixteen and taller, maybe different hair but the same eyes and smile. Still, he would be like them, shunning me for my sins. And I didn't care. They could all rot in hell if they thought a few months were going to change anything.

The hills gave way to forest and I breathed in the familiar pine smell. Post Falls, where the Langs lived, spread out from the banks of the Spokane River, supported by a saw mill. We pulled to a stop in front of a modern split-level, so new the lawn had yet to sprout. I sat sullen until my father opened my door and motioned me out with a sideways nod.

Brother and Sister Lang greeted us with hoots, hugs for the women, hard back-claps between the men. Luke was at work—he had dropped out of school the year before and was doing home correspondence—but the others paid me the same attention they always had, as though nothing had changed. Their honest smiles and teasing coupled with the fact that no one mentioned our reason for being there gave the entire afternoon a feeling of unreality: I could find no opportunity to respond with disdain nor protest some remark critical of me or my friends. They ignored my hunched shoulders and tight-lipped scowl. Sister Lang offered me lemonade and cookies, which I refused. "Good," she laughed. "More for me, then."

My parents left that evening, just as the sun slipped its last light through the close branches of tamarack. I shivered a little, hands tucked against my sides. I watched their car find its way up the unpaved road and then onto the highway, where my mother leaned out her window and gave a final wave. I desperately wanted a cigarette and wiggled my foot up and down to feel the sweaty cellophane slide reassuringly between sock and skin. My Levi's, split and frayed along the leg seams to fit over my hiking boots, hung as low on my hips as I could pull them. The back pockets were patched, an Ameri-

can flag on one hip, a peace symbol on the other. POW bracelet, knotted leather necklace beaded with bones: I must have
looked like the enemy. My one concession to modest attire
was the bra I wore beneath my knitted midriff shirt; I chafed
at the hooks biting my back.

Sister Lang took my arm and I stiffened. "Luke will be
home any time. Let's go make him some supper." She grinned
at me and started us both toward the house. I couldn't say no.

Sister Lang gave me a knife and set me to peeling potatoes.
Sarah hummed while she chopped onions, wiping her eyes
with the sleeve of her smock. They asked about my school, my
friends, the boys I liked. I marveled at the lightness of their
questions. Didn't they know? Hadn't my parents told them? I
shrugged answers—"fine," "okay"—and focused on the gritty
strips of skin dropping into the sink.

When Sister Lang reached her hand to my face I flinched.
She ran one finger behind my ear, smoothing back the strand
of hair that hung over my eyes.

"After dinner, Sarah can curl your hair."

I stood frozen, the knife and half-peeled potato in mid-air.
Even silent and unsaid, it was a hiss, a vicious whisper: *Leave
me alone.*

While Sarah chatted about Terry's new job, I drew the
blade slowly toward my thumb, wondering if I could hide the
knife, secret it away in my sock or pocket. And then what? I
couldn't imagine stabbing or slashing, only the knife between
me and whoever tried to get in my way. I'd only run if it got
too bad, but I'd need the knife; it seemed important, more a
key than a weapon. I could save myself with it, cut my way out
or in, open cans like the bums did—one hard stab and twist. I

could use it to fashion a pole, then find a string, bend a safety pin into a hook and fish the rivers to stay alive.

Luke's voice from the door jolted me around. He nodded, dipping his head without moving his eyes from my own.

"Howdy."

Cold water ran down my wrists and into the sleeves of my shirt. I turned back to the sink, steadying myself against the counter. His voice was deeper, his hands bigger. In his dirty work clothes, holding his thermos and black pail, he looked like a man—like my father and uncles coming home from the woods. Then the image of how I must look to him hit me: a girl standing with the women in the kitchen, scrubbing spuds. I pressed the sharp blade harder against my thumb, not so hard that the skin popped, just enough pressure to feel what was almost pain.

Luke pulled a chair away from the table and began unlacing his boots. I double-rinsed the potatoes, afraid to move from my place. I did not even know what the rest of the house looked like. Where had they put my bag? No matter which way I moved out of the kitchen, I'd have to pass by Luke, now working thick socks from his feet. From the corner of my eye, I could see his fingers move the cotton down his calves and over his ankles. How was it that a man's feet could be so lovely?

"Done?" Sister Lang took the knife from my hand and pointed it toward the refrigerator. "There's lettuce to be washed."

A salad. Carrots to cut, tomatoes and celery. I took her orders, steadied by the chores I'd always despised.

"What's for dinner?" Luke asked. I kept my head down.

"Steaks, potatoes and gravy," Sarah answered. "Chocolate cake for dessert."

He grunted, a small pleased noise. I listened as he moved down the hall. A door closed. His belted jeans clicked against the floor, water worked its way through the pipes. I imagined him beneath the hot spray, soaping his back and arms, suds running down his belly.

"Kim. Here." A bowl hovered in front of me. I'd forgotten the lettuce. Sarah stood grinning and before I thought to glare I felt the heat rise from my hips to my throat and face.

Finally, we settled in at the dinner table, where Luke prayed beside me. "For this and all Thy blessings, we thank Thee. We ask that You also bless Sister Kim, who has joined us here today."

I opened my eyes. For a moment I was twelve again, just come to the Sunday table. Some forgotten part of me responded to the memory, the easy laughter and affection, and I felt myself slipping back into that naive girl with her hair in tight braids.

No. I hated her. I never again wanted to be that vulnerable, foolish enough to believe in anything or anyone.

The knife was gone. The only weapon I had left was my bitterness, and I took deep breaths, feeling the fist in my chest tighten. It would be a fist, my heart, not an open hand. An open hand took what it was given. An open hand could be burned, branded. A fist took nothing—it kept its secrets.

I was wrong. I can't survive here, I thought. These people will try to kill my soul and call it salvation.

In God one finds love, absolute and unconditional, but not infinite. We believed that the gates of Heaven could be closed against a hardened heart—a "seared conscience"—and never be opened again, no matter how sincere the penance. Having no context for my sin, I could believe only that I had fired my soul in the worldly kiln to an impenetrable and lacquered armor. Even if I had wanted to regain my Father's house, I would find no ingress, no welcome.

Here were these lovers of God. I could never again be one of them. In this I found a dark and fitting comfort in place of absolution. I opened my eyes to the gravy bowl and ladled the congealing sauce over white bread, took more salad than I could eat. My first bite of deer steak brought another tremor of memory: sitting on the dark stairs while the women made dinner, taking in Luke's breath with the smell of hot grease and browning venison. I'd not tasted wild meat since we left the woods, and now it was all coming back and I couldn't stop it: the church in Cardiff, the late-night games of basketball, the wonderful float of near-sleep as I lay on the couch listening to the stove pop and the men play their music; the night they didn't find Matthew. My friends in Lewiston hadn't known me then, but these people had. They'd seen me that way, they knew who I really was. I shoved myself from the table so hard my iced tea rocked and spilled.

"I need to use the bathroom."

Brother and Sister Lang glanced at each other. Sarah pointed with her fork down the hall.

The room was still moist, the mirror streaked with condensation. My face looked disfigured, melting down the glass. Luke's clothes lay in a heap near the tub. I gathered them up and held them to my face, breathing in the dusty sweat, believing I could still feel the heat of his body.

I no longer knew what sin felt like. Guilt had been replaced by a simple and practical aversion to consequences. They would never know what I was doing—a thief, stealing this intimacy. They might never know what I wanted from Luke; I wasn't even sure I did. I knew I wanted his hands to touch me and could not imagine what I wouldn't let him do.

The boys at school had tried, snaking their fingers between the buttons of my Levi's, trailing their sharp tongues down my neck. I disliked their urgency, their little moans and pleadings. What I wanted was to feel again that which had possessed me in the church's dusky sanctuary: seduction, a pure longing so painful I bit my tongue to draw blood penance. It was still in his eyes, it might still happen. And what was that worth, to have him finally take hold of me in a real embrace? We were older, could plan a place, a time. Maybe then I'd leave, make my run for California.

The thought cleared my head. I'd never go back home to my parents, or even my friends. Why would I? I could be as free as I wanted to be. I could choose to go or stay. If I hid out long enough, even the cops would give up. I'd learned my lesson about hiding in small places. No more closets or apartments. I'd go to a big city, where I could run and be swallowed up by thousands of people who would never recognize my face.

I relaxed and flipped on the exhaust fan. The cigarette was nearly crushed, and I carefully reshaped it. The smoke lifted toward the ceiling. The last lungful I blew into the pile of cotton and denim like a good-bye kiss.

They didn't ignore me. They simply went on with their lives, offering me no opportunity or reason to object. Everything seemed absolutely reasonable: the errands and chores, the meals and after-dinner excursions into town for ice cream. The isolation from my friends served to remove both empathy and influence, and I no longer had my parents' constant suspicion to react against. If I acted sullen or shut myself in my sparsely furnished room, nothing changed—no one commented or demanded an explanation. Whatever void my emotional or physical absence created was filled with the camaraderie of family that existed whether I did or not.

I lay at night in my bed beneath the window, savoring my few remaining Marlboros. I thought of Patti and the others, imagining their encouragement: "They just want you to be their good little girl. They don't really give a shit about you." I wanted to hear Patti's gravelly voice, but I wasn't allowed to use the phone. I had to stay smart, be patient, or I'd end up in a place worse yet—St. Anthony. (I never doubted this consequence and still cannot bring myself to ask the question: Was it only a threat? Would you have sent me there, locked me in a place so far away I could never return?)

Evenings, we'd cruise through town, hot summer wind rushing us through our Dairy Queen treats. It was like this with the Langs: unrestrained in little ways, spontaneous, childlike. And maybe that's what I found with them, that lost part of myself. I was fourteen, and it wasn't the drugs or the music or the potential sex that drew me to the world; it was something else that even now I can only attempt to articulate.

My parents loved me, within reason, and that reason seemed dependent upon my obedience. They loved me, of course, even in rejection, and perhaps saw in their rejection the absolute and logical progression of their love. But such love is not unconditional, and what I yearned for was unequivocal acceptance, for the familial walls to prove themselves strong, beyond fracture.

I risked little with my peers, love never being part of our fragmented equation. Unlike my parents' love, the Langs' was not inherent nor assumed. If they were willing to take me in when my mother and father were unwilling to keep me, did it mean that their love was greater? If they accepted me without

derision the way I was—bad girl, delinquent, unrepentant—
then there was little more I could do to turn them away from
me.

They still acted as though I were that timid, backwoods
girl, lapping up praise like a puppy. And wasn't I? Brother
Lang smacked over the French toast I made him for breakfast.
Luke winked and grinned when I served him his coffee thick
with Cremora. Sister Lang and Sarah assumed me capable of
working beside them, and I forgot to resent their assumption.
Terry took me to see osprey along the river, their huge nest a
crisscross of sticks. I could not imagine why he wanted to
share with me their graceful flight and pinioned dives, nor
could I make sense of the joy I felt watching them rise with
trout spasming in their talons.

I can believe it was the land I missed, that part of me was
still fused to cedar and lupine. A tree will weave its new fiber
through strands of wire, lock its heart tight around a stray
bullet. I had left the woods wounded, wrenched from what
had sustained me since birth.

Some are born to the wilderness. Some come to the wilderness to be reborn. It was where my parents first found their
salvation, and where I would once again find mine.

We went to the river, the men to fish, the women to watch
from lawn chairs, their crochet hooks glinting over pale green
thread. How long since my parents had left? Two weeks?
Three? Soon the Langs and I would be moving to Spokane,
an hour away, where Brother Lang had been given the pastorship of a small church and its depleted congregation. Terry
wanted one last chance at the big trout, so we made a day of
it: fried chicken, potato salad, thick wedges of watermelon.

There was a rod for me. I rigged it without comment, still

unwilling to offer any semblance of gratitude. The river cut deep in front of us; beneath my feet, I could feel the familiar and delicate vibration of water. I cast and reeled in too quickly, then cast again, farther this time, relaxing into the rhythm and pull of the current.

Trees moved lightly in the breeze and I closed my eyes to listen to the murmur and shush of branches. The river's low thrum, the trees brushing—all I could hear or want to hear that summer afternoon with a family both mine and not mine. When the fish hit, I startled as though from sleep. The heaviness drew my line taut, then the reel began unwinding, playing out too fast.

"Tighten the drag a little." Terry was at my elbow. I did as he said, fearing that any more tension would cause the line to snap. The steady pull weakened and I regained a few yards, but then the fish turned, headed with the current downstream.

"Just let him go. He'll tucker out." I glanced at Terry, arms crossed, feet planted solid in the sandy soil. Luke and Brother Lang reeled in, and I registered their thoughtfulness, their desire to give me every advantage.

I steadied the butt of the rod against my hipbone and pulled the tip skyward before taking in the slack.

"What is it?" I asked, knowing I had never felt such weight in a rainbow or brookie. Terry shook his head.

"Sturgeon." Luke stood close behind me.

Terry grunted. "Don't think there's sturgeon in this river. Channel cat, maybe. Big, whatever it is."

The fish began another run. I was sure he'd take all my line, strip the spool clean. I worked the rod against my belly, arms already trembling with the fight. The force of his pull surprised me. Where was it he was pulling for? What place did he hope to gain? I imagined his passage deep in the river's cleaving. The line he drew seemed dead straight, as though the boulders and snags were impermanent, themselves fluid. I knew some fish would sound—nose down against a rock—and I half-expected the sudden cessation of movement, the stubborn, impossible draw.

But the fish did not stop. It ran until exhausted, then allowed me to exhaust myself hauling its weight upriver a few feet at a time until, rested, it could again make the air above its world sing. I didn't hear the men anymore, nor the women, whose quieter dialogue blended with the wind. I focused on the line, waiting for the fish to break surface, to give up some secret of itself, but in all my vision there was nothing save water and this invisible, incessant pulling.

Pointed shadows darkened the river. Nighthawks zig-zagged the sky, their sharp calls distant, peripheral. No one moved to pack the food, fold the chairs. No one moved to take the rod from my hands. They stood with me, Sister Lang pulling her sweater across her shoulders, Sarah leaned against Terry. So patient and clear, our seeing of nothing, as though that which we watched for expected our welcome.

Shade became darkness and still my line kept the light, reflecting the moon in a silvery strand. I could no longer see the spool itself and had no sense of what was left, how many yards of filament played out downriver. When the fish pulled, I gave. When he rested, I reclaimed what distance I could, my motions perpetual, uncalculated. I ceased to consider options, strategies. Time sank with the line and disappeared without end.

Near shore the water shallowed. How long had the fish been settled there, working his slow respirations, rocking in silt? A log, I thought. A trick of light. I lowered the rod and saw the shape disappear, then resume its place. I stepped back, stumbled, felt the line tense. Only then did I know my own exhaustion, the pain in my groin and arms. I straightened and began walking backward, afraid to take my eyes from that spot, intending to drag the fish from the river. Luke caught my shoulders from behind.

"You'll lose him. Use the rod. Use your arms."

I leaned against his chest, aware that I was groaning with each attempt to pull the rod vertical. The fish would not give, so solid I believed I had dreamed him, that it was stone I imagined undulating at my feet.

Then the line snapped, spitting back against my hands and face. Luke stood steady. I could feel the warmth of his stomach and thighs and knew he watched the river as I did, as though we might see the fish jump once, stitching the night down with its moonlit thread.

Brother Lang eased the rod from me and gave it to Terry. My fingers stayed curled like the hands of a hag.

"You were great, kiddo." They were all smiling, and then Brother Lang broke into a full laugh. "That old fish is going to remember you for a long time."

They walked with me slowly, matching their steps to my stiff shuffle. Already they were polishing the story—my story —of the battle. I heard told for me the length of my endurance, how the night came on and I stayed, never complaining, rock-solid against the fish. I crawled into the backseat, the soreness dulling to a kind of comfort, soothed by the warmth of their praise.

Pain is nothing that cannot be reinvented. Like so many things, it's a matter of perspective. The fish was a log or it wasn't. The rawness of my hands and the bruise in my side were wounds, or they were badges of courage. So many things depend on the stories we tell ourselves, or on the stories that others tell of us. The story itself can change, be enlarged, be diminished. I had already begun the story I would tell my friends of how I tolerated that summer with the Langs and came back unchanged: it was a map I intended to follow. But now my story had been interrupted. How did this fit in? It would sound foolish in the telling. I tried to revise what had happened to fit my narrative, but no matter how many ways I recited it, it came out the same: something had changed. I listened, and although it was all about me, it had nothing to do with the untidiness of my hair and clothes or how polite I was. What mattered was that I had stayed tough, fought it out. They were proud of me for doing this thing that I could never not do: dig in, hold on, fight the pull toward home.

That night, the air came in cool and silent through my window. I held the last of the tattered Marlboros, closing my fist harder and harder, then dropped them to the ground outside. Such a small and pathetic gesture, as though every sin could be rolled tight as tobacco and dropped a few feet into another world.

I lay back in my bed and allowed my bitterness its exit, with a breath let out the hate, let it drift from the window and into the dark. Believe that it is this easy. Believe that a young girl felt her new self descend like a cloak, a smooth and unblemished skin—cool, like a dampened sheet against fever. This is God, I thought. I whispered, "I am done. Forgive me."

The next morning I woke as I knew I would: joyful, radiant, washed in the blood of the Lamb. Surrender is no less sweet than the fight: absolution, pure submission, bliss in having no will that cannot be consumed, floating like Ophelia in the lovely waters.

I announced my conversion at breakfast and welcomed without self-consciousness their prayers. They laid their hands on my head and shoulders and gave thanks, and I felt the last of my old self spill out. I cried, great, gulping sobs that wrenched my guts, and they said this too was as it should be.

That day was no different in some ways. The men worked, the women cleaned, shopped and cooked. But I felt the prayers coming back to me and the songs filled my head. I tied my hair back and hummed. When I looked at Sarah, she smiled and I flushed with pleasure. I became once again reflective of the wishes and expectations of my elders, a steady moon of a girl.

I don't remember speaking of my parents then, though it would seem natural to assume we would have called them. What better news could they imagine? Their daughter had been reborn, had come back into the fold. Perhaps I could have gone home. But I did not call, nor do I know if the Langs did. I did not want to leave. I wanted to stay in this new life with these people who had made a place for the prodigal at their own table.

The church in Spokane sat directly across the alley from the parsonage. Dandelions and morning glories tangled thick around its foundation. Paint peeled from the siding. The remaining parishioners—five or six elderly women and men— hoped the Reverend Lang would crowd the foyer with newcomers and kindle a spirit of revival in their midst.

We polished the old oak pews and mended the hymnals with tape, cut the grass and trimmed the roses. I worked beneath the late summer sun, modest and hot in my long sleeves and borrowed, sagging skirt. The sanctuary held little light, and when I stepped into the shadowed room to escape the heat, the air was heavy with the coolness of wood.

While Sarah, pregnant with twins, took her afternoon nap

and Sister Lang attended Tupperware meetings, I found once again the plain chords they had taught me at Cardiff and played for hours on the old upright. They granted me this time alone, but little other. My privacy was a commodity I bartered for their trust. I had no money and was dependent upon them for my toothpaste and tampons (Sister Lang shaking her head), for the antihistamines I needed to subdue my allergies. Except for the church, I was allowed to go nowhere without them, but where would I have gone? I was no longer a runaway. I had no other friends. Even my parents seemed dead to me. Yet the more obedient my behavior, the tighter their surveillance. I accepted this, expected it. I had much to pay for. My debt was great.

Even greater was my need for Luke's approval. He had become more attentive, taking my hand when we walked to the store, reminding me to cover my knees when I sat. I had forgotten the modest ways and now I must relearn them. I shuddered at the memory of my first night with the Langs, at my grotesque desire for Luke, at my act of inhaling his smell. But the guilt could not override the stir of pleasure I felt even in memory: the warm musk, the dusky odor I associated with strong men and hard work.

Once again I spent hours on my knees, pleading with God for strength and purity of thought. Often I'd find myself, still kneeling, my head resting against the altar, surfacing from a dream of Luke. Even my prayers deceived me. Satan surely knew my weakness and found me unguarded even in this sacred place. I denounced His evil presence. My salvation lay in virtue, and virtue was never true if not tried: in the trial itself lay the merit. I pushed my thoughts forward, imagining our wedding night, when with the blessings of God and our elders he would draw from me a sacred and binding blood.

And I gave thanks for this: that somehow my virginity had

remained intact. I believed that even when I was lost to the world some part of me had resided in grace. Perhaps, all along, I had been saving myself for Luke.

"What's the answer?" I tapped my pencil against the table. "Do you remember the equation?"

Luke stared blankly at the paper, chin resting in his hand. He shrugged his shoulders and grinned.

I released a dramatic sigh of exasperation, then began ciphering in the margins. "If X equals seven, then . . ." Luke's index finger traced small, ever-widening circles on my knee, "then Y must be . . . Stop!"

"What?" One corner of his mouth curled into a weighted grin. I pushed his hand away. He slid the pencil from my fingers, so slowly the room darkened before I remembered to breathe.

It had been this way for a week. Each night we stayed up late and strangely alone, he a student of home correspondence schooling, I his tutor.

Each night he scooted closer until our shared breath lifted the book's pages. When his leg first brushed mine, I shifted, conscious of the heat between us. But this too became familiar, safe because it went no further. His hand on my knee I knew trespassed the boundaries of virtue, yet each night found it there again, until finally I gave in and reset my boundaries: no higher.

My choices seemed few to me then. I could not risk anger, I believed, which would surely turn him away from me. And wasn't anger itself a sin? I had been charged with getting him through his home schooling and was flush with the honor of such responsibility. If instead of knowledge I presented him with temptation, then it was my presentation that was at fault.

I must purify my own thoughts. I was the woman and as such was charged with yet another responsibility: with my patience and purity to diffuse the man's instinctive carnal urges into quiet domesticity.

I could tell myself these truths as they had been taught me. But what of the desire I myself felt rising like smoke from the friction of skin on skin? No one had ever given me the prayers to diffuse my own carnal lust; no one had spoken of the hunger of women. Surely it must be particular to my own perversion that this want grew in me.

I steadied myself with the rationale that we were nearly engaged. Another year, I promised myself, and we would be married, free to couple and lounge wholly naked, every inch of skin slick and revealed. Already, the names of our children were written in the margins of my Bible: David and Caleb, Jessie and Sarah.

I let my fingers touch the roughened skin of his knuckles, then felt the wedge of his hand between my legs, gently widening the space until his palm rested hot against my thigh. His eyes never left my face. I could see his mouth open a little, his white teeth, the tip of his tongue. I jerked when his hand brushed the crotch of my panties.

"Hey," he whispered, "you don't want to wake them up." He nodded toward the ceiling as though it were a window. They were sleeping, I knew, but God never slept. I closed my eyes, ashamed, afraid, unable to move.

Then the hand was gone. I opened my eyes to see him standing before me, once again grinning. "You'd best go to bed," he said, then left the room, leaving me to the light.

I shuffled the papers into order, then rose unsteadily. What had happened? Nothing. I ascended the stairs to my room—a doorless closet in the hall, really, just outside the real bedroom, where Terry and Sarah slept.

The sheets cooled my skin. I opened my Bible to the passage underlined in red: "There hath no temptation taken you but such as is common to man: but God is faithful, who will not suffer you to be tempted above that ye are able; but will with the temptation also make a way to escape, that ye may be able to bear it."

I must have faith, I told myself. I laid my glasses on top of my Bible and turned off the light. I could barely discern the stars out my window, but I knew they were there and kept looking into darkness until sleep took me and stars no longer mattered.

CHAPTER NINE

I stood at the kitchen sink, running hot water over the plates and looking out the window. The temperature had been hitting one hundred the last several days and air rose in snaking ribbons off the streets of Spokane.

The water scalded my hands, but I had learned not to mind the heat that turned my skin crimson. Sister Lang and Sarah could dip their hands quickly into the steaming rinse basin and pull out dishes sanitized and gleaming. In the bathtub each night I practiced, closing the cold water faucet down a turn at a time until only the hot ran over my palms.

For the last several weeks I had been watching the women carefully. I had much to know about keeping house and cooking, and always before I had resisted participating in any of the kitchen chores my mother had asked me to do. If I were to be a good wife for Luke, I must work hard to learn his preferences: how much salt he liked on his eggs, how much sugar in his coffee. I folded the sheets into tight rectangles, following Sarah's careful instructions. Each towel was doubled, then triple-folded and nested neatly in the closet. On my own initiative I had begun to clean the tub each evening after Luke's bath, wiping away the greasy smudges. Gathering his dirty clothes in my arms, I felt proud—so different from that other self, who might have shunned such a simple and loving task. Now I was fulfilling my duty, and the Langs surely must see how grateful I was, how worthy I was to be their daughter-in-law.

My every prayer had been answered. Even the problem with Luke seemed under control. Only once since that night at the table had he touched me in a bad way, and then just for a moment. We had finished his homework and stood to go to bed. As I'd turned toward the stairs, he'd slid his arms around me from behind and hugged me close against his chest. I could feel his heat at my back, his breath at my neck. I'd thought he might turn me toward him and kiss me. A kiss would be fine, as long as it went no further. I'd wanted him to kiss me, something he had never done. Instead, I'd felt his hands rise, cup my breasts, and then he was gone.

"Thank you, Lord," I'd whispered, for surely God had seen my weakness. I spent the rest of the night on my knees, imagining Luke at his own bed doing the same, our prayers rising to mingle like vapors above the sleeping town.

Yet instead of drawing us spiritually closer, that night seemed only to have made it harder for us to be together. Luke seldom looked at me across the dinner table, and he'd taken to sitting in another pew at church. I believed I knew why: only by separating himself from me could he gain control of his physical self. I bowed my head in understanding, comforting myself with the knowledge that he and I waged the same battle.

Perhaps what the Langs were discussing in private had to do with Luke and me. I lifted the plates gently, trying to cushion the clatter of glass so that I might hear the murmur of their voices coming from the bathroom. They were all in there —everyone except me crowded in the tiny space, leaning against porcelain, because it was the only room with a locking door.

I had been told to remain where I was and finish the dishes. Why? Had he told his parents of his sin, and of mine? Were they in there deciding what must be done? I shook my head. No. They were a family and needed to speak of things that I was not yet privileged to hear, and I must be patient. Suspicion was the work of the Devil.

This was not the first time they had closed themselves off. I had been asked to go outside just yesterday because, Sister Lang said, they needed to have a family meeting. I'd stepped out into the hot afternoon, squinting my eyes against the light. Family, family, I thought. I live here, eat, sleep and pray here. Isn't this my family?

"Lord," I prayed, "just let me be here. Just let me stay."

Was that Terry's or Brother Lang's muted voice? I strained to make out words, to detect some pitch or intonation that might calm me. I need not know the ways of the Lord, I thought, but more than anything I wanted to tiptoe across the kitchen and put my ear to the door. I watched the water filling the sink and leaned forward to catch the steam on my face, breathing in the moisture. Something was working at my guts, something dark and foreboding—the tremor of recognition I had been fighting to suppress.

Suddenly I knew what it was I was feeling, and I stepped back from the sink, grabbed the dishtowel and held it to my forehead and chin, wet with the steam and now sweat. It was all too familiar: the set of their mouths, the way they became silent when I entered the room. I remembered my mother leaned against the counter, the paper in her hands damp and curling, her quiet crying, her tears dropping into the scalding water as she read the letter from Lola.

The wave of certainty broke over me, threatened to consume me with panic. These people had saved me, had believed me worthy of love. If they were to refuse me, where would I go? If my desire for Luke had brought this on, I would purge myself. I would fast, shut myself away in a room without food, take only water and that so sparingly my body would know its true thirst.

The lock clicked. I could not bear for them to see my fear and kept my back to them as they filed by. There was nothing in the basin I could wash, nothing I could wrap my hands around and rinse clean. The screen door opened, sighed shut. Car doors slammed, an engine started. I spun around, suddenly afraid that I had been left. Sister Lang stood looking at me, and I was both embarrassed and relieved to find her there, hair tightly braided, familiar in her housedress cinched at the waist by a terry-cloth apron. Her ramrod back reminded me that I was slouching, and I tucked my shoulder blades and raised my chin, forgetting for a moment my misgivings. She liked to see me standing straight, my own braid hanging toward the floor like a plumb bob.

She moved into the dining room and motioned for me to follow. Already the heat had invaded the house, settling into the corners, sucking the breath from the morning. All the curtains were closed to shield against the sun, and the tempered light slowed our movement, as though sound and motion were somehow connected to the clarity of our vision. She pointed to a chair and I understood we would talk.

She began simply. "You should know," she said, "that Brother Lang has felt the presence of Satan in this house for some time now." I nodded in giddy agreement, aware that demons populated the very air we moved through. Only constant vigilance held them at bay; only prayer and purity kept them from burrowing like maggots into our souls, where they would fester and burst forth in a frenzy of vile destruction. When Christ cast out Satan's Legion from the possessed man, even the pigs in which the demons took refuge knew that it was better to hurl themselves from the cliff rather than be made monstrous by such evil.

I felt my jaws tighten, the saliva pool behind my teeth. Not until she reached out and pulled the dishtowel from my hands did I realize I had been stripping it between my fists, spotting the table with water. I rubbed at the spots with my palm, then looked at my hand, the creases damp and shiny.

"We've heard strange noises, the stairs creaking in the middle of the night. Evil stalks this house." Then she pointed her finger, the towel hanging down like a skin. "You," she said. "You have brought these demons into our home."

I watched the movement of her mouth. I could see her talking, but her words floated from her lips and into the air, mixing with the sounds of flies and Saturday traffic. I sat with my palm still open, feeling my body let loose its hold, feeling that part of me that wanted to rise screaming and begging instead drift slowly downward, inward, settling somewhere deep, unreachable. I could just as easily not be there. I could be anywhere I wanted—outside feeling the hot sidewalk through the soles of my shoes, or sitting at the piano, safe in the dark church. I began to hum a little to myself, rocking in my chair.

There was more. She told me she knew of my love for Terry, the husband of her true daughter. Hadn't I called him one day to the shadowed sanctuary? Hadn't I pressed myself against him and whispered in his ear the name of some dark familiar? In the church, she said, I had seduced him.

I was stunned with disbelief. Nothing had prepared me for this story of my life, a story that made of me a plotting adulteress, a betrayer of gross, unimaginable proportions. I shook my head, wanting to say *no, no, I'd never do that, I'd never* . . . but I had no breath to form the sounds, no chance of changing the vision Sister Lang had created of my lascivious nature.

There had been several times when Sarah had brought up veiled references to my sexual experience, her implication being that I had led a life of promiscuity. I never felt I had the right to protest, to set their thinking straight: I was a *virgin*, that magical designation that meant everything to a girl's future on earth as well as in Heaven. Once, over a meal at the K mart cafeteria, I had shyly asked Brother Lang if he would perform the ceremony at my wedding. I didn't understand the smirks and shared glances between the family members until Sarah said, "Daddy only marries virgins." I'd nodded, too naive to believe she meant her comment to be cruel. I could no more register that kind of intent than I could begin to understand how Sister Lang believed me capable of seducing Terry. I was fourteen years old and had been cast in the role of Jezebel, whose story I knew well: for her sins against the believers she was thrown down into the street and made to be eaten by dogs; only her skull, hands and feet were left to be cast onto the field like dung.

I don't remember how I found my way from that room. It's as though a shade were drawn, leaving only the silhouettes of bodies and their coarse movement visible in my memory: no detail, no emotion, no faces or fingers, just the dense and undefinable figures of people going on with their lives, and I somewhere among them.

I do know that I was shunned. Even though I continued to attend church, I sat alone in the long pew. I ate in silence, my throat constricting so that the food swelled in my mouth and I spat it into my napkin, afraid that if they saw my plate still full they might find more proof of my evil: demons feed not on flesh but on the spirit. Sleep became my only comfort. By some mercy I did not dream and welcomed the impenetrable darkness, feeling the water close over my head as though I were tied to a stone. And it is this I remember most: the sense of being anchored yet drifting languorously, like one drowned and made to love her own death.

The remaining days of the summer between my eighth- and ninth-grade years come to me in memory like smoke from a distant fire. Someone must have told me what day my parents would arrive to pick me up, and I awoke that morning, made my bed, packed my few belongings in a bag, then sat before my window and waited until Sister Lang called me downstairs.

I moved with my eyes down. I didn't think, didn't remember. What was in front of me commanded my full attention: dicing onions, grating cheese. Only when the car pulled into the driveway did I look up.

I greeted my parents kindly, as though they were old friends instead of blood kin. The dinner was served outside— a casserole and salad, a plain hamburger patty for my father— laid out on a cheerful, red-checked tablecloth. I ate and nodded in quiet agreement: Yes, the weather was good, the church was growing. No comment was directed toward me, no questions were asked. I had only to remain upright and silent not to shatter.

What my parents saw before them was a girl, modest and willing to acquiesce, a girl who bowed her head and said grace when asked. Were they stunned into the same state of unreality in which I found myself? Could this girl really be their daughter, the angry and spiteful child they hadn't seen for months? Changes so dramatic and seemingly sudden can hardly be reconciled except in retrospect, and all that is left to ground us are the expected and familiar motions of the present: the salt must be passed, the ice cream served, the coffee perked.

After the dishes were washed, I gathered my things and climbed into the backseat. We pulled away from the church, my family and I. The Langs were waving, and in the sharp light of August, I could see Luke's face, in his eyes nothing I recognized as regret or desire.

My brother was asleep almost immediately. His head rolled and nodded against the window until I pulled him gently down and pillowed his head in my lap. I had not seen the fields since late spring, and their golden color infused with the pink glow of twilight soothed me.

Nothing was spoken as the car glided silently across the prairie, its shadow growing and shrinking, absurdly deformed, finally swallowed by the earth's umbra. It was then that I felt it well up, the panic and overwhelming pain, and I began without reason to tell it, from the end back to its beginning, as though in the unraveling I might find the cause, the one offending stitch.

The road passed evenly beneath us. Nothing broke the rhythm of my story, no one questioned or interrupted. When it was done, I leaned back exhausted, not caring what they understood or what they doubted. I had spoken it, had brought it into the world, had made it real. In the rearview mirror I saw the small ruby glow of my father's cigarette, brighter as he inhaled, then fading. Nearly dreaming, I heard the only words he would ever speak of that summer. He said, "I was afraid something like this might happen." In his words I found comfort and I slept.

I do not know what meaning lay in my father's words that night any more than I know what drove the Langs to accuse me of harboring demons. I do know that most often the possibilities are too dark to contemplate even now. I bundle myself in the safety of ambiguity and allow the vagaries of language to protect me.

I see how my life is often defined by the events of that summer, how my emotions are fenced by fear and distrust. And what a fourteen-year-old suffering her body's own betrayal could not know about seduction I now understand: I seduced no one. I also know that I have no explanation for Sister Lang's accusation. Remembering how carefully I shut myself down that day, how I've allowed myself so little memory of time and circumstance, I wonder if there is some other horror I might not remember. Can I believe any of these people capable of sins greater than my own? Who would I blame? Luke, barely sixteen? Terry, who may never fully have known of his role in the condemnation? A jealous mother or wife? The father, the family, the church, the Devil Himself, God?

For years there remained only one answer, and that answer was that the blame lay with me. I came to distrust no one more than myself, and the loathing I felt for any passion that threatened to rise in me—lust or love, joy or decided sadness, anger, hate, hope—eventually honed itself into a dulled and protective sheath.

It was a covering I wore well: this new consciousness suited the life of a Christian. Kindness to others was no risk—I expected nothing in return. I found it easy to turn the other cheek when the slap itself produced no sting.

That night when I arrived home and took up my life like an old and familiar garment, I felt only an overwhelming relief. In this place I knew the boundaries, knew what I must do to be accepted and survive. I had learned my lesson: I could not run; I could never again believe I knew the world that well.

I woke the next morning to the sounds of my mother in the kitchen. Jumping up, I washed my face quickly, combed and tied my hair. When she turned from the stove I saw my own benumbed smile mirrored in her face. I felt a pinch of repulsion. "Let me," I said, and took the spatula from her hand.

My father and brother came to a table set with matching plates and flatware, coffee and milk poured, syrup heated. We bowed our heads and I offered up thanks for food and family. My mother began to cry softly. "I'm just so happy that we're all here together," she said.

Shame filled me, a hot and sickening infusion. What had I done to these people, the ones who really loved me? Nothing in memory seemed enough to have warranted my hostile behavior. I looked back on that other girl and shivered with disgust. That girl was no longer me.

As we cleared the dishes my mother turned to me. "You know we cannot trust you yet. Only time will take care of that."

I nodded in agreement and understanding. Of course. Why should they trust me? I had hurt them deeply, had nearly destroyed my family. I too would need time, enough to make clear to them how deeply that other daughter lay dead.

I was grounded, although it was not called such. Just as at the Langs', I could not leave the house without a chaperone, kept inside as though even the air might contaminate my fragile resolve. I read the Bible and prayed. I made up songs of grace and salvation on the piano. I attended church with my family four times a week and felt the eyes of the elders upon me.

Confession through testimony let me speak of my worldly experiences with the freedom of a voyager. Even as my mother and father listened to their teenage daughter describe the shame and degradation of her past, their eyes held the pride I remembered from before, when I was young, in that other life.

When asked to testify, I did so, but what the people wanted most to hear, I soon realized, was not just the part where I was reborn, but rather the part that they knew must have come before. They wanted to hear the horrors of drugs and sex: the story of loneliness and loss that was mine was not enough.

I had never shot heroin, had never found myself in the middle of an orgy. Never had I prayed to Satan or cast the bones of cats in the light of a black candle. I sensed their disappointment, and even I felt cheated. Marijuana seemed trivial in comparison, the Annie Green Springs I'd drunk after school little more than lemonade. Why hadn't more happened so that I could offer up even greater proof of my miraculous conversion?

The story I told became something outside of myself, something that had happened to that *other girl*. If my parents remembered what I had told them on the way home from the Langs', they never said, and without the reaffirmation of words to keep it alive, the summer became first an emptiness, a dark pause, and then the before and after of the story expanded until finally there was nothing left of that time in between to tell.

As I attempt to glean the telling moments of decision and awareness from the next four years of my life, from the time I entered ninth grade until I graduated with honors in 1976, I understand how difficult becomes the task of facing my own vulnerabilities and fears, resentments and regrets. And in seeing this I see also my inability to view even in retrospect that teenage girl as anyone innocent or without guile. Does some part of me still abide by that doctrine which insists that the child becomes responsible for the fate of her soul at the age of twelve?

Church filled every nook of my life. Instead of going to dances and movies, our youth group held dinners, put on skits, passed out tracts each Saturday and participated in church conferences all over the state. When revival came, I attended service each night. At camp meetings I searched out those my age who sat at the back, rigid with rebellion. I told them I knew what they were feeling, told them of my own dark times.

Among those followers of God who believed they saw the path my life must take was a quiet man who came to lead revival when I was sixteen. He was a stern but gentle speaker, not given to raucous condemnations or physical outbursts of praise. His dark suit and studied demeanor made him look more like a doctor than a preacher.

There was one night I had felt burdened, beset by some

melancholy I could not name. I had made my way to the altar and begun my prayers when he stopped in front of me and raised my chin.

"Daughter," he said. "God is with you." I nodded, and he continued. "You have a special calling. It is very strong. You will teach many."

He moved his hand from my chin to my head. The gentleness of his touch made me want to cry. "Pray with me, sister," he said, and I did, tilting my head back so he could cup it fully, feeling the balance of our weight between us. He spoke quietly, and the prayer he offered felt intimate, something only the two of us and our god need know.

"Dear Jesus, our sister stands before You to ask Your guidance in her life. We thank Thee, Lord, for the gift You have given, for the special ministry she will undertake. We pray she be given the faith and strength to accept Your will. In God's name we pray. Amen."

"Amen," I whispered, once again feeling my life held out to me as though it were a rare and precious thing. Healer, leader—a child who carried with her the promise of miracles. I felt drained, unable to walk from that room into a life not of my own making. My path was clear, my choices clearer: I could hear and obey; I could turn away and lose not only my own soul, but the soul of all those I might have saved.

But this was at a time when I considered myself incapable of choice. The exhaustion I felt I believed stemmed from a spirit made meek in the face of its Creator. I knelt at the carpeted altar, crying, praying until I lay prone in front of the preacher, who would not leave me until my spirit's thirst had been quenched.

It is often like this for those possessed of the Spirit: hours of speaking in tongues, singing and dancing, until finally your head lolls, your legs buckle. Later, you find yourself on the floor, arms still raised, covered by coats and prayer cloths. You feel the sweetness of surrender. You feel taken, ravaged by the very air—every breath, every pore, every part of your being a gift, perfectly composed and consumed.

When school started in the fall of my ninth-grade year, my mother drove me across town each morning so that I wouldn't have to attend my old junior high, where Patti and my other one-time friends still gathered at the corner to smoke. I was relieved not to have to deal with their scorn and pity. My new school had a reputation for being "clean," populated with students more interested in football and cheerleading than mescaline and Janis Joplin. My new classmates had already heard of me, of my past and my sudden transformation. I was surprised to discover they thought I was a narc, a teenage undercover agent who had bartered her way out of juvenile detention by selling her soul to *them*—the priggish parents who saw pushers on every corner, the principal, the pigs.

The distinction seemed of dubious credit, but I was secretly pleased to hear that my past reputation had preceded me. I had no desire, however, to be mistaken for a narc. Whether left over from my old self or ingrained in me by the code of family, one of the worst breeches of integrity anyone could make was to squeal, to rat, to be a toady. I went out of my way to assure the "rinks"—the dope smokers and neophyte hippies—that I was cool and would hold their confidence. My newfound jock friends were uneasy with my crossing over the clique lines, but they were aware that I had a mission: to recruit souls for Christ.

I invited my schoolmates to attend our youth meetings, led by a young minister and his wife who had about them an intriguing California aura. Reverend Dave, our youth pastor, wore his hair a little too long, the elders felt, and he had a way of moving his shoulders and head while playing his guitar that made them nervous. His wife had a heavy hand with the mascara wand, the women whispered—a bit too much glitter. Still, all this might be forgiven in the face of the fact that more and more teenagers were being drawn to the church.

"Jesus freaks!" the heathens shouted at us as they drove by, music blaring. We ignored them, joining hands in the park and praying beneath the limbs of gnarled elms, secure in our sacred circle, calmed by our combined voices. I wasn't alone anymore. Many of the popular kids from my school had heeded the call from the altar and joined me in the ranks of the born again. Bonnie was saved now, and Candy, Brent and Joe.

Together with Pastor Dave we started a call-in radio show, broadcast live from the studio of KRLC, the same station I had listened to all those long nights when my world was unraveling. We held the night spot from ten to eleven, catching the young crowd still tuned in by surprise. Between cuts of Christian rock (a new designation not all our congregation was comfortable with), we testified to the joy and love Christ had brought into our lives. When it was my turn at the mike, I spoke of my past.

"I know that there are those of you out there who are thinking, 'I'm so alone, I'm so scared.' You don't need to be scared. You don't need to be alone. You won't find comfort in drugs or alcohol. I've been there. I know. Christ is the only answer. Ask Him into your heart tonight. I'll pray with you."

Everyone in the booth would bow their heads; even the disc jockey, looking bored and a little incredulous, would lower his eyes.

"Dear Lord, You see into the hearts of everyone. You can see, even if I can't, the lost souls listening tonight. They need

You, Jesus. Touch them, Lord. Let them feel You come into their hearts. Let them know the joy of surrender, the joy of knowing You as their Savior. Let them be born again."

As I prayed, Pastor Dave and the others joining in with their own urgings toward salvation, I marveled at how far I had come. To every thing there is a season, I thought. Only God could know the reason.

Pastor Dave believed that if you were going to take away the activities of the world, you had to fill the void with more righteous choices. Instead of going to the school proms, we had banquets catered by the church matrons. We attended dressed to the nines—long gowns and stylish tuxedos, hideously large corsages and miniature boutonnieres. We did everything we could to mimic the ways of our unsaved peers without compromising the state of our souls.

In the keepsake photographs taken by our own Christian cameraman, we look scrubbed and virginal, happy in our abstinence. But every time I hear a zealous politician or clergyman declaring the church a protector of chastity, I remember the common aftermath of any teenage social function I attended, whether blessed or unholy: a mad scramble in the backseats of the fathers' Buicks or behind the church or in the closet where the choir robes hung down like a hundred satin wings. Even on the chaperoned bus trips to one Christian youth conference or another, straws were drawn to see who got first shot at the back, where lovers might pass their allotted ten minutes in seclusion behind the carefully draped garment bags and coats. The one difference between the manifestations of the hormonal ragings of those damned and those saved may be this: how deeply the afterglow is tinged with guilt.

What part of our trysting the attendant adults were privy to was met with punishment. For sneaking out of the girls' dorm and knocking on the boys' windows, we were made to spend the night not in our bunkbeds but on the cold seats of the bus, shivering without blankets or pillows. And then there was the "hot seat," a wired metal stool the offender had to sit on to receive her "jolt" of discipline.

I sometimes regret those years in the church, filled with guilt and perhaps even abuse, yet given the choices in my own life, even considering the summer with the Langs, I feel lucky to have escaped the chasm that so many of my junior high school friends eventually fell into. The last time I saw Maria, the girl whose filthy upstairs bedroom seemed such a haven from the prison I believed my life had become, she was working as a carhop. I did not recognize her, but she did me. Her front teeth were gone, and one side of her face was grotesquely swollen. "The old man," she said, shaking her head, dragging from her cigarette a final, sideways puff.

I never saw nor heard of Patti again but cannot imagine her life took any uphill turn. Of the others I was closest to, the ones with whom I chased the bums and smoked dope after school, the majority are dead, imprisoned or living with abuse. Larry died in the river, Dennis in a car wreck. The night Les and I were caught coming home from the party and made to lead our separate lives, those who had dropped us off robbed the corner store at gunpoint and were caught the next day. Most were sent to do time in juvenile detention, and I might easily have been one of them. I wonder if I could have faced the old storekeeper and his silver-haired wife, who had been so kind to me in the days when all I wanted from them was a few pieces of penny candy.

• • •

My father continued his night work, and my memories of him during those years are few. Only on Sundays did he seem part of the family. Other times, when my mother insisted that we ask for his approval of our activities, my brother and I waited for that window of opportunity to present itself: in the evening, when he rose from his bed and made his way to his chair, where, before leaving for the truck yard, he sat with his Bible and the plate of food my mother offered.

I seldom asked for privileges that might not be granted and knew well the boundaries of what events were considered acceptable. If I did question his decision, the reaction was immediate: there need be no reason but his word, and that word was no. I risked punishment if I opened my mouth again. I held my tongue but felt the resistance in me rise. In my room I would reach for my Bible and find the marked passage, Colossians 3:20: "Children, obey your parents in all things: for this is well pleasing unto the Lord." I closed my eyes and let the words settle into an intonation that separated me from the room, the house, the man in his chair whom I feared far too greatly to remind of the verse which followed: "Fathers, provoke not your children to anger, lest they be discouraged." I could hardly allow myself to contemplate its directive, for to challenge my father's knowledge of the Scripture, or to question his adherence to its dictates, would surely bring on his wrath.

My mother continued to rise before the rest of us, preparing our breakfast, packing our lunches, cleaning and ironing until she left for her shift at the grocery store. The cycle continued when she arrived home, when she fixed our meals and tended to the needs of her family.

Just as I had watched Sister Lang and Sarah, I now watched my mother, her seemingly perfect submissiveness, her quiet determination to keep peace and harmony between us. But I also wondered what secrets my mother hid, what stories she carried as deeply as I carried my own. She never complained about her life, never spoke of her own desires or emotions—she seemed to have no passion or need, no past or present of her own. I came to believe what she projected. I believed she needed nothing but her home, her family and her god, and something in me loathed her for it.

Eating the biscuits and gravy, roast and potatoes, fried chicken, eating from the cleanest dishes, sitting in the room filled with the food smells of my mother's cooking, I turned my back to her and ate what she gave. What I realize now is that what I wanted from her was not food or even harmony but a story, a narrative to give meaning to her life and mine. I needed my mother to tell me how to find happiness in submission, how to content myself with giving and serving and silence. If I could only find the secret—and surely she possessed such a secret—perhaps I too could be satisfied and happy.

I think back to my eighth-grade year, to that time just after I had run away from home. I had returned to school a hero, except to one girl, Lisa, who looked so much like me that the police had picked her up, thinking her the truant. In fact, she was skipping school but might have gone undetected had it not been for the bulletin put out on my account. It was my fault the cops had taken her in, my fault her father had whipped her.

She'd waited for me after school, and by the time I reached the corner where she and her friends gathered, I knew her intent. "She wants to beat you up," they whispered excitedly. "She wants to whip your ass."

I had no intention of having it out with Lisa, providing the leering crowd with a "cat fight." I crossed the street and kept on walking, only to have her follow me, throwing rocks at my back. Finally, I stopped and turned.

"I don't want to fight, Lisa."

"Chicken! Bitch!" The sides had been drawn, and I found myself being pushed toward her by the group at my back. Her supporters formed a wedge, and then we were a foot apart, circled by a loud and eager audience.

I was already in enough trouble. I didn't need to be hauled into the principal's office for this. I opened my mouth to say so, and she hit me. I staggered back. Arms caught me and stood me straight. I touched my lip and found blood.

There was something about seeing my hand glistening red that acted like a firing pin, sending me at the girl. I knocked her to the ground, pummeling her gut, twisting her hair in one hand to get at her face. By the time they pulled me off her, she was bleeding and retching onto the sidewalk. I wanted to kill her, and for years afterward the one confession I could always count on was my continuing desire to do so. I felt wild, unleashed, unable to control what had risen in me and exploded into fury. I jerked away from my friends, leaving them stunned and shuffling—half-ashamed at what they had seen—and walked home alone.

I hadn't tried to hide my swollen lip and bloodstained face from my mother, who stood at the sink, scraping carrots.

"What in the world! What happened to you?"

I shook my head and sat down at the table. While she dabbed at my mouth, I explained, for once feeling no need to lie. What had I done to provoke this? Hadn't I tried to avoid the fight? In her eyes I saw sympathy and anger. It was the most intimacy I had felt with my mother since I was a child.

When our eyes met, she pulled away. "You smell like an ashtray," she said, regaining her composure, drifting back into her controlled and authoritarian self. I shrugged. She knew I smoked. She smeared a bit of Vaseline on my cut, then resumed her place at the sink. There was a heaviness in her movement, a hint that something was working inside her, and I waited to see what would come of it. She ran her rag around the edge of a plate. "It's my fault, you know."

"What's your fault? The fight?"

"No, your smoking. God's punishing me through you."

What was she talking about? I knew she had smoked before, during those years in the camps. But why would God punish her now?

"But you quit smoking."

"No, I just told everybody I did. I lied."

She told me how she sneaked drags off Dad's cigarettes, plugging the crack at the bottom of the bathroom door with a towel. It was her secret sin—she was sure not even my father knew. And because it was secret—because she had allowed herself to believe that she could hide such a transgression from her husband and God—she was doomed to reap what she had sown: the proof sat before her, her own daughter bedraggled and bloodied like some barroom whore.

Would God lead me to sin, I wondered, in order to punish her, a woman who gave so much of herself there seemed nothing left but a shell? Even then, to think of her trying to hide, fearing the judgment of her family, made me want to reach out to her, rock in her arms and let her feel the kindred circle of mine, make her feel what connected us—something more than weakness and sin, something more than cigarettes: it was the overwhelming sense of guilt and despair brought on by our inability to see ourselves as worthy of love.

I did not realize then what bonds there were between us. Nor did I consider these things when I was living in her house as the good daughter, fighting the bitterness and disdain I felt for her desire to please us. The struggle was constant: I knew I must subjugate myself, just as she did, to my father's will, and then to the will of my husband; I also knew that I could no more imagine myself leading my mother's life than I could imagine going against my father's authority. Perhaps, just as my father had sacrificed his desire for the woods in order to take up his duty to God, I must give up my desire to control my own life. I must remember the cause of the Fall of Man; I must remember the perverse desire of Eve. I must learn to submit to my duty as a woman, don the veil of my sex, follow the teachings of Paul: "The head of every man is Christ; and the head of woman is the man. The woman is the glory of the man. For the man is not of the woman; but the woman of the man. Neither was the man created for the woman; but the woman for the man." If I wanted to honor my family and my God by attracting a righteous man to wed, I must remember.

I must remember how deep and insidious was the nature of my weakness.

The fall after I returned from the Langs I began dating Tom, a young man from church. His initial courtship filled my need to be loved and desired, and I found myself calculating my every action in order to gain his admiration. Our need to spend every waking hour together wore at my mother's patience and my father's stony authority. What I know now they undoubtedly saw then: Tom was proprietary, jealous beyond reason. He guarded my every move, chose my wardrobe, flew into rages if he found me talking to another boy, whether friend or suitor. When I was invited to a pool party at the house of a church member (the Assembly of God allowed swimsuits covered by long T-shirts for girls taking part in mixed swimming), he ranted over the phone at me: he had to work and I couldn't go without him. It was improper. The other boys would see my body, *his* girlfriend's body, and I'd be responsible for their lust. Was that what I wanted? Did I want them to look at me, to want to have sex with me? That was it, wasn't it? I was a prick-tease, a loose, two-timing prick-tease.

I cried. I pleaded my innocence and promised obeisance. I did not go to the party.

Perhaps because he seemed already to own me, or perhaps because my chastity with Luke had, finally, been perverted into something unimaginable, I didn't resist his sexual advances. I separated myself from his desperate fumblings, numbed myself to whatever pleasure and emotion I might have felt. My only desire lay in pleasing him, in being whatever it was he needed me to be.

Often, after evening service my friends and I would meet at a local restaurant to drink 7 Up and eat fries sodden with ketchup. One night, because Tom was working late at his afterschool job, I left my parents' car in the church parking lot (driving it a recently awarded privilege) and caught a ride to the cafe with two male friends from the church. We spent several hours talking and laughing with others our age, and I felt an odd exhilaration brought on by saying what I wanted to say without feeling Tom's silencing gaze. I was still flush with my freedom when the boys dropped me off at the church.

Tom was waiting for me in his pickup. The boys must have seen as I did the set of his face: more than sullen, closer to fury.

"Do you want us to stay?"

"No. It'll be okay. Thanks."

They drove off slowly while I stood between my car and his pickup, wishing that I were back at the restaurant with its smiling waitresses and fluorescent lights. One lamp shone over the lot, illuminating a single corner with its glow. I watched moths flit across its beam, the shadows they cast huge and distorted.

"Get in." His breath escaped out the cracked window and disappeared. I made my way to the passenger side, opened the door and pulled myself onto the stiff seat.

"So, did you fuck them?"

"What?"

"You heard me." The whites of his eyes caught and reflected the light.

"I didn't . . . We went for a Coke." I kept my hand on the door handle, thinking I could make it to my car before he caught me.

"Bitch."

"Don't call me that. I didn't do anything."

"Whore."

I shook my head. He'd called me names before—*stupid, dumb, cheap* when he thought I was flirting—but never had he used words like these.

"Tom, nothing happened. They gave me a ride, that's all. Ask everyone else who was there. Ask . . ."

"Liar!" He lunged across the seat, pinning me against the door. He was strangling me, crushing my throat with his fingers.

"You slut!" He hit my head against the window until I screamed. Then, as though someone had dragged him backward by his shirt, he fell away, staring at me. In his eyes I saw horror, not at what he had done but at what I had driven him to do. I was monstrous.

I fumbled at the handle and fell onto the asphalt. The door slammed, the engine shrieked alive and he was gone. I listened to the squeal of his tires around corners, the sound growing more and more distant, finally fading away altogether, until all that remained were the sounds of the city.

I can hear the mill, I thought. There's the train and the river. I didn't care that someone might find me, ear pressed to the ground like a Hollywood Indian. I didn't care that he might come back, or that my parents might be planning my punishment for coming in past curfew. This is what mattered —me, by myself, just outside the light's perimeter, blending with the night.

No one knew what had happened, not even my mother, who may have read in my face some pain but did not ask, giving what she could by admonishing my coming in late with words instead of grounding. The next day, when Tom came to the door with flowers, I took them without smiling and placed them in a vase, then folded my hands in front of me and waited. I believed I loved him, and that he loved me. Why else would he have acted so passionately? Why else would it hurt so bad to imagine his absence? The high-necked blouse I wore to cover the marks on my neck also served as a reminder of subservient modesty. I would not anger him again, would not cause him to question my loyalty. If I failed to make him happy, as I had that night by consorting with other boys, he would leave me.

My mother said I was too young to get so serious. The retort was easy. "*You* were only sixteen," I said. "Why isn't that good enough for me?"

Sixteen seemed to me an age when something should happen, something that might change the way people looked at me, the way I saw myself. I thought of my mother's marriage, Sarah's life with Terry, how all I ever wanted was to be given to Luke and left to spend the rest of my life in bliss. But that was not to be, and so I went to the department store and had my ears pierced.

I drove home, my earlobes swollen with heat, fear of my father's reaction adding to the feverish feeling. My hair was long enough to cover the small gold dots. Maybe he wouldn't notice.

But my mother did, and when she pulled back my hair and took in the twin punctures, she looked first as though she believed we were both doomed, and then she smiled a small smile and shook her head. "Kim, Kim, Kim. You better hope your daddy doesn't find out."

There was something of the conspirator in her after all.

A few months later, I sat in Tom's pickup after school, feeling the calm afternoon bend and mutate. My house faded and narrowed as I stared at it through the windshield. Nothing seemed familiar. "I want to date other girls," he repeated. "I just think we're too young to get so serious."

I sat frozen, refusing to believe what he was saying. "Kim, you can keep the ring. I think you should have it."

A huge bawling noise rose from my throat. I ran across the yard and threw open the door to my house so hard the windows rattled. I heard him gun his pickup out of the driveway, spitting rock and filling the air with the smell of burned rubber.

My mother soothed me. It was for the better, she said. She washed my face with a cold rag and left me in my bed. "Stupid, stupid, stupid," I whispered to myself again and again. I was ruined. No man would ever want to keep me.

CHAPTER TEN

As the shiny newness of my conversion faded, leaving me with little more than the present by which to define myself, I found I longed for those times with Les when she and I believed we owned the few hours around midnight, when we walked the empty streets of Lewiston. I saw little of her, having left her behind with the cast-off remnants of my past life. One of the few nights we spent together she had stroked my hair. "Don't worry, Kim," she said. "We'll get you back." I'd shuddered beneath her hand, feeling that dark sister in me rise, and at least for a moment I felt suspended between two worlds—half novitiate, half sibyl.

I drove to her house one spring afternoon, full of what Nan called piss 'n vinegar. It was a feeling I hadn't had for a long time—a kind of itch that started from the inside and worked its way out so that I jerked with the urgency of it.

Lewiston was turning green, green and daffodil-yellow, the sky so blue and clear it made your teeth hurt to see it. I recognized the restlessness I felt, and it scared the hell out of me. I wasn't content, and nothing was more dangerous to a Christian.

Les was home, and she must have read in my eyes what I could not say. Her parents were gone, so she grabbed her Marlboros and we headed down the road. On the way, we picked up a few others, friends I hadn't seen since the old days.

They got me to smoke a cigarette, and the rest came easy. I rolled down the window of my parents' new Toyota, cranked the rock and roll and ripped through the back alleys of Lewiston at forty miles per hour.

Les was beside herself, happy and laughing in that way I remembered—a kind of seize-the-day, open-mouthed guffaw that made me brave. The skunky odor of pot filled the car, but I decided not to worry about consequences. One day was all I wanted; one day to feel free again, in charge of my own life.

Coming around a corner too fast, Lynyrd Skynyrd blaring, smoke wafting from the windows, I lost control in the gravel. The rest seemed a movie in slow motion: the car fishtailing, my frantic counter-steering, the trailer house that filled my vision as we skidded through someone's herd of plastic lawn deer.

The car stopped, nestled against the trailer so tight the poppies bent their broken necks into my open window. I didn't wait to see who might appear to survey the damage done to the manicured yard. Tires spitting sod, I swerved back onto the road, suddenly aware of the silence coming from the backseat.

"You okay?" I asked.

"Jesus Christ!" Les blurted. I could tell by her voice she was pleased. Here was the old Kim back, heedless and even more valuable with her new driver's license.

But I'd had a scare, and the thump of my heart reminded me of the precarious state of my soul. What had I been thinking? God had let me have this close call, had let me know who was really in charge. I drove straight back to Les's, dropped her and the others off without a word of explanation and marked the speed limit—a solid twenty-five—all the way back home.

By the time I pulled into my driveway, the guilt and fear had set in. I wasn't surprised by the absence of my mother, still at work, my brother still bobbing over numbers at the elementary school. I was relieved. I could take a shower, wash the smoke from my hair, pray the sin from my soul. But where was my father's pickup? He should be in bed, sleeping his daytime sleep.

The silent house had a heartbeat of its own, pulsing with space. I called my mother at work to let her know I was home. I waited fifteen rings before hanging up. I called my best friend from church, Bonnie. No answer.

The panic crept up from the base of my skull, making my scalp tingle and tighten. Had I seen anyone since I'd left Les's? Was I too dazed to notice who else existed in the world besides me? Where was everyone?

The Second Coming. Blood to the horse's bridle. Antichrist. 666. The Beast. I'd seen it all only a week before, in a film the church had shown: Christ had returned, taking the faithful to their heavenly reward, leaving those inconstant Christians (like me!) to suffer unspeakable torture at the hands of Satan and His legions. *Revelations*—the Rapture, and then the Tribulation. The faithful would receive their rewards and be removed from this time of terror, while those of us left faced a world given to unprecedented war and demons set loose upon the face of the earth.

I ran outside, searching the streets. The air, heavy with the drone of bees and the smell of cherry blossoms they clung to did nothing to alleviate my fear. Of course Christ would come on a day steeped in perfection, a day when everything seemed new and sweet and full of earthly promise. In the quiet of mid-afternoon, no cars passed, no mothers stood in their yards pinning shirtsleeves and pants legs to clotheslines. I got back into my car, closed the door. I knew where I must go— to my grandmother's house. Nan couldn't drive, never went anywhere but where we took her. She was certainly born again and free from sin. If she did not come to the door, then I was lost. Christ had returned for His true bride, and I had been left behind.

I scanned the houses along the street, peering into the windows of strangers. No one. I glanced into my rearview every few seconds, but no one followed me. My heart raced and it was all I could do to hold off the wave of panic I felt swelling beneath my breastbone. *Turn a corner. Go up Eleventh Street. Get to Nan's, then you'll know.* I calmed myself, my mantra the names of streets and avenues: Burrell, Airway, Bryden, Thain.

Turning off the car, I sat for a moment, frantically studying the house and its windows. No light, no movement. I opened my door slowly, unwilling to fracture the sealed space. The comfort I normally felt walking toward my grandmother's home had turned to dread.

I reached the porch, pressed my ear to the door, hoping for the sound of her ever-on TV. The silence convinced me. *She's gone. Everyone I love gone. All of them taken but me.*

"Oh, Nanny, Nanny," I cried, calling for her as I had when I was a child, slumping against the threshold. I drew up my knees and rocked, thinking I wouldn't leave this house, I'd find a way in and hide as long as I could, live off the jugs of water and cans of peaches and beans Nan had stored in the basement. I'd find a way to live until I could convince God that I'd withstand any torture, like Joan of Arc at the stake, if He'd only come again for me.

The door opened and I fell onto the soft carpet of my grandmother's living room.

"Well, Kim honey. What in the world?"

I jumped to my feet and stood staring at her in disbelief. Behind her the television projected its silent story, the actors' mouths moving in a pantomime of speech. Instead of dark-suited men reeling off news of the Second Coming, Eddy Arnold and Eva Gabor pointed in astonishment at a pig.

"What's wrong with the TV?"

"Why, nothing. Are you okay?" She peered into my face, her forehead arched in concern. I couldn't take my eyes off the black-and-white screen, off the grimacing faces of those people mired in mud to their kneecaps.

"Kim, what's wrong?" She was pulling at my arm, pinching a piece of skin between her thumb and finger. I detached my gaze from the television and moved it to her. Her eyes were gray, the same color as Eva and Eddy and their worrisome pig. No one else I knew had eyes that color. I moved my face closer to hers, looking for the slate-blue corona around each iris. "Nan? Nan?"

"Sit down, Sister." She pushed me toward the couch. "I'll make us some tea."

"Nan, why is the sound off?"

"The sound?"

"The TV."

She studied the screen for a moment, as though she had forgotten its existence.

"I turned it down because I was taking a nap. You woke me up."

I listened to her move through the kitchen, the familiar tick of cups and the discordant shuffle of her crippled leg. Was I crazy? My guilty conscience had done this to me. I was being punished.

The warmth of the sugared tea relaxed me. Looking at my grandmother—the round body and twisted foot, the hair bound up in toilet paper to keep its style while she slept—I managed a smile. We switched the channel to *Dialing for Dollars* and turned up the volume, hoping that our phone number would miraculously be chosen and I could answer when the call came, ready with the Word of the Day, ready with my grandmother's address and Social Security Number so that they could mail her a check for $300 and she could make one last trip to Oklahoma, she said, before she was too old.

When I saw my father that evening, on his way to work, lunch pail in one hand, heavy gloves, thermos and notebook of logged miles in the other, I saw too that his hair was shorter. I should have known—every four weeks, same day, same time, my father visited the barber. How could I have forgotten this ritual?

I felt comforted seeing him there, absolutely predictable, stepping into the dusk with the confidence of a man blessed with night vision. I often imagined him in the heart of the night, driving his truck full of wood chips down the river road, the moon riding the water beside him. What did he see during those hours when the rest of us slept and only the animals had eyes to mark his passage? What did he think while his family dreamed? He could just as easily have been asleep in his bed; his presence would have been no less felt.

I wished for his vision that night as I lay staring into the dark, trying to discern the pair of hands reaching out to me—Jesus' hands, delicate, mutilated, decoupaged and lacquered, beckoning to all those lost. I knew they were there, on the wall where I had hung them, but all I could see without my glasses was a small star of light reflected off the sleeve of Christ's white robe.

What was I feeling? What had come to take the place of that afternoon's consuming need to reject, at least for a moment, the life I had chosen? Not guilt, not even contrition. I was angry, resentful, like a child beaten for spilling her milk.

For the first time since the beginning of my summer at the Langs' I wondered, What if it's not true? Maybe there would be no Second Coming. Maybe, like Mrs. Steiner had said in mythology class, all people believe the same—that their god is the only god. Could the Greeks really have thought Zeus existed, that they could be punished by pestilence and disease if they disobeyed or were disrespectful? Would they have viewed my beliefs and fears in the same way that we perceived theirs—as nothing but primitive superstition and ignorance?

I worked at these questions the way I had once worked at my father's riddles, testing each word for truth, weighing the logic, taking into consideration the perspective. Why would God leave me in terror if I were honestly trying to be good? Man could only strive toward Christ's example of perfection; as humans, we were inherently flawed—and so the hourly battle to keep our robes spotless. But if we were doomed by our Maker to sin, it seemed to me that the rules of the game were woefully unfair: the chances were good Christ would come during the time when you were successfully walking the straight and narrow, but what if He dropped from the sky during the one second or hour when your guaranteed failure was manifesting itself?

A Sunday school teacher once told us that even cheating the telephone company out of a dime was enough to send us to Hell. If Christ were to return at that moment, before we had time to hang up, acknowledge our sin and repent, we would be doomed to burn in Satan's eternal fire.

And the pain that would be endured! For years I had listened, petrified, as one preacher after another detailed his version of perpetual punishment: a lake of fire into which the unsaved and unforgiven were cast screaming and writhing; souls tearing their hair, gashing themselves with bloody nails, forever devouring each other's flesh with the teeth of cannibals.

The preachers gloated on the details. They loved to see the congregation bent forward and shivering, some with fear for their own souls, others with a kind of eagerness, as though they yearned to imagine what punishment awaited those who had spent their earthly lives drinking and fornicating while the forgiven had denied themselves the body's pleasures. *Burn, burn!*

I knew that even to question God's purpose was a weakness, a sin. To question his existence, hiding in one's heart a broken faith, some fundamental doubt, would most certainly be enough to bring on damnation.

I closed my eyes against my thoughts. I imagined the fingers curling over the gaping wounds, the hands turning into fists, the fists themselves curling against wrists and drawing away, like the feet of the Wicked Witch disappearing beneath Dorothy's fallen house.

No! I threw back my covers and fell to the floor. *Forgive*

me, forgive me my doubt. I will never question, never again ask for reason. Let only my heart lead my steps and never my mind. But even as I prayed, I knew something had changed. The driving fear seemed dulled, my actions mechanical, too well learned. For many nights to come I would find myself beside my bed, kneeling on the floor and praying to a god I was no longer sure would listen. I had betrayed Him with my thoughts, unable to control the workings of my brain any more than I could the desires of my body.

Slowly, over the next several weeks, the tenor of my prayers changed, settling into a kind of contract, an acquiescence of both faith and reason: if God could not take me while I searched for some truth, if the quest itself were a sin, then so be it. Whatever faith I had left, compromised as it was, was mine. I possessed it, had forged it. It was all that I could offer any man or god.

The full realization of this washed over me in the early hours of one morning's prayers, and I felt as I had when baptized—fully submerged and floating, touched by grace. I fell into sleep, sagged against my bed, where my mother found me later that morning. She woke me for school, tenderly and without question. What I carried with me to the table, where I ate in silence, must have seemed to her a necessary burden. What my father saw as he handed my mother his empty pail and sat to unlace his boots, I'm not sure, but there was something that passed between us, understood and determined, and I knew then that what came after that morning would be between the two of us—me and my father, who saw things so clearly.

The week before graduation, I stood in front of my father, waiting as he considered the request I had just made of him.

A friend's parents owned a summer house on Coeur d'Alene Lake and had invited our class to come for a graduation party. Everyone was going, including my new boyfriend, John, a 230-pound running-back and leading scorer on the football team, who did not attend our church.

I explained carefully, trying to control the tremor in my voice: I would not drink, of course, I never did, the parents would be there, it wasn't really a party, more of a supervised camping trip, boys on one floor, girls on the other. I'd gotten straight *A*'s on my report card and hadn't missed curfew for months. Surely he could trust me.

He considered his plate for a moment, then said, "Let me think about it."

Three days later, he said no.

"Why not?" All movement in the house ceased. Even the kitchen was silent, my mother as paralyzed by dread as I was.

My father hadn't been home long, settled into his recliner with a plate of biscuits and gravy, two strips of bacon and a tumbler of milk. His socks hung off the ends of his feet like deflated balloons.

His mouth continued to work its bite of biscuit, but a twitch had gone through his shoulders. He settled them with a slight shift of his back and looked at me without raising his head.

"Because I said so."

The arbitrariness of his answer made me furious, but I could not risk showing my anger. I opened my mouth but nothing came out. Nothing I could say would change his mind now. He kept looking at me, sucking the bacon from his teeth, his fork poised above his plate and dripping white gravy.

Fighting back tears, I ran to my room, nearly knocking my mother over. She was standing in the hall, and it was her I wanted to scream at. How could she cower there, eavesdropping, folding the same towel again and again, more of a child than I was? Why wouldn't she defend me, help me?

That day at school, while the other girls talked about what clothes they would bring, who would bunk with whom, I seethed. He was making me a freak again, someone strange, shackled like an animal. John listened while I cried, comforting me against his hard chest. I told him to go anyway, but all I could think of were my friends around the campfire, laughing and listening to the slow lap of water, John there with his strong arms around someone, but not me.

There's no reason, it's not fair, I thought again and again. More than anything, I wished my father would talk to me. Other parents discussed things with their kids, actually *talked* about decisions. Here, I could perceive no way in which my feelings mattered. Here, it was all yes or no. My sense of injustice gave me courage. I'd ask one more time. Surely he'd see how badly I wanted to go, how harmless a thing it was.

When I told my mother of my plans, she shook her head. "I wouldn't, Kim. You know your father." The consternation in her voice made me even more determined. To be a grown woman and live in a house with fear as the ruling principle, to be afraid of waking your husband's wrath . . . I had never seen my father enraged, yet there was some danger that lurked beneath his calm exterior, and we were all subject to it. "As long as you live in my house," he had told me, "you will abide by my authority." That authority included the physical punishment meted out during my childhood, and certainly I feared the power of his hand. He no longer whipped me, yet I still quivered whenever I caused his anger to rise. It wasn't the discipline that frightened me: even as a girl I had learned to grit my teeth and not cry when a parent's belt or switch or open palm blistered my backside. I could survive being grounded or having privileges taken away. What I could not bear was being made mute by tyranny; it was my own anger welling beneath the surface that threatened to consume me.

The morning of graduation, I once again stood before my father, half-regretting my decision, nearly deaf with the pounding in my ears. I focused on the bands of skin exposed between pant cuff and the top of his socks—pale and hairless where his boots rubbed, almost pretty.

"No," he said, and with his eyes warned me I had already gone too far, a look on his face that usually scared me into sullen obedience.

"But Dad, please, I want to go so bad . . ."

"No."

All the disappointments of the past years, all the resentments, the swallowed protests rose in my throat. I had one thing to barter, and even as I spoke it I knew how little it was worth.

"I'm eighteen. What if I go anyway?"

He looked up from his plate, every muscle in his body tensed, solid. "Then you take your things and you never come back."

I let the words sink in. Maybe it was what I'd wanted all along—a reason to leave. Years before, I had run away out of hatred and defiance, but all I felt now was the sense of a sudden and clear path opening before me, free of boundaries and punishment, fear and tongueless subserviency. I was not surprised by the ultimatum. The position of the father must be recognized and honored; by challenging him, I challenged not only the authority of the family head but the authority of the church as well. Such usurpation would not be tolerated.

I felt a sudden and overwhelming desire to be rid of it all: the sin and guilt, the constant answering to mother, father, god. I let my eyes meet his and did not look down, letting the

seconds pass, letting the look on his face—stony and impenetrable—settle into my memory. When I turned away, I passed
the kitchen, where my mother stood stunned and silent. The
pain on her face stopped me for a moment, but I knew that
any hesitation would be seen by my father as weakness. I did
not want him to think that I was any less resolved than he
was, that I felt anything like regret.

From the phone in my bedroom I called my best friend,
Bonnie, asked if I could stay with her and her family for a few
days, then began to take inventory of my possessions. Only
then did I realize how insubstantial my physical presence in
that house had been: a poster that read MAKE LOVE NOT WAR,
hung on the back of my door because someone might find it
offensive; a purple alarm clock; a few bottles of perfume; a
basket of stuffed animals; a box marked KEEPSAKES, full of
letters and trinkets from boyfriends; Barbie dolls still clothed
in the straight suits and pillbox hats Glenda and I had dressed
them in that year we lived in Whispering Pines; a 7 Up bottle
with its neck melted and stretched; the peace-sign patches,
torn from the pockets of my old 501's and hidden away; the
POW bracelet I had worn that year I turned fourteen, when I
thought myself as much a prisoner as the man whose name I
bore on my wrist; a picture album, which I opened then
quickly closed, stung to tears by the photographs of family;
my Bible, my name on its cover glinting like a reminder of my
remonstrance; the print of Christ's bloodied hands, which I
left hanging on its single nail.

I made a small pile, added to it my curling iron, tooth-
brush and a bottle of Prell (little pearl floating in its thick
green sea), and in a few trips carried it all to my 1967 Chevy
Impala, the one thing I truly owned, bought and paid for with
the money I had earned at afterschool jobs.

As I backed out of the driveway, I searched the windows

for my mother's shadow. What had I left her to? A husband brooding and immovable; a younger son who would spend years of his life trying to make up for the pain I inflicted, trying desperately to be the good child; a house suddenly and without warning emptied of a body, a daughter, a soul.

And silence—this surest of all, for my father was a man taught well the stoic art of burying that which is most deeply felt, and my mother could recite the words of Paul the Apostle: "Let the woman learn in silence with all subjection. But I suffer not a woman to teach, nor to usurp authority over the man, but to be in silence." Any utterance against my father's authority, public or private, he would see as treason.

Perhaps because of the chaos of their own young lives this was the only way my parents knew to save us: an ordered and structured hierarchy, a familial chain of existence and command that guaranteed our physical and spiritual survival. Only *I* refused to understand its worth and reason. Once again, it was I who had torn the carefully woven fabric of family.

May 29, 1976, one week past my eighteenth birthday, I wrapped myself in lavender satin, hung the gold cord indicating my induction into the National Honor Society around my neck and marched down the aisle to the bombastic blaring of "Pomp and Circumstance." I knew that by then every invited family member and friend had heard what I had done. I didn't care that they were out there, that my mother and brother were somewhere in the crowd, pale and withdrawn, that my father may or may not be watching me from the bleachers.

I accepted my diploma, listened to the pep band play its ragged rendition of "The Way We Were," watched the ice sculpted into an enormous red-white-and-blue "76" melt into its metal pan. The night was beautiful—full of damp-earth smells and the high call of nighthawks. I looked around me. It was the same field where I had seen my first football game, the same lights that had dazzled me into a state of astonishment.

In five years, the only thing that had changed about the setting was me. The world went on its way whether we thought it wicked or not, impervious to our sense of its contagion. And all these people around me—teachers, friends, parents, toddlers screaming for their siblings, babies oblivious to the delirium of the day, sucking their syrup-sweetened pacifiers—did they know they were doomed? How many had sat in their places before them? Generations of Lewiston seniors had found their way to the stage without ever once fearing that the paper might disintegrate in their hands, the earth might shudder beneath them, the sky crack open, the cemetery only blocks away give up its ghosts. I wanted to believe my life might continue. I wanted to be part of a community, a family, that believed the next day or year, the next son or daughter, held the promise of something other than inherent imperfection and destruction.

My father left Lewiston that evening and drove the 120 miles to Coeur d'Alene Lake, but this was northern Idaho, on a body of water larger than some counties, and even after hours of searching, the only speeding ticket of his life flung on the seat, he never discovered the one cabin where I slept.

I knew of this only later, and I was stunned, not by fear of what might have happened but by the action itself, that I was able to elicit such a reaction from him. What would he have said to me? I could not imagine anything other than bitter confrontation, could not imagine that he would ever suggest compromise. If he had found me, would it have been as it was years before, when his eyes were enough to command me to follow?

But he did not find me, there on the shore where I sat next to John around a campfire, gagging down half a beer from the six-pack one of the boys had brought. I hated the bitter, grassy taste, but it seemed the thing to do my first night of freedom. I waited for some panic to set in, some sense of loss and sadness. But all I felt was air and space, room to move and breathe. I wasn't even sure I missed them.

I felt a pang remembering my mother's face, and if I let myself, a twinge of guilt every time I thought of Greg coming home to find our father settled deeper into his chair, our mother brittle as rime. I wondered when I would ever see my little brother again.

My boss at the pharmacy where I worked after school needed someone forty hours a week, and I would begin looking for an apartment the minute we got back from Coeur d'Alene. I had lost all sense of the future I'd planned: to attend college and become an English teacher. I looked around at the other seniors, still bound to their parents, chained by someone else's rules. For once in my life, their lives seemed more pathetic than my own.

CHAPTER ELEVEN

I leaned against the counter, bored and restless, the feather duster loose in my hand. Children rode by on their bicycles, wild with the warmth of June. Sundays never seemed right anymore. I hadn't been inside a church since I'd left home. The final, outward break from doctrine had been simultaneous with my break from family.

Still, all that time once filled with singing and prayer now seemed without purpose and threatened to expand into a feeling of loneliness. I did not want to be lonely. Lonely filled me with panic. Even at work I felt cut off, closed up in a box of glass and metal, surrounded by aspirin and splints, lotions, greeting cards and Russell Stover chocolates—everything anyone could ever need to feel better or encourage someone else to. Anymore, the only thing that made me feel better was being with John.

At first, just having my own apartment seemed like heaven. I painted the walls shell white, decorated them with pastel landscapes from K mart instead of the juvenile posters I might once have chosen, and carefully arranged in the cupboard the few pots and pans my boss and his wife had given me. On the wall across from my bed, I nailed the walnut gun rack my great-uncle Clyde had made as a gift for my graduation. In it rested my .22 rifle, my Ithaca shotgun and my father's Winchester 30.06.

I had found the Winchester leaned in the corner of my grandmother's closet, where it had been for years, ever since my father, still recovering from his back injury, had pawned it to his brother for a fifty-dollar loan. I loved the swirled grain of its stock, the smooth comfort of it against my cheek. Its smell of Hoppes gun-cleaning fluid brought back a run of emotions, which I let my mind sift through, discarding those images too specifically linked to my family or the Langs. I savored only the sensations of those times, warm as a tightly banked fire. If I let my mind's eye wander, allowed myself to remember and miss what existed beyond the smells and warmth, I'd feel it in the pit of my stomach: loss, regret, an overwhelming sense of sadness and longing that would devour me from the inside out. I kept the rifle as I would a funeral token—a flag folded and tucked into a tight triangle; a clutch of crushed flowers, dry and dusted. It symbolized for me the metaphorical death of my father: I could imbue it with whatever nostalgia I chose.

When John wasn't working as a carpenter's apprentice, he took me into the mountains. He had promised that in the fall he would lead me to the breaks of the Salmon River, where pheasant and chukar made tunnels through thistle; we practiced our aim on the hundreds of ground squirrels whose burrows mounded the high meadows. But he had gone camping for the weekend, and I was stuck behind a plateglass window dusting Bag Balm.

I imagined him wading the shallows of a mountain stream —the breeze still cold off the higher snow fields, the fish smell of fresh water, the pitched hum of insects waking to the sun. Nothing felt more right than being surrounded by pine and cedar, fir and spruce, the tamarack that bared its branches in winter like a common town tree.

Even better was to be with John in the woods. I loved his love of the forest, his knowledge of animals, his accuracy with a rifle. I loved pleasing him with the accuracy of my own marksmanship. I loved the way he spread his flannel shirt on a bed of needles and covered me with his body. I loved looking past his head and seeing the sky, not just a piece of blue, but the whole of it from horizon to horizon. I loved the way the ravens called as they passed over, not a warning or hoarse caw of fear, but a cry of acknowledgment: *there, there.*

Standing at the counter, longing for the presence of ravens, it came to me that I could go into the woods anyway, by myself. Tomorrow was my day off. I could go fishing, take my .22, find the squirrels and shoot them. I would cut off and bring home the wiry little tails, as John did, proof of my good eye and independence. But I wouldn't go into the closest mountains. Instead, I would go to the Clearwater, back into that place from which I came.

The next morning, I loaded my fishing rod, tackle box and .22 into the car and drove the river road east. It felt strange at first, doing something like this without a male companion, but as I left the city I felt the uneasiness lift. I was on a road I knew well. The river, slowed by dams and straightened by dikes at Lewiston, quickened upstream. Even though the

North Fork no longer ran free, the Middle Fork still flowed in below the dam and lent to the Clearwater River a remnant of its remembered current.

As I came into Orofino, the sight of Dworshak Dam stunned me. No matter how large I remembered it, its enormity didn't seem real. I had felt the power of the river, had seen it tear away trees and float entire buildings during spring thaw: I tried to imagine the workers detouring the water in order to pour concrete and anchor steel. It seemed an impossible task.

I crossed the bridge at Greer and wound my way up the mountain. The grade ended abruptly, spilling out onto a flat expanse of cultivated fields, already green with new wheat. In the distance the trees formed a protective circle and the hills rose even higher into dense forest and alpine meadows. Even if the river and its canyon had become something foreign, the Weippe Prairie had not.

I rolled down my window and breathed in the rich smell of damp earth and early flowers—balsam root, dog fennel, lupine and camas—that floated on the heavier perfume of pine. The tears that stung my eyes surprised me, and I let out a loud "Hah!" It was a good noise, a sound of skepticism and control. It worked. I shook my head and tried to remember the road I would follow through Weippe and on into Pierce, the series of turns I would need to take in order to reach Reeds Creek.

At first, Pierce didn't seem much different. There was Kimball's Drug, the Confectionery, the old Clearwater Hotel. But as I drove slowly down Main Street, I realized what I wasn't seeing: people. No old-timers sat in the hotel window, pinging empty Folger's cans with spit. No women stood in the doorway of Durant's Dry Goods, testing the warm weather with bare arms and pinned-up hair.

The school, I knew, had been closed and condemned, the

children bussed to the new building, halfway between Pierce and Weippe, pledging allegiance with the Weippe Gorillas, the team we had once considered our arch rivals. But the post office—it should never be empty. Just then a dog barked and a woman bellowed for it to shut up. I relaxed my grip on the wheel.

Everyone is at work, I thought. Later, on the way home, when I come back through, it will be different. I picked up speed, heading toward the hollow, fighting the sense of urgency rising in my chest.

Pole Camp was gone. Only the shop remained, a dustier shade of red, but still standing. I pulled off the road and stared at the clearing where our circle had been. I looked closer and saw the house that Clyde and Daisy had built, the one with a genuine foundation. The forest had closed it in, but the windows were curtained, the burn barrel still upright. I searched the clearing for the stumps our trailers had rested on, the outhouse, anything that might verify that my life there had been real.

There—behind the lightning-struck yellow pine, we had had our secret place. There my cousins and I had eaten thick butter-and-sugar sandwiches, quarreled and made up, come for solace and pity after a whipping. I wondered if at twilight the elk still came into the meadow—beyond where the wash shed had stood—to eat the marsh grass and whistle their calves in.

A few miles farther, I passed the Jaype mill, whose name I had always heard as initials—J. P.—still huffing out its smoke. A solitary loader swung its jaws over a deck of logs, lifting six or seven at a time and placing them precisely between the hard metal ribs of a rail car. The familiar activity was a comfort, and I drove on toward Cardiff, where the church and parsonage stood skirted by a bog of mud. I did not slow to look. I wanted the woods. The creek would be there, the meadow where I had seen the fawn, the hollow with its sheltering trees. No matter what I did, no matter how many times I left, I could always come back to the woods.

I hardly noticed the clearcuts behind the stingy buffer of trees left standing along the road. The logging didn't surprise me. I expected to see raw stumpage and slash piles, the knee-deep gouges left by skidders. This was part of the life there, the sound of saws as familiar as the wind through the trees. But this wasn't the forest. The trees could fall but the *forest* would somehow remain, always out there, always removed and separate from what we called timber.

I turned onto the dirt road that paralleled Reeds Creek, my old Chevy chattering across ruts, working my way back to where I knew the branches shaded the deeper holes and fat trout wallowed in silt. The hollow lay just across the meadow, hidden behind the thick grove of pine. Already the sun had crested and begun its slide behind the mountain, and I knew the house would be dark and cool.

The creek seemed changed, shallower and muddier (had it ever been the strong clear flow I remembered?), and as I wound my way back, the water thickened. Within a mile the current was dead, dammed by a mass of slash.

I stared at the mound of roots and limbs, at the bulldozed wad of dirt and stumps. Fingers of water had found their way through, following the curve of branches, seeping between rock and wood. Behind the mound the ground was scraped and pitted. A sheen of oil slicked the stagnant pools.

"No, not here," I whispered. "Please, not here." I stepped slowly from the car. Insects skimmed the surface of the water, yet the water remained still—there were no fish to rise.

It was as though I had been hit, as though I could taste the blood in my mouth. I reached into the backseat, loaded my rifle and shot. A small explosion of dust erupted from the slash. I shot again, then emptied the .22 as fast as I could pump. I pulled all the ammunition I had from my pockets, reloaded and shot again, pulled the maps and Kleenex from the glove compartment until I found the last box and aimed and shot until my ears rang.

I hated it. I hated the dozer that made it, the man who pushed it there, the company the man worked for. No one was innocent. I slumped against the car and cried. Something had broken—whatever thread it was that tied me to my life there. The water that had fed me, cooled me, cleansed me had been choked off, turned to sludge.

Alone in the woods, the air and sun still unchanged, the throaty trill of a meadowlark reached me, and I felt an over-whelming sadness—not just because of the creek, but because of the flood of memories and feelings that swept over me. It was as though seeing the creek this way had released all the emotions I had tamped down and buried since we left the house in the hollow.

What I mourned was the loss of myself: that girl who had fished long into the warm summer afternoons, who had be-lieved in a world held solid by family and the encircling pres-ence of trees. I wanted it all back: the red shack; my brother still a comrade who would accompany me into the darkest glens; my mother in her apron, bent over pies, listening for the dieseling idle of my father's pickup; my father bringing in the cedar-scented air, a man for whom the world had made itself simple.

I knelt and gathered the dirt in my hands. It sifted through my fingers like powder. The land had been scavenged, scraped, then burned to sterile ash. I knew nothing could ever grow there—not in my lifetime, not until the wind and rain had covered the scar with sediment deep enough to nurture the seeds that might fall from the few remaining pines.

I left the creek, following the dirt road back to pavement. I would not go to the hollow that day; I could not bear what I might see. Instead, I drove the road slowly back toward Pierce, past the bunk buildings of the Clearwater Timber Protection Association, past the wide curve in the creek where I had been baptized. Then Cardiff, where the parsonage with its creosote-stained siding squatted silent and cold, even though the sun shone brilliantly off its tin roof.

This time I stopped. I rolled down my window and studied the parsonage and the church. How small they seemed: the plain building, now looking dispatched, settled into disrepair, seemed an unlikely place to have ever contained the warmth I remembered, the loud singing and boisterous praise, the preachers twirling like dervishes down the aisles. I knew that inside the doors of the church was a wall of obsidian, built by one of the elders as a gift to the congregation. Many times I had studied its makeup. The black shards reflected my face in broken whorls, and when I reached to touch the fractured image I felt the cutting edge of glass.

The double-seated outhouse still stood tilted between the house and church. Did the rope swing still hang from the cottonwood limb above the creek, the one only the boys were allowed to sail from? Beyond the creek lay the railroad and the trails of coyote and bobcat.

Where were those skulls now, perfectly matched, incisors gleaming? Did the Langs carry them in their gypsy caravan, stashed with the hymnals, cushioned by tea towels and aprons? They would be picking cherries somewhere in Oregon, camped in a canvas-walled tent, singing their songs of faith.

I let myself miss the Langs as I had known them then, and

felt with a nauseating intensity the shame and betrayal they had left me with. Times before, on a day such as this, the sun greening the leaves, warming the stone flies to hatch and swarm the creeks, Luke and I might have found ourselves alone in the church. In another place, another time, it might have been called first love. Whatever it was I felt then was lost to me now.

I thought of the life we had all lived there for those few years. So little of it seemed real, so little of it made sense outside the world we had created for ourselves. I pulled onto the road and drove the miles back to Pierce, its windows and sidewalks still faceless, then on to Lewiston, to my apartment empty of anything that felt like family.

Sitting on the kitchen counter that night, smoking, flicking ash into the sink, I let the cool air from the open window draw the cloud of my breath away. Outside, the locust trees hung heavy with their sweet blossoms, drawing the bees in clusters that wove and bobbed through the branches like dark drowsy spirits. I had nothing to attach the trees' fragrance to, no memory I might later recall and feel the rhythms of life continue.

That night was one of many I would spend alone, balanced at the window, smoking and looking into the night for some sense of what my life might be made of. For the next fifteen years, there would be no place I could find that gave me comfort, no place I believed I might be sheltered from the world— no sanctuary, not in the arms of a lover or the house of a friend, not even in my own bed, there least of all, for it was there that the fear set in and the dreams found me, and always I was running, trying to hide, trying to find the place of safety I had left, the way back a dim and impossible memory.

CHAPTER TWELVE

My father's arms encircle me as he snugs the rifle into my shoulder, pressing me against his legs. He steadies my left elbow, extended and trembling with the barrel's weight. I lay my cheek on the cool wood, breathing in the camphor of gun oil.

"Steady," my father says. "Don't hold your breath. Aim like you're pointing your finger."

The target—a red circle crayoned on butcher paper and tacked to a stump—seems more distant with one eye closed. I know in a moment my arms will collapse, that the rifle will fall from my hands. Imagining the lovely brown stock caked with mud makes me shudder. I focus on the wavering bead and touch the trigger. The still afternoon explodes into pain, sharp and burning, spreading from my shoulder to the tingling tips of my fingers. My ears ring as the shock reverberates across the meadow.

He moves from behind me, loosens my hands, cradles the rifle against his chest. He pulls a Camel from his pocket and smiles, a full, eye-wrinkling grin, holding the cigarette between his teeth. He is proud of me.

He nods toward the target. "Let's go see," he says, and I move after him, my shoulder numbing, still feeling at my back the cool air of his absence. It is 1964. I am six.

I am twenty, my father's age when I was born. He, my brother and I sit in the pickup, parked somewhere in the Clearwater National Forest, drinking sweet tea from a thermos, waiting for dawn. Nearly a decade after moving to Lewiston, we have come back to hunt my father's country.

It has been two years since I left home on graduation night, and we have barely spoken since. Two years on my own have given me the courage to believe that I'm independent enough to forge a new relationship with my father based on love and respect rather than on authority and obedience. I want to be welcomed into his home again. I want him to stay in the room when I enter to visit my mother. I want him to stop getting up from the table when I sit down. More than anything, I want a family that will not shun me.

I know that our truce will not come via apology—we both hold firm to the decision we made that day—and so I've found another alliance: I've asked him to hunt with me, to show me the land he knows. He logged it, punching through skidroads now grown over with chokecherry and alder. The thicketed draws, the stands of cedar, the meadows lush with tall grass and lupine are landmarks he lived by, familiar beyond simple memory. He has moved through this landscape, taken it inside of him, worked in the bone-deep cold of its winters, hauled from its heart millions of board feet. He has found the water sprung from rock and filled his hands with it, so cold it seemed molten.

I crave his intimate knowledge of the woods and want to show him what I have learned. I'll point out the deep-cut track of a running deer (*twin divots at the back—it's a buck, then*), name for him the birds that cross the sky (*flicker, evening grosbeak, pine siskin, and that one you call "camp robber"— it's really only a gray jay*). Given the chance, I'll prove my marksmanship, but not with the rifle I've carried for the last year. I've given the Winchester 30.06 back to him, cleaned, oiled and polished—a token of peace. Maybe here, I think, in the woods, we can come to some understanding of the ways we share.

Sitting next to him in the pickup's cab, I feel light-headed and girlish, once again a visitor in my father's territory, beset by the need to act properly, to show myself worthy of his command. I try to keep my arms and legs close, conscious of every brush of cloth between us. I try not to breathe too fast and give away my nervousness. Greg sits on my right, six-foot-three and solid, touched by the light coloring of our Grandfather Barnes—dark blond hair that will prove itself red as he matures, his beard and mustache the color of fox. Between the two men I feel both protected and diminished, the daughter, the sister, always in need of safeguarding. When the silhouettes of trees notch the horizon, we pull on our hats, savoring the last of the heater's warmth before stepping out into the frosted morning air. My father checks for matches, drops a few shells into his shirt pocket. He turns a slow half-circle, squints at where the sun colors the clouds, smiles at us and heads for the cover of timber.

For a time, we keep to an old dirt road, then turn onto a game trail that leads us along the flank of a high ridge. My breath wisps out and evaporates, and I keep my eyes on the path, intent on keeping up. Already, my shoulder is numb with the weight of the Marlin—a lever-action 30.30, heavy and homely compared with my father's Winchester. I swing it around, cradle it in the crook of my left arm.

My father is a tall man, long-legged and lean, unhurried and efficient in his movements. He keeps our pace steady, as though he has no intent of simply hunting but will lead us directly to where the deer stand exposed, stunned by our arrival into stillness. We should slow down, I think, listen. There might be bucks stripping alder only a few feet away. The farther we get from the rig, the farther we have to carry what we kill. The thought of half a carcass on my shoulders makes me groan. The muscles in my thighs ache with the climb. Sweat wicks into my long johns, and I am thankful for the overcast sky, gray and cool as gun metal.

I've been told my father can outwalk any man, can walk for days without tiring. Beneath a towering larch, he stops just long enough to strike a match. Golden needles drop around him, catching in his hair. His hands seem sometimes possessed of their own grace, like the wings of a raptor, finely boned and beautiful. He is strong, his chest and arms surprisingly large, so that when he rolls up his sleeves I find myself staring, seeing the muscle there tense and release, and I feel all that he has held back and is capable of.

No matter how carefully I step over twigs and loose rock, my presence is betrayed by the thud of my boots, the crack of dry limbs echoing through the quiet. A raven flies before us, calling its disgruntled warning. I watch its blackness against the sky and see the head pivot to follow our movement. He knows something we don't, I think. I think that ravens are our attendants through the forest—dusky harbingers, impartial jurors, marking our progress, patient as fate.

I see my father's back, the straight shoulders, the way he

moves: in the swing of his legs the hint of a swagger. I sense the rhythm of his stride and begin to hear its song, its smooth cadence. I bring the rifle around to rest behind my neck and drape my arms across its barrel and stock, like a woman carrying water.

Only a few miles into our hike and already I want to stop for a drink of tea. I want to rest. I try to discern the hour by the muted light of clouds. I hum out ragged bits of old songs —"Going to the Chapel of Love" and "I'll Fly Away" and something by Bobby Goldsboro.

My father's sudden stop startles me. I nearly run, thinking we've surprised a cougar or bear. He points to me, freezes me in my tracks, motions me to his side. My eyes follow his to a dense jumble of slash and tall brush.

Even with his direction, at first I cannot see the light-dappled back of a deer, motionless in the frosted undergrowth. My father's hand is a brushstroke through air as he silently traces the hidden head and legs. I nod, finally able to see the doe where she stands fluid as mercury.

I step back to give him room, but he shakes his head. He has given me the shot. I should be grateful, but instead I feel patronized, instantly aware of his expectation, his judgment of my every motion. This will be his test of me, his way of making me prove up. The action, which normally comes easy —*snug the butt of the rifle tight against your shoulder, elbow up and out*—seems awkward as I lay my cheek to the stock. The deer raises its head and I think she has sensed us, but she dips again, browsing in fern and the shriveled leaves of mullen.

I aim for the killing spot, just behind the shoulder, a point at which I know the bullet might puncture the lungs or pierce the heart, but now I'm not sure I want to kill the doe. We're not here for meat; we're here because a daughter and her father can speak to each other only in a code made up of action and reaction. The forest, the trail, the deer are backdrop and props for the little war we wage, and if only a few hours ago I believed our outing an innocuous attempt at reconciliation, I feel our roles settling upon us: the powerful father, the willful daughter, each intent on gaining some edge over the other, even here, in the wilderness, in this ritual of blood.

The shot echoes across the ridge. I lever in another cartridge and aim again, waiting for leaves to move, for shadows to separate. What I see is the deer's white flag of a tail disappear into the thick undergrowth. I turn to my father pulling smoke deep into his lungs. He looks at me above the still-lit match and raises one eyebrow. I glance at my brother, who is studying his boots.

Before I can protest, my father turns and moves away. Greg shrugs his shoulders and follows him. I want to tell them I meant to miss, or that anyone can miss a shot. I think, Quit walking, listen, but the distance between us lengthens until I fall far behind.

I hate my weakening legs, my slow finger against the trigger. I hate the doe, who believed us trees solidly planted in the bank, and I hate that I made of her some symbol of resistance. I think I might hate the man in front of me, my father, who carries his burden so easily, as if it were nothing, the rifle slung over his shoulder. I wonder what he is thinking, and as has always been the case between my father and me, I think he can discern the reason for my every action. He wanted me to shoot the deer, and because he wanted me to, I wouldn't. *But it was you who started it*—I want to say—*you're the one who insisted I take the shot. It wasn't a gift, it was a test, a trial.*

By the time we crest the ridge, I'm somewhere between tears and fury, both unacceptable shows of emotion. I swear silently that I'll never subject myself to this again. My father slows, then stops. He pulls a cigarette from his pocket with two fingers, lights it, scans the ridge. I long for a cigarette of my own, but I cannot imagine smoking in front of my father. I kick mud from my boots, glad for the moment's rest, already planning a hot bath when I get back to my apartment, where I can be free of my father's reckoning.

He turns his gaze on me. "Now," he says, "you lead."

For a moment I feel between us the steel-blue shock of recognition: he is the father, I, the daughter. His job is to teach, mine to be taught. No matter how many years pass, no matter what conciliatory gestures I make, nothing will change. I look to my brother, who shakes his head and looks away.

I hate this, this *lesson*.

It was *I* who had thought to save *him*, to rescue him from his television and easy chair, to remind him of the life he had left behind. I wanted him to remember what his life was like before his all-night runs hauling wood chips from one mill to another; before his stride of open country turned to the cramped steps of a man shuffling from bed to table, from the door of his house to the door of his truck, between the close boundaries of manicured hedges, back and forth, cutting the same swath so it might be watered and grow to be cut again.

But now it is I who must walk for hours toward what I think might be our beginning. The men follow me, my father half-smiling, my brother wary and observant, knowing that he might be called upon to take my place. If there are deer, I do not see them. The air darkens. How long will he let this go on? "Learning the hard way," he'd say, "makes them remember."

What I learn is this: I am lost, and he will not lead me out. We could walk for miles, spend the night shivering in our clothes beside a fire of pine branches, more smoke than warmth. He'd let us, I think, just to prove . . .

I want to spit my anger at him. I want to cry and sink to the ground. I want him to gather me up in the circle of his arms and carry me to a place of comfort, as he did when I was a child. I stop, close my eyes, take a deep breath: "I don't know where we are," I say.

He settles onto a log and unwraps a chocolate bar, breaks it into thirds. I crouch on my heels, unwilling to give in to exhaustion, to let him see me beaten. Greg walks a little ways off to pee, an excuse, I think, to give us all the room he can. My own bladder is full, but I can't bear the thought of fighting my way off the trail and into the brush to gain the privacy I would need to squat.

"You haven't been watching," my father says. "The treadmarks on the road run a certain way. Notice that."

I nod, tired beyond remembering. I let the chocolate melt on my tongue. He crosses his legs and points, his cigarette deep in the V between two fingers.

"See the ridge? That tallest snag? Tamarack. Been there long as I can remember." The dusky horizon seems a solid wash of trees, none distinguishable from the other.

"You look down too much. You've got to see it all, forward, backward, sides. You get lost in here, it'll be a long time before someone finds you."

You could, I think, but I keep my eyes on the blank sky and say nothing.

"You won't always have the sun, or even stars. You have to make your own map. Memorize it." He rises, unhurried, lifts the Winchester to his shoulder and begins to walk us out.

• • •

In the late heat of August, I stand with my mother at her kitchen window, watching my father mowing their lawn. He is nearly sixty now and paces himself, pausing to pull a cigarette from his pocket before pushing toward the next turn. My mother worries about his heart, but I still believe he could march for miles. When he stops to empty the bag, he sees me and nods, the distance between us only a few yards—a distance we still cannot cross.

I think of that hunting trip, the dark way back, without horizon, without stars, the bead of my father's cigarette our only light, his face luminously floating. I could barely lift my feet as I shuffled through downed limbs and stumbled over rocks, yet he moved through the night as though his life depended on silence. I wonder if he would remember the walk out as I do, those places where he slowed so that we might rest: beside the antler-stripped alder; along the bank of a creek rimmed with ice; beneath the drapery of a single cedar missed by the sawyer or left to seed, a tree so large the tips of our fingers would not touch had we measured its girth. During the silent drive home, the road a dark ribbon unfurling before us, we drank the still-warm tea, sweetest at the last. If he had touched me then, reached across and patted my knee or squeezed my arm, the wall between us might have fallen, his rigid authority and my bitterness dissolve into the shared and necessary experience of the elder and his charge. I might have come away from that trek in the wilderness believing my father's instruction a map I could follow. I might have believed the hand that held fire could heal any wound.

CHAPTER THIRTEEN

One early spring day in 1971, a year after our move from the woods to Lewiston, my great-aunt Edith pulled her new Buick into my grandmother's driveway. I stood waiting on the porch in the short-sleeved blouse and pedal-pushers Nan had bought me, feeling shy at the bareness of my skin.

We were going a few miles upriver, to Spalding, where I had often seen the Nez Perce boys climbing the bridge to get to the high, arching top from which they'd make their graceful dives. This outing, however, was not to watch the divers but to witness the end of the log drive on the Clearwater River.

Every spring for forty-three years the loggers and mill-hands who worked for Potlatch had gathered at the headwaters of the North Fork to begin the arduous task of running herd on the logs as they were pushed into the river. In the early years, an extensive network of wooden flumes carried the logs, but new equipment and roads had replaced the primitive system. The operation had come to include motor-powered boats and a floating cook shack and bunkhouse called the wanigan, but the work—the snagging and gathering of the mill-bound timber, the dynamiting of water-soaked deadheads—belonged to the men willing to risk their lives for the adventure if not for the company.

They worked in their calked boots and woollies topped by canvas, stepping catlike across islands of logs nested tight in the eddies. The dangers were inherent and well known: a log could roll, pinning the man or sending him into the high and icy rapids. A greater fear was having a jam break loose with little warning, crushing the lumberjack, burying him beneath a solid raft of timber.

My father never worked the drive because he did not work for the company, but my great-aunt's husband, my uncle Ed, who was killed in the woods, had. For her, watching the drive was something to be done in remembrance of her husband, but that was not our only reason for being there: this would be the last of the log drives, the last in the entire country. Dworshak Dam was almost complete. There would no longer be clear passage for the river or the logs it carried.

I watched the familiar shapes of the boats appear and waved as the men went by. They rode the wanigan like old cowhands, legs braced wide, cleats sunk like spurs into the tough wood floor. I might have felt a pang of nostalgia at witnessing the death of yet another part of the life I knew, but what I remember most is the sun on my face and bare shoulders and the way the warm breeze wafted easily across my newly shaven legs. I remember the powdery perfume of the two women I stood between and how I felt happy in their company. They seldom talked sin and treated me as though I were just a normal girl, taller than some, given to slouching, but little different from the others my age who crowded the banks of the Clearwater.

The house in the hollow is gone now, torn down by the company, the yard a pasture for pack mules. Headquarters—the store and saw shop, the log-lined swimming pool where I took my first lessons and nearly drowned beneath the panicked body of Janet Gardner—is a ghost town, boarded up and then burned. Only a few of the circled houses and the company's shop building remain. The forest has taken the rest of it, granted it a covering of meadow grass. Elk graze where children once waited in snow to their elbows for the school bus, the chains on its tires clanking so loudly they could hear it coming over the rise a mile away.

My father says that even the deepest pockets of the forest are not the same anymore. He says that no one who wasn't there can imagine the wilderness as it once was. Even as he moved through the draws and worked his way down the ridges, leaving space like an open wound behind him, he felt the loss. "It was just gone," he says: the joy he once felt following the deer to their beds, the pleasure of pulling from a cold stream trout deep-bellied and prone to fight. Even the logging became little more than a day's work.

I wonder when it died for him. I wonder what forces it took to kill it.

During the eighteen years since leaving home, I have made my way through a maze of jobs: bank teller, pharmaceuticals

technician, secretary. I've sold life insurance and served cock-
tails. In 1979, three years after graduating from high school, I
started taking courses at Lewis-Clark State College in Lewiston, where I met my husband, the poet Robert Wrigley. He
reminded me of my love for language, and as I read the books
he gave me—the poems of Richard Hugo, William Kittredge's short stories, Ivan Doig and Guthrie, Westerners de-
fining for me a life I recognized—I began to believe I might
once again feel at home in the world.

Where we live with our children, above the Clearwater
River at Lenore, the land is dry and barren, scoured by canyon
winds. In the fall, in the big eddy below our house, steelhead
rest in deep pools. They have threaded their way from the
mouth of the Columbia, the ocean a dream of salty warmth.
Patches of white algae inflame their sides; their backs are mottled with it. Between them and their home beds is the dam,
rising up from the river like the blank face of an indifferent
god. Those that escape the hooks and nets are taken at the
hatchery, their bellies slit, eggs and milt mixed in stainless-
steel tanks. The eggs hatch, the fry are released and begin
their journey back.

Before the dam, people here judged their lives and land by
how close the water came: to the fence, above the track, over
the road. It found its own sweet way, slowly filling the school
well, rising just enough to catch the postmistress's milk cow
by its hind legs. Fishing boats were pulled higher up the bank.
Children were double-warned. Those made desperate by the
hard winter's cold took to the eddies, leaning far out over their
gunnels to snag a sodden log. Bucked up, stacked in the kiln
of July and August, it would steam and crack into free, burn-
able wood.

I miss the river's sudden, animal heaving, waiting to see

how high it might come. High as '48? Higher than the year early thaw sent snow melt crashing down Big Canyon, knocking the supports from under Peck Bridge, toppling it into the stew of barn boards and fencing? I sometimes long for the dam to collapse into the churning water, to sink into the ancient flood plain. I long for the river and its course to be as they once were, the way I remember before the dam, when my life seemed bounded only by the sawtoothed horizon.

I think of how long we search to find that place we might call ours, where we might feel we have found a home: the perfect house in the perfect town; the secret hollow; that place in the heart we call love; that state of grace we call salvation. Yet it is easy for me to intellectualize my parents' quest for a new life, to cast my father as the villainous male, an extension of the patriarchy that doomed my mother to victimization. I know that they will tell me it was nothing but the call of God, nothing but the Truth, that drew them to the church. And I remember that call. I have felt the purging and radiating calm of being born again. I have spoken in tongues, have healed and been healed. I have seen demons cast out and watched a man live forty days without food. I saw the paleness of my father's face that morning after the demon had found him. I remember these things without doubt, beyond reason, just as I remember my mother's hair, her movie-star beauty and the way my father looked at her when he came from his work of cutting and falling, taking only the best trees, the ones he could sell and keep his soul alive.

Even now, more than two decades later, I can see the Langs as though they sat beside me. That summer when I chose their house as my cell, I came to believe myself saved, that they had pulled me from the brink of hell. Did some part of me also believe as they did that I had brought the demons that lurked beneath the stairwell?

What was it that sometimes swept over me, knocked me to the floor and caused me to sing out in another voice? Even now, if I close my eyes and listen hard enough, the rhythms come back to me, the surge and lilt of vowels and consonants: *glossolalia*—"an ecstatic utterance." In the woods above our canyon, Nez Perce once went alone to fast and pray, to have their visions. There are times I long to search out their *weyakins,* their sacred places, to hear the dry rattle of snakes and feel the bloodletting vines of berries, to be purged, to dream in the tongues of animals.

I watch my children at Halloween as they carve their jack-o'-lanterns and crayon the green skin of witches. I haven't yet told them of their grandfather's demon, nor of my own night fears—how sometimes I wake and believe I see in the doorway red eyes winking. Voices whisper damnation, promise salvation, voices of angels or devils or perhaps only the past. My husband comforts me, saying, "It is only the light of a candle, only the wind in the mouths of pumpkins that you hear."

I sometimes believe I can excise the past from my soul, consider it as my father once considered a stand of timber— test each memory for soundness, recognize the true ring of unbroken, concentric circles. I could say my father only imagined the demon roaming our house; I could say that the words I spoke in tongues were the unintelligible mutterings of exhaustion. I could say that no memory is more or less sound, no story more true than the one before: my father loved the land and his wife, his family and his god; my father feared the chaos of his own nature and delivered us from the wilderness into a life I am still aswirl in.

I carry it all with me, in the quiet pools and strong currents of my being. I fill my hands with the black dirt left by the river's birth. I believe that what I hold in my hands is memory: like the river, it takes what it touches, carrying it along until all that remains is the bed over which the water flows.

So it is that I have chosen to remain here, above the Idaho river whose feeding brooks once ran beneath my window, whose waters I drank from my hands. All that I am and have ever been the river has known. It is the map I follow back to understand what has shaped me: my family, the camps, the church; the preacher's son whose initials I carved into the spongy bark; his family I believed loved me—back past the dam and into what remains of the forest, to where my father's voice once rose in laughter, back to that place where I sang with the soul of a child.

About the Author

Kim Barnes's stories and poems have appeared in numerous journals, including *The Georgia Review* and *Shenandoah*. She coedited, along with Mary Clearman Blew, *Circle of Women: An Anthology of Western Women Writers*. She lives with her husband and children above the Clearwater River in Idaho.